Lisa —

As you prepare
for your Rx-Care interview,
may the insights here give
you stirrings for your soul.
Peace to you, my friend ... your
continue to discern God's
for your life and ministry

Love,
Jimmy

Leading the
Congregation

Leading the Congregation

Caring for Yourself
While Serving Others

Norman Shawchuck
and
Roger Heuser

Abingdon Press
Nashville

LEADING THE CONGREGATION:
CARING FOR YOURSELF WHILE SERVING OTHERS

Copyright © 1993 by Abingdon Press

Library of Congress Cataloging–in–Publication Data

Shawchuck, Norman, 1935–
    Leading the congregation : caring for yourself while serving others / Norman Shawchuck and Roger Heuser.
        p.   cm.
    Includes bibliographical references and index.
    ISBN 0-687-13338-6 (alk. paper)
        1. Clergy—Office   2. Pastoral theology.   3. Christian leadership.   I. Heuser, Roger.   II. Title.
BV660.2.S49   1993
253—dc20   93-18258
                                                                                CIP

Scripture quotations are from the New Revised Standard Version Bible. Copyright © 1989 by the Division of Christian Education of the National Council of the Churches of Christ in the USA. Used by Permission.

Excerpts from *On Leadership*, by John W. Gardner, reprinted with the permission of The Free Press, a Division of Macmillan, Inc. Copyright © 1990 by John W. Gardner.

Excerpts from "I like youngsters," by Michael Quoist, reprinted with the permission of Gill and Macmillan Ltd.

The poem "The Prayer 'Soul of Christ,'" from *The Spiritual Exercises of Saint Ignatius: A Literal Translation and a Contemporary Reading*, by David L. Fleming, reprinted with the permission of The Institute of Jesuit Sources. Copyright © 1989.

The Time Management Matrix, from *The Seven Habits of Highly Effective People*, by Stephen R. Covey, © 1989 Simon and Schuster, is reprinted with the permission of Covey Leadership Center, 1-800-331-7716.

Excerpts from *Unstable at the Top*, by Manfred F. R. Kets de Vries and Danny Miller, reprinted with the permission of New American Library, a division of Penguin Books USA Inc. Copyright © 1988 by Manfred F. R. Kets de Vries and Danny Miller.

Excerpts from *Servant Leadership*, by Robert K. Greenleaf, reprinted with the permission of The Robert K. Greenleaf Center. Copyright © 1989.

Excerpts from *The Fifth Discipline*, by Peter M. Senge, reprinted with the permission of Doubleday, a division of Bantam, Doubleday, Dell Publishing Group, Inc. Copyright © 1990 by Doubleday.

Excerpts from *Letters to Dolcidia* by Carlo Caretto. Copyright © 1991 by HarperCollins.

94 95 96 97 98 99 00 01 02 — 10 9 8 7 6 5 4 3

MANUFACTURED IN THE UNITED STATES OF AMERICA

For Alvin Lindgren,
friend, teacher, mentor, guide,
who taught us the foundations
for purposeful church administration—
and inspired us to go beyond.

To Verna, my best friend, who never complains about the long hours and many weeks apart while I am holed up in my North Dakota writing shack working on "another book." *Norman Shawchuck*

To Gayle, whose genesis in my life has been a gift of pure joy. *Roger Heuser*

And to our twins Macintosh, whose smiley faces beckon us enter the workshop where words are crafted into ideas, and ideas are woven into books.

To Ona, Roger's mother, whose compulsive personality, knowledge of the church, and interest in this book combined to give us one great proofreader.

Contents

Acknowledgments

We gratefully acknowledge Peter F. Drucker for his pervasive influence upon our thinking and writing. He is the master without peer in the fields of leadership and management. We trust this writing is faithful to all he has taught us.

We are indebted to our students, clients, and colleagues who have interacted with us in the shaping of ideas for this volume. We have learned from them, and this book is a result of our having been their students.

To the following graduate students—Tyler W. Daniels, Kenneth Henson, Justin Orrell-Jones, Kim Rinker, Iann Schonken, Paul Stoecklein, Patricia Terrell, and Kirsten Wyatt—who made their contributions in the necessary details of research. A special thanks to Paul Stoecklein, who helped in proofreading, in tracking down many of the sources, and in constructing the index. And to Phyllis Burns, Coordinator of the Graduate Programs at Southern California College, who managed the countless details necessary for the graduate program while Roger was on sabbatical to work on this book.

Finally, we acknowledge Paul Franklyn and Linda Allen, our editor and copy editor, and John Robinson, designer, whose dedication to this book has truly made it far better than our own limited skills would allow.

Chapter One

Why Is It So Tough to Be a Church Leader?

The best metaphor for our world of today is astronauts speeding through the cosmos, but with their life-supporting capsule pierced by a meteorite fragment. But the Church resembles Mary and Joseph traveling from Egypt to Nazareth on a donkey, holding in their arms the weakness and poverty of the Child Jesus: God incarnate.[1]
Carlo Caretto

In virtually every segment of American society the people cry that leadership has fallen on hard times. Since the 1960s, a pervasive mistrust of leaders has crept into the very fiber of the American ethos. A feeling pervades that our leaders are not to be trusted. Robert Greenleaf describes this condition as "a time when holders of power are suspect and actions that stem from authority are questioned. Legitimate power has become an ethical imperative."[2]

The Social Context of Religious Leadership

This trend toward holding leaders in distrust has not developed in a vacuum. In three short decades the American populous has learned that even our nation's top leaders will act surreptitiously in order to achieve their desires, in war and in peace. The seemingly endless Vietnam war; the failure of Lyndon Johnson's "Great Society"; Watergate, culminating in the ignominious resignation of Richard Nixon; Ronald Reagan's campaign promise to balance the national budget in four years, only to lead America into the largest federal deficit in history; the Iran-Contra affair; and the disheartening televised portrayal of the U.S. Senate throughout the Anita Hill-Clarence Thomas hearings. All of these and more have disappointed and disenfranchised the

American people.[3] In line with this, Warren Bennis suggests, "We emerged from World War II as the richest and most powerful nation on earth, but by the mid-1970's America had lost its edge. . . . America lost its edge because it lost its way. We forgot what we were here for."[4] Bennis is saying that the vision that once united Americans to a common sense of unity and volition has been lost.

The same is true on a worldwide scale. Globally we perceive a pervasive inability for persons or governments to lead. The conventional wisdom for leadership is no longer working. The problems of the world are too complex, too interrelated, and the speed of change sends entire societies hurtling deeper into chaos. The solution to one problem only sets up the dynamics that create an even worse situation. The people know—and cry, "What shall we do to be saved?"

Within this cry we observe an unseemly element of wanting to be rescued, of making someone else responsible for solving our problems, of wishing for a parental figure who will make everything come out in our favor. However, such infantile hopes for salvation without accepting personal responsibility or plying personal effort should not dissuade us from the fact that there is in every institution today a need for leaders, and the call for such is appropriate.[5] John Gardner summarizes a global sentiment when he writes, "A great many people who are not given to juvenile fantasies want leaders—leaders who are exemplary, who inspire, who stand for something, who help us set and achieve goals."[6]

Indeed, people desire leaders who can motivate them to volunteer their energies toward a collective effort. However, such leadership requires vision and the courage to lead the organization toward that realization of the vision—even when the way is uncertain. Are there such women and men among us today? Apparently not many.

Even great leaders, like Mikhail Gorbachev, often fail. Gorbachev had a vision, but it was too limited. He stumbled on the step of never being able to envision a Soviet Union without communism. His vision was that of a reformed communism, while the vision of the populace was for an entirely new system. Because of this, Gorbachev was ultimately outdistanced by the desires of the people. Boris Yeltsin assumed leadership, not necessarily because he was more intellectual or politically astute than Gorbachev, but because he was more in touch with the people's antagonism toward the prevailing ideologies and structures and their desires for change. Clearly, Gorbachev possessed the courage, but he failed to understand the ascending forces within the Soviet Union. As a leader, Gorbachev began well, and he set in motion the very forces that eventually would undue him. However, he did not end well; he became lost somewhere along the way.

Quite beyond the need for the leader to possess a compelling and expanding vision and the courage to lead, leaders in a turbulent environment must also possess the willingness to place themselves at great risk. We are not suggesting that leaders should place the institution or the cause at risk—but to place themselves at risk. Great leaders see the cause as paramount, and themselves as servants of it. There is little place in the world today for leaders who are not willing to risk comfort, security, popularity, and even life in pursuit of the vision.

For some time before his assassination, the word was out that Martin Luther King, Jr., was a marked man. Many of his friends and advisors counseled him to "cool it" a bit, for the sake of his own safety. A nation run mad, having tasted the blood of John F. Kennedy and Robert Kennedy, like a vampire would surely thirst again. To these warnings King responded with renewed zeal, refusing to give up the cause or to become less public. As a result, he died for a cause, a vision for his country.

How similar to King's legacy is that of César Romero's, slain Archbishop of El Salvador. While administering the sacraments in a quiet, little chapel in San Salvador, Archbishop Romero was murdered in cold blood. The wealthy wanted him in their pocket, and the young Marxist priests wished he would bear arms with them. Ultimately, Romero died for the cause of the poor in his country, being caught between two different factions. As with Martin Luther King, Jr., Romero risked life, itself, for the good of the more noble cause.

The examples of King and Romero serve to remind us that even religious leaders are no longer immune to the burdens of leadership. No generation of American religious leaders has ministered to more complex or confusing conditions than today. What a sobering commentary on the social context in which religious leaders live and work today.

As church leaders, we are greatly influenced by our social context. Societal values impose tremendous pressures upon the thoughts and behaviors of clergy. Even as the clergy seek to change society, so also society seeks to domesticate, or do away with, its clergy. For leaders, the society is no longer a safe haven, and perhaps it never was—at least not for its greatest leaders, such as Jesus, Paul, and Martin Luther King, Jr.

In addition to the social environment, the ecclesial context also makes it tough for leaders to lead.

The Ecclesial Context of Religious Leadership

Church Leaders Have Not Escaped the Distrust of Followers

As leadership in secular institutions has done, so leadership in religious organizations has fallen into greater distrust and skepticism. And, regretfully, not without due cause, for here as in society the expectations and desires of the people have been too often disappointed. In recent years, several highly visible religious television personalities have used their position to deceive and sway their followers to serve their own unethical ends. These travesties cause people, inside and outside the church, to hold all religious leaders in greater suspicion.

Henri J. M. Nouwen describes a certain style of religious leadership as the main reason for many people's having left the church in recent decades in France, Germany, Holland, Canada, and the United States:

> One of the greatest ironies of the history of Christianity is that its leaders constantly give in to the temptation of power . . . even though they continued to speak in the name of Jesus, who did not cling to his divine power but emptied himself and became as we are. The temptation to

consider power an apt instrument for the proclamation of the Gospel is the greatest of all. . . . With this rationalization, crusades took place; inquisitions were organized; Indians were enslaved; positions of great influence were desired; episcopal palaces, splendid cathedrals, and opulent seminaries were built; and much moral manipulation of conscience was engaged in. Every time we see a major crisis in the history of the Church . . . we always see that a major cause of rupture is the power exercised by those who claim to be followers of the poor and powerless Jesus.[7]

In the same vein, James MacGregor Burns states, "All leaders are actual or potential power holders, but not all power holders are leaders."[8] The search for power in position has been part of the Christian tradition since the time James and John sought positions of power in Christ's kingdom.[9] Dallas Willard, however, defines Christian leadership as power without position. While position is not incompatible with power, position is just not necessary, for authority has power that comes from the person.[10]

The metaphors for leadership most often used by Jesus—Servant and Shepherd—seem not to fit well with current understandings and practice of church leadership.[11] There are compelling reasons that fuel the frustration: lost hope, and even cynicism, of large and growing numbers of people toward organized or institutional religion. Recent studies have demonstrated a trend away from organized religion in favor of a more personal, individualized relationship with God. In one recent study, nine in ten people said they believed in God, seven in ten prayed for guidance at least once a week, and half regularly pray before meals. Yet, only 51 percent belonged to a church or synagogue.[12]

However, there is another appealing side to the picture. Many faithful Christian leaders—in highly public places and at the grass roots level—live out their call with integrity and resolve. The followers of such leaders are blessed to experience leadership built upon a sure foundation.

Pressures That Can Victimize the Leader

Even well-intentioned leaders can be victimized by the nature of the ministerial profession. Derek Tidball points out:

There are thousands of ministers today who continue to function more or less in a traditional way and who gain much job satisfaction in doing so. . . . Maybe some of that contentment is due to the fact that they do not have very great ambitions. . . . Some of the satisfied try to [bury] themselves in the frantic life of the flock. And since they are adored by their flocks they derive warmth from them and a degree of insulation which protects them from harsh winds of the outside world. In this way [however] they actually cease to be shepherds. Instead of leading the flock to richer pastures, they become caretakers, befriended and pastored, themselves, by the flock.[13]

In many places, effective religious leadership has been replaced by management of the status quo. Managing to get by does not seem to be a bad alternative to the heavy demands placed on a pastor who chooses to lead in the spirit and pattern of Jesus. Pastors can eventually wind up as caretakers, or settlers—insipid and lukewarm—a peculiar clergy disease which the desert fathers called *acedia*.[14] Described as the "devil of the noonday sun" or "spiritual sun stroke," *acedia* was a common malady among monks, priests, and laypersons who lived under the desert sun. They were persons who experienced spiritual boredom, a loss of passion, wandering about listlessly with no goal in mind.[15]

Acedia, as a clergy condition, still afflicts many religious leaders— those who have lost their passion. No longer does the "fire burn in the belly." With hardly more than a whimper, such pastors settle down to get by until a better appointment or call comes along, or until their pension kicks in. *Acedia* is an old word for an old sin widespread. Leaders in their middle years are especially vulnerable "when life has been daily for a long time and promises to be exceedingly daily for a long time into the future. . . . A person in the grip of *acedia* has drifted so far out of the current of things that from where he [or she] lies motionless by the shore he [or she] hardly bothers to watch life go by."[16] Colleagues who succumb to *acedia* should be neither scolded nor scorned; they need our compassion. Ministry is a tough, lonely vocation with few immediate rewards.

But the plight of church leaders who languish under *acedia* is nothing compared to the temptations and struggles encountered by others who have decided to give ministry their very best effort every day. The forces of evil unleash relentless fury—or alluring temptations—upon these leaders, day after day. The struggles described in the accounts of

Jesus' temptations in the wilderness continue to this day—in the lives of men and women who daily go forth to meet the fray.[17] Saint John of the Cross, in the 1500s, observed that the clergy of his day were uniquely afflicted by three spirits: the spirit of fornication, the spirit of blasphemy, and the spirit of scruples and complexities.[18] The meaning for these storms and trials is sent by God to those "whom afterwards [God] purposes to lead into the other night (though not all reach it), to the end that, when they have been chastened and buffeted, they may in this way continually exercise and prepare themselves, and continually accustom their senses and faculties to the union of wisdom which is to be bestowed upon them in that other night."[19]

Is it different today? Instead of the "cold sins" that chill the spirit and dull the senses, many among us have succumbed to the "warm sins" that excite the passions, such as adultery. Urban T. Holmes observes: "What we fail to realize is that the pastor or priest who succumbs to the sins of passion is fallen in the same manner as a fallen soldier. These are the demons that threaten anyone who sets upon the path through chaos. Some will lose."[20]

Many of our colleagues in ministry are not faring very well in this milieu. It will do us no good to deny or ignore this fact, nor should we flagellate ourselves. The truth is that we are hurting enough, almost as reflections of the hurt and confusion in the social context to which we wish to bring hope. Pastors face increasing numbers of lawsuits because of their own passions run wild. The divorce rate among clergy continues to climb. There are probably more religious leaders serving time in prison than at any time since Stalin and Hitler attempted to expunge the clergy from their societies. Only this time the forces that imprison clergy are from within themselves. Something seems to be going wrong in the clergy profession. To survive in ministry unscathed seems to be the exception rather than the rule.

The Congregation Makes Leaders Act as Managers

The Differences Between Leadership and Management

Leadership and management can hardly be separated; yet, they are not the same. Broadly speaking, *leadership* is seeing to it that the right things are done; *management,* on the other hand, is concerned about doing things the right way.[21] More specifically, Bennis and Nanus describe the difference as follows:

> By focusing the attention on a vision, the leader operates on the emotional and spiritual resources of the organization, on its values, commitment, and aspirations. The manager, by contrast, operates on the physical resources of the organization, on its capital, human skills, raw materials, and technology.[22]

James M. Kouzes and Barry Z. Posner summarize the difference between leaders and managers as "the distinction between getting others to do [management] and getting others to want to do [leadership]."[23] John Gardner distinguishes the differences in at least six respects. Leaders are those who are characterized as follows:

1. They think longer term—beyond the day's crises, beyond the horizon.
2. In thinking about the [congregation] they are [leading], they grasp its relationship to larger realities [for example, the community] . . . of which they are a part, conditions external to the [congregation], global [and environmental] trends.
3. They reach and influence constituents beyond their [congregations], beyond boundaries. . . . Leaders' capacity to rise above [local conditions] may enable them to bind together the fragmented constituencies that must work together to solve a problem.
4. They put heavy emphasis on the intangibles of vision, values, and motivation and understand intuitively the nonrational and unconscious elements in leader-constituent interaction.
5. They have the political skill to cope with the conflicting requirements of multiple constituencies.
6. They think in terms of renewal. [Managers tend to think in terms of maintenance.] The routine manager tends to accept organizational structure and process as it exists. The leader or leader/manager seeks the revisions of process and structure required by ever-changing reality.[24]

Leadership and management must both be included as valued contributions within an organization. Each is necessary for ministry effectiveness. For example, if a visionary leader cannot manage people and structures, the vision remains a "wish dream."[25] On the other hand, if a leader emphasizes action and implementation without vision, there may be much sweat and activity—with none of it tied to any sense of purpose or direction. George Odiorne calls this the "activity trap":

> The Activity Trap is the abysmal situation people find themselves in when they start out toward an important and clear objective, but in an amazingly short time, become so enmeshed in the activity of getting there that they forget where they are going. . . . Once-clear goals may evolve into something else, while the activity remains the same—and becomes an end in itself. In other words, the activity persists, but toward a false goal. . . . Meanwhile all this activity eats up resources, money, space, budgets, savings, and human energy like a mammoth tapeworm. . . . While it's apparent that the Activity Trap cuts profits, loses ball games, and fails to achieve missions, it has an equally danger-ous side effect on people; they shrink personally and professionally.[26]

A problem in many congregations, especially those in decline, is that they are overmanaged and underled.[27] Many congregations talk of wanting a leader but exert great pressure to make the pastor into a manager, because managers can be domesticated, but leaders have a vision and a passion that cannot be fully tamed.

Too often what a new pastor finds when coming to a congregation is that their personal vision for ministry is a far cry from the expectations the congregation holds for his or her work among them. Stanley Hauerwas and William H. Willimon express their concern about the effect of this clash of expectations upon the pastor's life and ministry:

> Cynicism, self-doubt, and loneliness seem to be part of a pastor's job description. . . .
> When some seminarians graduate . . . and go to their first churches, they often complain that these congregations are woefully backward, conservative, and ingrown. . . .
> How can this young pastor use all the good things he or she has learned in seminary when the congregation could not care less? . . . No wonder there is such shock and frustration among many newly ordained clergy. No wonder there is such bafflement within the congregations because these clergy do not seem to know what their job is. The congre-gation watches in befuddlement as the pastor manages to do everything but plan worship, preach well, teach, and build up the congregation. Pastor and congregation become hostile to each other because of such radically different expectations of what a pastor's job really is.[28]

These, then, are some of the basic conditions that help to weave the social and ecclesial fabric that surrounds the pastor's efforts to lead effectively: the distrust of leaders, the pressures to maintain the status quo, the tendency to become caught in the activity trap, the congregation's desire to have the pastor act as a manager and not a leader, and the clash of expectations between the congregation and the pastor.

PART ONE

The Leader as a Person

PART ONE

The Leader as a Person

Introduction

A violin is a musical instrument that is both sensitive and strong. It is sensitive in that it is affected by the slightest touch, and it is strong because its strings can withstand a good deal of pressure. A violin must be continually and properly tuned to be played well, for if it is not, even the finest violinist cannot call forth beautiful music from it. . . . When ministers are in tune with themselves, they can touch people in beautiful ways, but when they are out of tune with themselves, not even the Lord can make music with them.[1]

Michael Cavanagh

Too many church leaders rely almost entirely on their *persona*, the public front that is well conditioned to look good in every ministry situation. This is "leadership by rote," the pastor going through proper actions and responses to the varied, relentless demands of ministry. C. Welton Gaddy describes the inner war that eventually led up to his personal acknowledgment of a severe depression: "More than once I have stood in a pulpit and delivered a sermon in a style that exuded confidence and authority, some would even say power, while my mind was confused, my rubbed-raw emotions hurt like third-degree burns, and my spiritual life seemed to be sagging severely, on the verge of hitting bottom and splintering into a thousand pieces."[2]

This section of the book, "The Leader as a Person," views the leader from the inside out. At the very core of our inner life lies buried what we often most strenuously avoid. However, it is also the core of us that we long most ardently to nurture and sustain. It is about the precious treasures that lie hidden in the fields of our heart and how to guard those treasures.

The section is about taking care of the inner life. Our penchant for "ignoring the self," says Michael E. Cavanagh, "is analogous to an ambulance driver ignoring and mistreating the engine of his [or her] ambulance, even though he [or she] does so because he [or she] is busy transporting people to the hospital. Sooner or later, the ambulance is likely to run out of gas or fail mechanically and threaten the safety of the very people the driver is trying to help."[3]

The care and feeding of the pastor's interior life is not auxiliary to ministry—it is the foundation of ministry. Without this all leadership effort is sterile, without compunction, and ultimately leads to boredom and insipidness.

The leader is the one fundamentally responsible for what happens inside of himself or herself. When you are alone, what happens? What thoughts occupy your aloneness? To what extent have you kept your early promises to God, and how well has God kept promises to you? How has your call been strengthened, and how has it been tested (Acts 5:40-41)? Specifically, what are the means by which you nurture your own awareness of God within your secret self?

Relying on skills and public persona will last only for a season. The leader's interior life is a far more crucial indicator of what counts. Many pastors become casualties by running away *from* themselves, and *from* God, and *into* their work. But the call of God is first to be a person of prayer, and one who sets up housekeeping in the Word (Acts 6: 2,3). What matters most in being a Christian leader is the interior life, because "the greatest and hardest preparation is within."[4] There is no other way. There are no alternatives to the interior journey of the leader. How we take care of ourselves ultimately relates to and greatly influences our leadership effectiveness.

> Abide in me as I abide in you. Just as the branch cannot bear fruit by itself unless it abides in the vine, neither can you unless you abide in me. (John 15:4)

Chapter Two

The Interior Attitudes of the Leader

The great malady of the twentieth century, implicated in all of our troubles and affecting us individually and socially, is a "loss of soul." When soul is neglected, it doesn't just go away; it appears symptomatically in obsessions, addictions, violence, and loss of meaning. Our temptation is to isolate these symptoms or to try to eradicate them one by one; but the root problem is that we have lost our wisdom of the soul, even our interest in it.[1]

Thomas Moore

To be led by the Spirit into the wilderness, there to do business with the temptations that are peculiar to Christian leadership, is the inescapable path to freedom from those temptations. To remain true to our call, we must continuously examine our inner motivations and desires in the light of three attitudes that Christ taught as the foundation blocks of all Christian leadership: to be as children, paupers, and servants before God and the people.

The Leader as a Little Child

Childlikeness: The First Quality of Religious Leadership

The eager disciples asked, "Who is the greatest in the kingdom of heaven?" (Matt. 18:1). To their utter amazement, you can be sure, Jesus put before them a little child, and as they listened he said, "Truly I tell you, unless you change and become like children, you will never enter the kingdom of heaven. Whoever becomes humble like this child is the greatest in the kingdom of heaven. Whoever welcomes one such child in my name welcomes me" (vv. 3-5).

29

The disciples asked a sincere question, for their teaching had conditioned them to believe that when the kingdom of God was established, there would be a hierarchy of greatness among its inhabitants. The hearts of the disciples were filled with ambition; they wanted a kingdom that would bring the honor due them in this new career. After all, they had left their previous vocations and families and immediately followed after Jesus. These aspiring disciples thought that the children would only "waste" his and their time. Besides, what role could children possibly play in this new enterprise? How could they keep up with the competition?

Jesus' surprising response to the disciples' question was sincere, for he came to announce a reign of God in which there is no hierarchy and no superiority. His response must have shocked and offended them. Time after time, and to the very end, they raised the question of greatness in the Kingdom (see Matt. 18:1-5; 20:20-21; Mark 9:33-37; Luke 9:46-48). So deeply did this question concern them that Luke poignantly paints it on the canvas of the Last Supper. Jesus had just announced his passion—they knew now that the time was near—and a great dispute arose among them as to which one of them was to be regarded as the greatest. But he said to them, "The kings of the Gentiles lord it over them; and those in authority over them are called benefactors. But not so with you; rather the greatest among you must become like the youngest, and the leader like one who serves" (Luke 22:25-26). To the very end they raised the question, and to the very end Jesus gave the same answer: The greatest will be as the youngest, and the leader as the servant.

When Jesus urged childlikeness as the model for leadership, he meant it as good news, not bad news. Childlike spirituality (not to be confused with infantilism or a childish psychological state) is a way to lead church leaders into the Kingdom with an attitude similar to a child's; one who opens the self to this reality as a gift, and one who lives and ministers as the least in a service to all. This is childlike spirituality and authentic leadership within the Kingdom.[2]

Like the aspiring disciples, many religious leaders tend to take themselves far too seriously. They are devastated by the slightest criticism and are jealous of their "position" in the congregation. Children take their *play* seriously, but not themselves. They are transparent without shame.

God wants everyone to be like youngsters, whom Michael Quoist describes in his book *Prayers for Life:*

I don't like old people unless they are still children.
I want only children in my kingdom . . .
Youngsters—twisted, humped, wrinkled, white-bearded—all
   kinds of youngsters, but youngsters . . .
I like children because my likeness has not yet been dulled in them.
They have not botched my likeness . . .
I like them because they are still growing, they are still improving.
They are on the road, they are on their way.
But with grown-ups there is nothing to expect any more.
They will no longer grow, no longer improve.
They have come to a full stop.
It is disastrous—grown-ups think they have arrived.[3]

Jesus calls religious leaders to childlikeness that they may learn to allow God to carry them through the tough places, to teach them the lessons they need to learn, and to imbue them with the playful creativity needed to lead the congregation into an unknown, and often uncertain, future.

Jesus combined childlikeness and humility in his own life and ministry: "The higher we rise in the kingdom the more we shall be like Jesus in this humbling of himself. Childlikeness such as he exhibited is an invariable characteristic of spiritual advancement, even as its absence is the mark of moral littleness. The little man, even when well intentioned, is ever consequential and scheming—thinking of himself, his honor, dignity, reputation, even when professedly doing good."[4]

Carlo Caretto journeyed through his entire life and ministry to experience the freedom and presence one might experience as a little child in the care of God. He often prayed, "Spirit of God, reveal yourself to me your child." And he reminds us that "it is our privilege, not our punishment, to become child like—Christ like—in and through our leadership positions." His search for childlikeness is chronicled in his letters to his sister, Dolcidia, a Catholic nun. In these letters he repeatedly requests her prayers that he might become "little, little, little. Small,

small, small." Carretto's understanding of childlikeness as one of God's gifts for leadership is beautifully described in a letter dated March 23, 1955:

> "If you do not become like little children you shall not enter the Kingdom," and that's not easy for those who have been complicated by sin. To become little children means to increase our feeling for God's fatherhood over us, it means to think and act as little children do towards a father they love. He looks after everything, he resolves everything and so on. When does a little child ever worry about tomorrow? Never: the father takes care of it. Isn't that right, sister? . . .
>
> . . . All our plans, even on the road to holiness, are perfectly useless: the real plan is in His hand and we need to go to Him like children seeking love.
>
> I want to become little so that I can run more swiftly towards the great final fire. Go on, my sister, no holding back, just trust in the immense mercy of One who immolated His Son to save a slave.[5]

The Leader as Pauper

Poverty of Spirit: The Second Quality of Religious Leadership

"Blessed are the poor in spirit, for theirs is the kingdom of heaven" (Matt. 5:3). With this promise Jesus introduced the Beatitudes—the attitudes that are to shape our thoughts and lives. For those early disciples of Jesus, each one was called by Christ, having renounced everything. However, Jesus calls them "blessed," not because of their privation or their renunciation of things, for these are not blessed in themselves. As Bonhoeffer suggests, "Only the call and the promise, for the sake of which they are ready to suffer poverty and renunciation, can justify the beatitudes."[6] Do we dare to believe that those who do their little part to bring the kingdoms of the world under the reign of God are to stand as paupers amid the riches of wealth, power, prestige, and worldly wisdom? Yes, in our better moments we do believe. Contemplating the wonder of our call, we realize our impecunious condition. Inherent in our call to ministry is the realization that we are not by nature equipped to bear this burden of leadership that God has laid upon us—we all embrace our calling as paupers.

> Consider your own call, brothers and sisters: not many of you were wise by human standards, not many were powerful, not many were of noble birth. But God chose what is foolish in the world to shame the wise; God chose what is weak in the world to shame the strong; God chose what is low and despised in the world, things that are not, to reduce to nothing things that are, so that no one might boast in the presence of God. He is the source of your life in Christ Jesus, who became for us wisdom from God, and righteousness and sanctification and redemption, In order that, as it is written, "Let the one who boasts, boast in the Lord." (I Cor. 1:26-31)[7]

It is hard to desire littleness and nothingness, obscurity and benign respect, in a world obsessed with possessions and positions. It is hard to choose a pauper's station, when everyone around us is scrambling for upward mobility. The temptation that afflicts us as leaders is not that of monetary wealth. Only a fool would choose a profession in the church if the goal were to become rich. Indeed, the "to be rich temptations" among most clergy are not for money but for admiration, respect, adulation, prestige, and power. These are the riches that must be guarded against, if ever we are to experience the freedom of being poor in spirit. God means this poverty as a gift and blessing, not as a practical joke upon those whom God has chosen as leaders in the church.

The desire to be poor in spirit is planted in the deep soil of our inner being, but so is the desire to be popular or magnificent. These conflicting desires and motives reside side-by-side in our deepest interiority—and they do battle with one another, each seeking to gain ascendancy over the other. Richard Foster fears that "within all of us is a whole conglomerate of selves. There is the timid self, the courageous self, the business self, the parental self, the religious self, the literary self, the energetic self. And all of these selves are rugged individualists. No bargaining or compromise for them. Each one screams to protect his or her vested interests. . . . No wonder we feel distracted and torn."[8]

How, then, are we to deal with this invitation to paupery? Carretto says that "it all depends on the spirit in which it is tackled." We empty ourselves of material gain like Jesus in order to take on the physical conditions of a slave. "Poverty . . . nowadays is not just a religious virtue but has become a sign of contradiction in the world. . . . The Gospel can no longer be preached by the rich, it goes against the dignity of the [call]. . . . How will it be possible, sister, to preach [to the world] in the future unless we get down to the bottom of the social ladder and give a genuine, clear, simple witness to poverty?"9

The spirit of poverty embraced by the Christian minister, according to Nouwen, is *the way of the cross,* as *downward mobility* vs. *upward mobility.* Life is often dichotomized between winning and losing, and making it to the top is applauded.10 What a difference is God's way, the Word of God coming down to us and living among us in order to serve us, not seeing divine equality (and power) as something to be exploited. The minister is set apart as a living hermeneut in the midst of a world gone wild in its pursuit of the way of comfort and upward mobility; a way that can never be satisfied, for one gain only increases the ravenous desire for another. The leader, as pauper, stands as a sign of hope that by seeking the way of the cross every human passion may be satisfied and every longing filled.

The words of Carretto and Nouwen are burdensome, possibly too heavy for us to bear. It is said that Bishop Walpole, to a friend who was weighing a call to ministry, adds a reminder of what motivates our ministry: "If you are uncertain of which of two paths to take, choose the one on which the shadow of the cross falls."11 This is the way and spirit of poverty, to which every Christian leader is called. A promise filled with promise.

The Leader as Servant

A Desire to Serve: The Third Quality of Religious Leadership

The body, and the senses, must conspire with the mind. . . . The intellect is powerless to express thought without the aid of the heart and liver and every member. . . . It is always essential that we love to do what we are doing, do it with a heart.12

An essential condition for religious leadership is that we love to do what we are doing and do it with hearty abandon. The desire to be a leader must burn like a fire in the leader's belly. Alone, the desire to be a leader is not enough. There are other conditions and disciplines, certainly. However, unless you greatly desire to be a leader—you won't be. You might occupy the office, but you won't fill the role.

The desire to serve others must be stronger than the desire to lead—so that leadership becomes a means of serving. Being a servant-leader, says Robert Greenleaf, "begins with the natural feeling that one wants to serve, to serve first. Then conscious choice brings one to aspire to lead. That perhaps is sharply different from one who is leader first, perhaps because of the need to assuage an unusual power drive or to acquire material possessions. For such, it will be a latter choice to serve. . . . The leader-first and the servant-first are two extreme types."[13]

With so many shadows and blends falling between the two extremes, what is the difference between the leader-first and the servant-first? Inherent in the call to "servant-first" leadership is to make certain other people's highest priority needs are met.[14] The best test, but difficult to administer in evaluating one's own "servant-first" leadership, is to ask if "those served grow as persons? Do they, while being served, become healthier, wiser, freer, more autonomous, more likely themselves to become servants? And, what is the effect on the least privileged in society; will they benefit, or, at least, not be further deprived?"[15]

Choosing to be a servant leader in a materialistic and power-grabbing society is always difficult since it runs counter to the values of leadership for the sake of power and position. To become a servant leader, therefore, requires the desire to reflect through our leadership that which we see in God:

That God is beautiful is no secret. It is written on every flower, on the sea and on the mountains. That God is immense is secret. All you have to do is look at the universe . . . what is the secret? Here it is: God is a crucified God. God is the God who allows himself to be defeated, God is the God who has revealed himself in the poor. God is the God who has washed my feet, God is Jesus of Nazareth. We are not accustomed to a God like this.[16]

No one chooses a life stance of childlikeness and paupery out of a desire to rule or to be adulated or to gain position and honor. And yet, more than a few end up this way. The poignant question of Paul is applicable here, "You started out so well, what caused you to stumble?"

The answer comes by examining one's motivations. Does the desire toward service continue throughout the long haul? Or do we succumb to the ever-present temptations for popularity, power, and position? Religious leadership, as mentioned in the first chapter, is fraught with its own unique temptations, which leads us to a fourth essential condition for religious leadership: self-examination.

The Leader and the Interior Life

Self-examination: The Fourth Quality of Religious Leadership

Socrates said, "The unexamined life is not worth living." To look after and care for the soul, according to Socrates, was more important than money, honor, and even reputation. The first duty was "to know thyself. . . . For once we *know* ourselves, we may then learn how to *care for* ourselves, but otherwise we never shall."[17] Even the fantasy character Alice in Wonderland asks the question, "Who *in the world* am I? Ah, that's the great puzzle!"

One of the greatest dangers stalking all religious leaders is that of becoming so busy or so bored, so proud or so depressed, that the things they desire most, as well as their actions, go unexamined.[18] Because we want it so much, we assume it is right for us and that we are therefore doing it well.

An essential practice for being an effective leader is, therefore, that one must continually examine one's own life. First, examine the character and structure of one's life when out of the public eye: Who am I? What thoughts do I entertain? To what private and secret activities do I give myself? Second, examine the quality and character of one's life and work when one is in the public eye: What are my values and behaviors as a leader? To what do I give myself? What are the true results of my leadership?

Without exception the Reformers sounded the call and set the example of self-examination. Martin Luther taught that the last activity of each day should be to examine one's motives and actions of the day, and then give the day to God and go to sleep, that while we are out of the way in the hours of this momentary death, God may finish our work, doing for us as we sleep what we could not accomplish in our wakeful hours.[19]

Calvin tellingly describes the need when he says that "without knowledge of self there is no knowledge of God . . . [and] without knowledge of God there is no knowledge of self."[20] John Wesley modeled self-examination as a continuing essential for the religious leader. In his early years he set aside time in every day for the "examination." Later, he began the practice of setting aside each Saturday for self-examination. Finally, in his later years, he developed the habit and inner clock to pause for the first five minutes of each hour to examine the hour past.[21]

Problems enough are evident in congregations whose pastors are confused over their roles as a leader. There are more and deeper problems when a pastor forgets he or she is a person.[22] The study and practice of leadership begins with our interior life—it is our own identity and self-understanding that influences all other leadership behaviors and relationships.

Congregations expect competent church leaders, but they also want pastors who possess inner character and integrity—a congruency between what they profess and what they do. For a variety of reasons, the journey inward is resisted by many. Some are afraid, others are too busy or feel guilty for taking the time, as the urgent demands and problems press in on them.

Bill Hybels, pastor of Willow Creek Community Church, Barrington, Illinois, describes the temptations that were his, as his congregation grew, to not take the necessary time for reflection and self-examination. The results culminated in Bill's spinning into burnout and near breakdown.

In a dramatically honest history of the church, he describes the efforts for growth and the results from growth: "The ministry can be a dangerous business. It is possible to become addicted to fruit bearing. There starts to form in one's head the following formula: more effort + more time = more fruit. If energy can be translated into someone's transformation, then it has to be worth it."[23]

Coming out of the experience, Bill and the elders of the church agreed that because the congregation was so large and demanding, and Bill carried so many pressures and concerns, it was essential that he begin to share the teaching load with other staff. In addition, the elders decided Bill and his family should be away from the church two months a year. During this time he rests, relaxes, and prepares his sermon schedule for the coming year.

The interior life of the leader does indeed work its way out in all other aspects of ministry. The Christian leader "must not be a slave to one's own unexamined passions. Otherwise the souls entrusted to one's care may be subject to manipulation by the supposed career, whose passions are projected on to the relationship."[24] These foundation blocks of Christian leadership—to grow into childlikeness, to journey toward being poor in spirit, to desire leadership in order to serve, and to continually examine one's private and public life—form the vortex of effective ministry. They are not barriers to leadership; they are doorways to freedom. They are not to be enjoined with gloom and doom, but with spontaneity and joy. The possibility of each is given to us as a promise from God.

These promises of God are described in the chapters that follow, through the interior concerns that we label as the call to ministry, the spirituality of the leader, the leader's personal vision, and the managing of one's own effectiveness.

"O Lord, give me beauty of my inner soul, and let the outward person and inward person be the same."[25]

Chapter Three

The Leader's Spirituality

Ministry is service in the name of the Lord. It is bringing the good news to the poor, proclaiming liberty to captives and new sight to the blind, setting the downtrodden free and announcing the Lord's year of favor (Luke 4:18). Spirituality is paying attention to the life of the spirit in us; it is going out to the desert or up to the mountain to pray; it is standing before the Lord with open heart and open mind; it is crying out, "Abba, Father"; it is contemplating the unspeakable beauty of our loving God.[1]

Henri J. M. Nouwen

> **Spirituality:** The means by which we develop an awareness of the Spirit of God in us and the processes by which we keep that awareness alive and vital, to the end that we become formed in the Spirit of Christ.

The Relentless Demands of Ministry

Nouwen aptly observes that we are so obsessed by activity that we have no time for prayer and no time to attend to our own wounds. Likewise, "Our demon says: 'We are too busy to pray; we have too many needs to attend to, too many people to respond to, too many wounds to heal.' "[2] Jesus and his disciples experienced a whirlwind of ministry demands. Mark describes their rat race to the extent that so many people were coming and going that Jesus and his disciples did not have time even to eat (Mark 6:31). Even the promise of a few days of rest was dashed by the throngs who pressed themselves into the cherished aloneness that the weary disciples sought.

Jesus' response to Martha stings us, as we slug it out with the relentless demands of our ministry: "Martha, Martha, you are worried and distracted by many things; there is need of only one thing. Mary has chosen the better part, which will not be taken away from her" (Luke 10:41). Do we really want to be at Jesus' feet when there are so many other things to do? Must we be distracted by the many urgent things waiting for us to do? And when the demands are not so pressing? Nouwen speaks for many of us when he says: "It seems that when there are no deadlines to meet, I organize them for myself. . . . Something as simple as a language course can play demon with me. Why speak different languages if my heart remains dry and angry, upset and lonely?"[3]

The clergy profession, says William R. Nelson, is a balance between knowing "what it means 'to do' ministry and at the same time 'to be' God's person."[4] Without an awareness of this balancing act, it is too easy for pastors to slip among the company of shopkeepers, which may be a noble endeavor but not fruitful for pastors who "are preoccupied with shopkeeper's concerns—how to keep the customers happy, how to lure customers away from competitors down the street, how to package the goods so that the customers will lay out more money. . . . I don't know of any other profession which it is quite as easy to fake it as in ours."[5]

Why all this clutter (even of important or noble things) in our lives? Are we helpless pawns, caught in the jaws of an unrelenting fate? Of course not. One can hardly think of another profession in which the leaders have so much "space" to call their own or more freedom to set their own schedule than that of the parish pastor. Sooner or later we must admit that we tolerate or initiate this clutter, because it serves an important purpose for us. As stressful as it may be, it keeps us from having to face a reality we dread even more—that of coming home to ourselves.

For a variety of reasons, leaders resist giving themselves to being formed within a spirituality of Christian leadership and ministry. Some are afraid; others see no need. Yet others are preoccupied with giving themselves to the work of the church, the ministry being their only thoughts, their only care. Active leaders are needed in the church, but not to the exclusion of intimacy with God.

We serve a church that honors frenzied activity and long hours. We are recognized and rewarded for our doing, and not for our being. This is a condition of our own making. We want people to see us as busy achievers, the hub of the church's activity. Even as we scurry around with our "fuel gauges" on empty, we would rather have the secretary say, when someone calls for us, "I would really prefer not to disturb him just now; he's busy—meeting with someone," than to say, "May the pastor return your call this afternoon? She's spending the morning in prayer." Or for it to be known that we are away for three days of serving—on the "judicatory's board of finance and administration," than that people might hear, "The pastor is at a retreat center spending three days in silence and prayer."

How different from us stand those great Reformers and initiators of God's kingdom: Luther, Wesley, and the others. Wesley left us two brief written insights into his spirituality. The first he wrote about his own discipline: "Here then I am, far from the busy ways of men. I sit down alone;—only God is here, in his presence I open, I read his book; for this end, to find the way to heaven."[6]

He was there, every morning at 4:30 or 5:00 A.M. for his daily retreat, a daily practice for over fifty years. The second brief writing was penned to one of his lay pastors serving a small parish, who complained that he was too busy to find time for prayer and reflection. Wesley sent this reply: "O Begin! Fix some time each day for prayer and scripture. Do it; whether you like it or no. It is for your life! Else you will be a trifler all your days."[7]

Spirituality Supports Ministry

Spirituality for the leader is found in Jesus' invitation to his disciples: "Come to me, all you that are weary and are carrying heavy burdens, and I will give you rest. Take my yoke upon you, and learn from me; for I am gentle and humble in heart, and you will find rest for your souls. For my yoke is easy, and my burden is light" (Matt. 11:28-30). This can also be true for us if and when we practice what Jesus did. After being baptized by John, Jesus spent a month and a half in solitude and fasting while being tested in the wilderness. Throughout the remainder of his life, Jesus often spent time alone, praying through the night before attending to the needs of his followers the next day. It was out of a leader's wilderness preparation that Jesus was so effective in his public life of service. The same would be true for his early disciples as they too passed through their own wilderness preparations into the maturity and vision that a disciplined spirituality birthed in them.

Therein lies the secret of the easy yoke, according to Dallas Willard. In order to effectively follow Jesus in public ministry, we must also follow Jesus into the lonely desert and mountains to be alone with God. It is true that "a successful performance at a moment of crisis rests largely and essentially upon the depths of a self wisely and rigorously prepared in the totality of its being."[8] In other words, "We who are appointed by God to heal others, need the physician ourselves.[9] This necessary relationship between the leader's private solitude and public ministry, according to Nouwen, can only be nourished "when we have met our Lord in the silent intimacy of our prayer" which will enable us also to "meet him in the camp, in the market, and in the town square. But when we have not met him in the center of our hearts, we cannot expect to meet him in the busyness of our daily lives."[10]

This connection between spirituality and ministry is demonstrated in the meeting between Jesus and a demoniac boy. When the disciples asked Jesus why they could not cast the demons out of the boy, Jesus said that this kind could come out only through prayer and fasting (see Mark 9:29). The delights of prayer, fasting, contemplation, caring for the least privileged—are these, more than good intentions, actual practices at the center of our ministry?[11]

The extent one is willing and able to weave the spiritual delights, or the means of grace, into one's own private life will determine one's ability to minister effectively—on the spot. These "on the spot" episodes, according to Willard, "are not the place where we can, even by the grace of God, redirect unchristlike but ingrained tendencies of action toward sudden Christlikeness."[12] The church leader who desires to follow Christ must "accept his overall way of life as [his or her] way of life totally. Then, and only then, we may reasonably expect to know by experience how easy is the yoke and how light the burden."[13]

Ministry and spirituality are intertwined in the scriptural analogy that is apparent in Numbers 7:1-9. The congregation brings its offering before the Lord—in covered wagons. "Then the LORD said to Moses: Accept these from them. . . . So Moses took the wagons and the oxen, and gave them to the Levites . . . according to their service." Depending on the weight of their load, each Levitical order was given an allotment of wagons and oxen. We might apply this physical allocation to the spiritual "weight" of the ministry that we each bear, and say, "According to your burdens, so shall your covered wagons be." God allocates the tools that are needed to accomplish the task.

Any ministry that we can do in our own effort is probably not worth the effort. Any ministry that is beyond our effort requires that we abandon ourselves to the mysterious action that God is able to work in us, and then through us. But this involves a stripping away of the last vestige of hope that we can somehow accomplish the task on our own. Stripping ourselves is not easy. It entails giving up the gifts that are dear to our personality, and that have got us through thus far. It requires giving up our busyness, surrendering the helm, and staying—waiting—without making plans, without making any provision, until we come to our nothingness.

It is a painful thing to enter a ministry that is beyond our own capabilities; and many there be who will never "cast their nets into the deep waters," preferring to fish in the pool, to navigate on their own, rather than to risk the deeps where all may be lost. Perhaps even more terrifying than risking the loss of those things dearest to us, we might discover the wonder of God—who is Almighty. Peter discovered that he certainly was in over his head out there in the deeps; while kneeling on the greatest catch he had ever made, he moaned, "Get away from me, Lord, for I am a sinful person." Had anyone asked him, he would have said, "It is a fearful thing." And for this reason many of us play all around God, being careful not to let God get too close. A friendly visit once in a while? Yes! An abandonment to a consuming fire that will strip away everything that we hold trust in—our education, skill, personality, position, everything? No! At least, not yet!

But this is the invitation of the Spirit to all who accept the call to ministry as a leader. It is a costly spirituality. But in calling us, God has already planted the possibilities of this spirituality within. We have only to give ourselves to it. Carretto describes this penetrating spirituality as "Suffering [which] is the great treasure of life, especially when it is spiritual suffering, mature and solitary, lightened a little at a time. Everything else is like a preparation, but altogether more superficial, light and insubstantial."[14]

We may look at such spirituality and join Peter's dirge, "Get away from me." Or we may see it for what it is: God's way of providing the "covered wagons" to sustain us in our ministry.

Spirituality Renews Vision and Restores Energy

Some years ago, Shawchuck conducted a retreat that was held in a New England monastery. The monastery seemed to be almost totally bereft of priests, and those who were in evidence were elderly and gloomy.

On the office door was posted a long list of events to be conducted by Father George. Late one night, Fr. George and Shawchuck sat down for a visit. Shawchuck commented that the monastery seemed almost empty and that nearly the entire list of events were conducted by Fr. George. Fr. George leaned back in his chair and began to reminisce.

For many years the monastery flourished. The number of men in the house grew to a large number. Facilities were often expanded to meet the needs of the growing community. Then, after many years, no new persons sought entrance into the community. As years passed, those who were there grew old and tired. Some died; many left for residence in another house in Europe. Finally, all that remained were eight or ten old men and Fr. George (in his forties).

From its inception the community was organized around a spirituality requiring the priests to pray together three times a day. As the number of able-bodied persons declined, the community reduced its prayer and worship discipline, complaining that with the added responsibilities each remaining person had to assume, there wasn't time for so much prayer.

Finally the few remaining older men decided to give up the daily prayer routine altogether. They were old; they had prayed enough.

By now Fr. George was carrying the weight of the maintenance of the properties and the necessities of the older men. In order to meet the financial needs, Fr. George began scheduling more and more retreats and seminars, which he led for outside groups.

For a while Fr. George maintained a daily prayer discipline, but it was not the same, for the other brothers were no longer praying with him. Finally, he stopped his daily prayers and gave himself entirely to his work.

After a couple of years, he found himself tired, lonely, and bitter. Only his commitment to the care of the older men kept him going. But now he was too tired to spend the many long hours each day conducting events, and his mind had grown dull; study was difficult and fruitless.

Everything turned from bad to worse. He worried about complete collapse of the entire operation.

Then he recalled the joy and strength he used to receive from the times of prayer with his brothers. Though there were none who would now pray with him, he would begin to spend a half hour each morning in prayer. Once again he would contemplate the beauty of the sanctuary.

After some time, it seemed that his recall of materials studied previously was clearer, and new ideas came with less effort. He decided to increase his prayer time to include a half hour after the evening meal. Again, after some time, it seemed he was more able to lead his many events and care for the house with fewer hours of preparation. He decided to increase his daily prayer time to two hours a day. His entire life and work took on a new meaning and vitality. He now knew God was working with him.

The conversation ended with Fr. George saying, "What you see me doing in my long days and nights is only possible because I have returned to the discipline." Then he quoted a statement accorded to Martin Luther, at the height of the Reformation: "I am so busy that unless I pray more hours every day I won't get my work done."

Indeed, there is a unique spirituality for leadership and ministry. The apostles were not being trite when they said, "It is not right for us to leave the ministry of Word and Prayer." They had discovered that the greatest service they could offer the church was their prayers; unless the Word lived in them, they could not birth it in others.

The Spirituality of Jesus: A Model for All Religious Leaders

It is not platitudinous to say that all you need to study in order to gain a good grasp of the topic of spirituality are the means that

Jesus employed to support his inner self and his work. Herein lies the heartbeat and backbone of spirituality for Christian ministry. As we consider the substance of Jesus' spirituality, consistently ask yourself this question: If Jesus, being the Son of God, felt he needed this to sustain his ministry, can I hope to respond fully to my call without it?

Jesus turned to these elements of the spiritual life here, on earth, as he lived out his ministry. This is who he was, and who he calls us, each one, to be. We have come to call these the spiritual *disciplines,* but a careful study will quite convince us that, for Jesus, these were his spiritual *delights.* In these he found his deepest delight. More specifically, what can be said about the elements of Jesus' spirituality?

The Three Elements of Jesus' Spirituality

1. He carried out his ministry within the context of a small, intimate, covenant community. The Gospel writers make it clear that as soon as Jesus announced his mission and ministry, he set about to form a community with whom he would live and minister. Why did he do this? He did it because he felt the need to relate to an intimate community whom he could count on being there when the going got tough. He recruited those whom he wanted to be with him. He did not create this community for the others; he formed this community for himself. He felt the need to live out his ministry within the atmosphere of a small community, banded together, closer than brothers.

And from within this community of twelve others, he formed an even more intimate relationship with three. It was this more intimate group of three persons whom he desired to be with in the moments of his highest ecstasy (the transfiguration) and the moments of his deepest agony (the passion in the garden). There were moments in Jesus' life that he felt were too personal to share with a group so large as twelve, and then he relied on these three. Jesus would choose many others to work with him, but *these* he chose to be with him. With no others would he have relationships of such intimacy and pathos. They lived *together* in solidarity.

2. Jesus established a rhythm of public ministry and private time. "But he would withdraw to deserted places and pray" (Luke 5:16). "He made his disciples get into the boat and go . . . [and] he went up

on the mountain to pray" (Mark 6:45). "He went out to the mountain
. . . and he spent the night in prayer" (Luke 6:12).

It is clear that Jesus ordered his life and public ministry around a
rhythm, a discipline, of moving from public ministry to solitude and
prayer. He went *to* ministry from solitude and prayer, and he went
from ministry to solitude and prayer. Even though he had his community, he continually found those "lonely places" where he was with
God alone.

3. *Jesus taught by example that six "graces" were vital to his life and
ministry: prayer, fasting, the Lord's Supper, the Scriptures, spiritual
conversation, and worship in the Temple.* These he incorporated into
the fabric of his life in order to sustain his ministry.

Prayer: "And going a little farther, he threw himself on the ground
and prayed that, if it were possible, the hour might pass from him. He
said, 'Abba, Father, for you all things are possible; remove this cup
from me; yet, not what I want, but what you want" (Mark 14:35-36).
Jesus demonstrated that prayer was vital to his life and ministry. And
he taught it as vital to the ministry of those whom he called, teaching
them that some things can happen only by prayer (and fasting).

Fasting: "He fasted forty days and forty nights" (Matt. 4:2). Jesus
fasted as his final preparation for going public in his ministry. Obviously he felt it important to the work he was to do.

The Lord's Supper: "I have eagerly desired to eat this [meal] with
you" (Luke 22:14). This meal was for him. It is striking that as his last
free act before his terrible passion and death, Jesus chose to eat with
his community. He wanted to be remembered by his friends: "Whenever you eat this meal, remember me." He also knew that the meal
was a healing and restoring event: "Whenever you eat this meal, you
will re-member me—you will put the body back together again."[15]
The Lord desired to eat with his community often. Luke was greatly
impressed with the "grace" Jesus found in common meals together, so
Luke's theology is referred to as a "meal theology."

The Scripture: As a boy, it was said of Jesus, his parents "found
him in the temple, sitting among the teachers, listening to them and
asking them questions. And all who heard him were amazed at his
understanding and his answers" (Luke 2:46-47). Matthew's comment
about Jesus' teaching after the Sermon on the Mount was that "the
crowds were astounded at his teaching, for he taught them as one

having authority, and not as their scribes" (Matt. 7:28-29). Two disciples on the road to Emmaus, after the resurrection, discussed their conversation with Jesus: "Were not our hearts burning within us while he was talking to us on the road, while he was opening the scriptures to us?" (Luke 24:32). Shortly after this incident, Jesus met with his disciples and "opened their minds to understand the scriptures" (Luke 24:45).

Spiritual Conversation: The Gospels are filled with serious conversations of a spiritual nature that Jesus had with his twelve disciples, and others who were curious and serious about life's choices. Serious spiritual conversation was part and parcel of the concrete ways Jesus expressed and shared his spirituality with others.

Worship: "He went to the synagogue . . . as was his custom" (Luke 4:16). "So [Jesus] continued proclaiming the message in the synagogues of Judea" (Luke 4:44).

A Spirituality for Religious Leadership and Ministry

From the example of Jesus' life, and from sifting the renascence of literature in spirituality, we are able to summarize and suggest the fundamentals of a spirituality for the religious leader: a spirituality of waiting; a covenantal, communal spirituality; a holistic life-style of spirituality; and the examen of consciousness.

A Spirituality of Waiting

In a society that honors frenzied activity, we, as religious leaders, often feel guilty, or of little value, if we are not running the maze with all the rest. In such a milieu, we often become ashamed even to admit that we "wait" upon the Lord. And many of us don't.

There is a waiting that is merely stalling or procrastinating. This is not the waiting that pastors need to build into their spirituality. The waiting needed is an active waiting. It is not sitting with empty heart and head or succumbing to *acedia*, the devil of the noonday sun. It is waiting in loving attentiveness to the loving Lord. So important in Scripture is this discipline of waiting that almost no story of one called to leadership fails to show the necessity of waiting upon God for effective ministry. The waiting periods may be brief, such as

Jesus' regular retreats to a quiet place to converse with God. They may be a bit longer and in most surprising places, such as Jonah's three-day retreat in the belly of a fish. Living in the spiritual disciplines might seem to be wasting time for many busy pastors. However, for the Desert Fathers, the spirituality of waiting was "wasting time with God." The worried and hassled leaders who wait on God "shall renew their strength, they shall mount up with wings like eagles, they shall run and not be weary, they shall walk and not faint" (Isa. 40:31).

The idea of waiting passively is so foreign to busy church leaders that a clarifying word might be in order. Carretto describes it as the ability to "walk standing still. That is, be terribly active and at the same time totally passive. Incline your will, but keep still before God. Don't move. Don't even move your lips, listen in silence. It's up to Him to speak, it's up to Him 'to carry you.' It's not easy, I can assure you, because silence frightens us and stillness seems like a waste of time to us."[16]

A Covenantal, Communal Spirituality

One of the main reasons for living in covenant with a small group of other pastors or religious leaders is that *the community does your faith when you cannot do for it for yourself.* We should not take lightly the poignant words of Jesus to his community on the night of his deepest agony, "Pray for me." To whom can you confess your sins and lament your failures? With whom can you be in covenant around the temptations that beset you in ministry and the disciplines you so sorely need—but cannot seem to master? With whom can you "let your hair down" without fear of criticism? There is probably only a small group of other clergy or professional church leaders whose experiences track your own, and who are neither appalled nor angered by your confessions.

A covenantal community is not an escape from a fear of being alone. The community helps us to risk gazing into our real selves. The one who seeks fellowship as an escape from oneself is not desiring community, but only a temporary diversion. Dietrich Bonhoeffer urges: "Let [the one] who cannot be alone beware of community. . . . Let [the one] who is not in community beware of being alone. . . . Each by itself has profound pitfalls and perils. One who wants fellowship without solitude plunges into the void of words and feelings, and the one who seeks solitude without fellowship perishes in the abyss of vanity, self-infatuation, and despair."[17]

The days together must be in balance with the days alone, or both experiences will suffer from neglect. We engage in a struggle of constant repair to the covenant, says Walter Brueggemann, to avoid two temptations that dog a covenant spirituality: "On the one hand, to grow so close that one disappears into the other. On the other hand, to grow so distant that the other has no voice in the self. Either way is death. . . . The dominant agenda of spirituality is to keep covenant, to live in the tension between freedom and community."[18]

We know there are (some rare) exceptions, but generally the religious leader must be a part of a community of other pastors, or have no such community at all. The alternative to belonging to such a community is too often loneliness, anger, desperation. The example of Christ and the witness of the church's founders and the reformers is that we are to live within small groups who are in covenant regarding ministry and life.

We often say that the group of clergy to which we belong is our covenant community. It is true we are in covenant as the clergy of a given church. Our ordination vows are covenantal in nature. It is also true, however, that this community is too large and impersonal to offer us the sense of daily support and connectedness we seek and need. This can come only from a small group meeting regularly in covenant.

A Holistic Life-style of Spirituality

It is said that Ralph Waldo Emerson commented on a pastor's sermon: "He had lived in vain. He had no word intimating that he had laughed or wept, was married or in love, had been commended, or cheated, or chagrined. If he had ever lived and acted, we were none the wiser for it. The capital secret of his profession, mainly, to convert life into truth, he had not learned."[19]

The spirituality of the leader must not be exclusively dedicated to, nor separated from, those activities that relate to his or her role. The separation of professionalism from spirituality is, as Nouwen points out, "one of the main reasons for the many frustrations, pains, and disappointments in the life of numerous Christian ministers."[20]

Neither should spirituality be separated from all of human experience. Our relationship with God must have something to do with our own families, friendships, politics, conversations, bodies, exercise, and travels. A holistic life-style of spirituality stresses the connections among the leader's varied interests, responsibilities, and experiences.

The Examen of Consciousness[21]

Integral to a spirituality of leadership is the daily exercise of discernment in a person's life. How am I experiencing the drawing of God through God's love and presence? How is my human nature tempting me, luring me away from God? Welling up within each of us are urges and movements, some for good and some not for good. Nevertheless, these spontaneities happen in all of us. The primary concern in the daily examination of consciousness is not in the morality of good or bad actions. The examen is noticing how God is moving and affecting us. Often, such movements are so deeply imbedded in our affective consciousness that they go completely unnoticed. However, these unconscious motivations influence and determine our actions. Therefore, *consciousness* is prior to and more important than our actions, events, or conditions.

The *examen of consciousness* is a time of prayer, perhaps fifteen minutes once or twice daily,[22] and is concerned with what happens in our consciousness prior to our actions, events, or conditions. John Wesley advised the morning and evening hours for such a review:

Be serious and frequent in the examination of your heart and life. . . . Every evening review your carriage through the day; what you have done or thought that was unbecoming your character; whether your heart has been instant upon religion and indifferent to the world? Have a special care of two portions of time, namely, morning and evening; the morning to forethink what you have to do, and the evening to examine whether you have done what you ought. Let every action have reference to your whole life, and not to a part only let all your subordinate ends be suitable to the great end of your living. Exercise yourself unto godliness.[23]

The daily examen is an intensive exercise of discernment in the leader's life. It is not a striving for self-perfection. The daily examen is "an experience in faith of growing sensitivity to the unique, intimately special ways that the Lord's Spirit has of approaching and calling us. . . . Examen assumes real value when it becomes a daily experience of the confrontation and renewal of our unique religious identity, and how the Lord is subtly inviting us to deepen and develop this identity."[24] The process is an experience of faith in growing sensitivity to God's design for our life, and in the patterns of God's daily dealing with us. This precise grasp of our faith identity seeks to make the examen an intensely personal experiences, as a specific person with a unique vocation and spiritual journey.

The examen is a time of *contemplative prayer.*[25] Without contemplation, the examen is futile. The aim of this contemplation for the leader is the developing of a heart—a consciousness with a discerning vision. It is a gift from God (see I Kings 3:9-12). It is listening to God, being open to God's revealing of ways that are so different from our own (see Col 1:27; Isa. 55:8-9). Without the intent of a discerning heart for vision, the daily examen is fundamentally misunderstood.

Based on the writings of St. Ignatius of Loyola, five steps can be identified to help the leader develop an inner listening in discerning the congruence of everything in his or her truly Christ-centered self.

1. Prayer for enlightenment. The daily examen is not self-introspection through memory recall or a review of the leader's calendar. The prayer for enlightenment "is a matter of Spirit-guided insight into my life and courageously responsive sensitivity to God's call in my heart."[26] It is a petition for enlightenment, asking God for help that we may see ourselves a bit more as God sees us. It is far too easy in this technological, global world of ours to become a victim of our own human, natural powers. The Christian faith transcends human experience and capabilities in the discovery of ourselves as mystery.

A prayer: "Help me to be aware of those times when I have been blind and deaf to your presence and to your gifts of love. Help me to see and hear you more clearly, that I may respond more fully to your love and call to my life. Amen."

2. *Reflective thanksgiving.* After a petition for enlightenment, the leader can rest, thanking God for gifts given even in the most recent part of the day—recognizing that even the smallest gift soon grows to include an awareness that all is a gift. Becoming too involved with ourselves and our work, we too easily deny our true selves as paupers, making demands for what we think we deserve or taking for granted all that comes our way. "The stance of a Christian," says Aschenbrenner, "in the midst of the world is that of a poor person, possessing nothing, not even himself [or herself], and yet being gifted at every instant in and through everything. . . . Only the poor person can appreciate the slightest gift and feel genuine gratitude. The more deeply we live in faith the poorer we are, and the more gifted: life itself becomes humble, joyful thanksgiving.[27]

A prayer: "Thank you, God, for all the ways you make yourself present to me—through persons, events, situations. Thank you, Lord, for accepting my love for you. O God, how great you are! Amen."

3. *A personal examination of actions.*[28] This step does not lead us to examine whether our most previous actions are good or bad—it is not making a list of vices and virtues. Rather it is an awareness of our interior moods, feelings, urges, and movements of the Spirit since the last examen—all of which can be discerned in order to recognize the Lord's call at the most intimate core of our being. The important questions for us to ask are: What has been happening in me and to me? In what subtle, affective ways is the Lord with me? How do I recognize him? What has God been asking me and of me? What changes need to be made, and which ones now? What is God's personal challenge to me?

Often there may be one area in our hearts where God is seeking to bring about a conversion. God is "nudging us in one area and reminding us that if we are really serious about [God] this one aspect of ourselves must be changed. This is often the one area we want to forget and (maybe) work on later. We do not want to let [God's] word condemn us in this one area so we try to forget it and distract ourselves by working on some other safer area which does require conversion but not with the same urgent sting of consciousness that is true of the former area."[29] With God's help, we probe this closed-off area of our hearts in an honest attempt to be open with the Lord, and to stay with this moment in which we are personally experiencing the Lord as God confronts us here and now.

In order for such reflection to take place, it is necessary to have an interior quiet time and a place for ourselves—a place where we can be alone with God.

> **A prayer:** "I really do love you, my Lord, in spite of the ways I have missed your presence and have not responded to your love actions in my life. Help me now to be conscious of the ways that I may become sensitive to your desires in all my ways. Amen."

4. Contrition and sorrow. The spiritual song (the Magnificat) of the leader is mostly magnanimous. But Christian joy can be without depth until it is touched by sorrow. Living in a sense of wonder-filled sorrow, our inner, sinful tendencies need to be converted into joy and gladness.

Since the last examen, the leader's sorrow springs from a lack of courage and honesty to respond to the Lord's call. Such sorrow is not of shame, nor depression or weakness. Mindful of shortcomings, the leader's heart has solid footing in the person and work of Jesus Christ.

> **A prayer:** "I'm sorry, God, for failing to respond to your love and for my mistakes and failures. But I rejoice in your generosity and gladly receive your many gifts—and heartily eat at your table with joy and celebration. I'm not worthy of the many gifts you give me, through your constant love. Amen."

5. Hopeful resolution for the future. This final step grows out of the previous four steps. The present discernment of the immediate past helps us to set a concrete course for the immediate future. Now there is a possibility of renewed vision and sensitivity. In the light of my immediate past and present discernment, how do I view the future? In my interior listening, what am I hearing for what lies ahead? Am I depressed, fearful, anxious, peace-filled, angry, hope-filled or excited?

It is in trusting God more completely and in allowing God to lead us, in spite of our weak efforts and present circumstances, that we experience hope in the future. As Paul asserted in his letter to the Philippians, "But this one thing I do: forgetting what lies behind and straining forward to what lies ahead, I press on toward the goal" (3:13b-14a).

A prayer: "Be with me, Lord, ever helping me to respond more authentically to your love. By your help I will love you better from this moment on. Amen."

These, then, are the fundamentals—the substance of the leader's spirituality: waiting before the loving Lord, covenantal community, a holistic spirituality, and the examen of consciousness—all of which are sustained by the means of grace.

The Means of Grace

None of the fundamentals of spirituality for leadership is possible without reliance on the means of grace. The means of grace become the life stream of spirituality for leadership and ministry. Without them, there is no spirituality.

The elements of Jesus' spirituality have been long described as the instituted means of grace—the graces taught by Jesus in word and deed as the means by which we make ourselves open and available to the grace God is always seeking to pour into our lives and upon our ministries. Jesus taught us to order our lives and ministries around these "instituted" means of grace. He taught us that our ministry depends on them, even as his did. We see in the means of grace a rhythm of conversation and silence, community and solitude, eating and fasting, waiting and action.

In addition to the *instituted means of grace*, the church (especially the groups led by the Reformers) pursued the *prudential means of grace*—those things that are simply prudent in the life of the Christian. The "prudential means of grace" are (1) Acts of Mercy: do all the good you can, to everyone you can, whenever you can; (2) Avoiding all harm: avoid doing all the harm you can, to whomever you can, whenever you can; and (3) Attending all the ordinances of the church (worship, baptism, etc.). These fundamentals of spirituality for the religious leader are illustrated in figure 3.1.

Here, then, is a model for us in the ordering of our lives—now that we have accepted the call. It is a model originated by Jesus' actions in the Gospels. And it is available to us for our well-being and leadership effectiveness. What matters is what we do with it—one can imagine that John Wesley would respond, "Oh, begin!"

We often believe that the experiences we confront in ministry cause us to feel, act, and respond in certain ways. To a far greater extent than most of us are willing to consider, however, our interior world creates our contextual reality. *The quality, character, and results of our ministry are a reflection of our spirituality, projected on the screen of the organization we lead.*

In the prayer below, John Wesley expresses this struggle between the daily demands of ministry and his own spiritual life. David Fleming updates the language of Ignatius, in the prayer that follows Wesley's, that each minister might use during her or his time of examen:

Deliver me, O God, from too intense an application to even necessary business. I know how this dissipates my thoughts from the one end of all my business, and impairs that lively perception I would ever retain of your standing at my right hand. I know the narrowness of my heart, and that an eager attention to the earthly things leaves it no room for the things of heaven. Oh, teach me to go through all my employments with so truly disengaged a heart that I may still see you in all things, and see you therein as continually looking upon me, and searching my reins; and that I may never impair that liberty of spirit which is necessary for the love of you.[30]

THE PRAYER "SOUL OF CHRIST"

Jesus, may all that is you flow into me.
May your body and blood be my food and drink.
May your passion and death be my strength and life.
Jesus, with you by my side enough has been given.
May the shelter I seek be the shadow of your cross.
Let me not run from the love which you offer,
But hold me safe from the forces of evil.
On each of my dyings shed your light and your love.
Keep calling to me until that day comes,
When, with your saints, I may praise you for ever. Amen.[31]

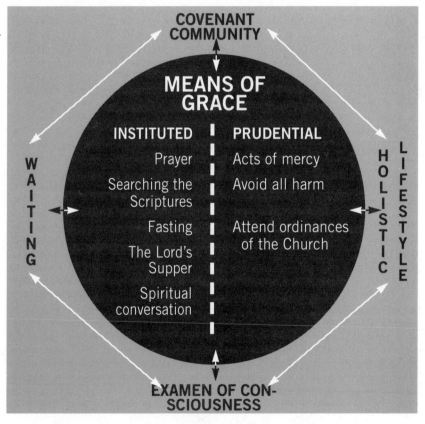

Figure 3.1

Fundamentals of a Spirituality for the Religious Leader

Chapter Four

The Leader's Call

I could have sold most anything
But you called me to be a pastor,
And here I sit among the people:
Pushing prayers,
Swapping jokes,
Trading self-esteem for longevity
Begging for building funds,
Rustling a Catholic now and then
Hawking the urban problems
Picking pockets with committees and boards
Pirating among the open pulpits
Auctioning God to the lowest bidder.
Lord, just exactly what was it you had in mind when we talked
so long ago? Would you please go over it just one more time?

Currently, the gulf between the "ordained" and the "laity" is narrowing considerably. We celebrate this trend as a second reformation correction, a return to the teachings of Scripture regarding the work of the ministry. Peter made it clear that all believers "are a chosen race, a royal priesthood, a holy nation, God's own people, in order that [they] may proclaim the mighty acts of him who called [them] out of darkness into his marvelous light" (I Pet. 2:9). No matter how humble, every believer has a gift to offer. The laity are capable of assuming far more responsibility than the clergy have been willing to accord them.

John Bueno, founder of Latin America Child Care, provides for the care and education of 65,000 children. In doing so he works with thousands of workers—all poor and many uneducated by North American Standards—but they carry on the ministry in a fashion that has captured the imagination of the American continents. Bueno says, "The mission of the Church will be accomplished by the *one talent workers.*" It is true, however, that the ministry of these willing workers is held together around the vision and leadership of its founder, John Bueno, and his leadership team, Byron Klaus and Douglas Petersen.

Every follower of Christ is called to serve. However, not everyone is a church leader. The call to a station of leadership is not given to those who are necessarily more spiritual, or even more gifted. God follows no set pattern in calling those whom God has chosen to be leaders in the church. (Actually, it seems God resists following set patterns for just about everything.)

The Call to Leadership

The development of ministry in the Old Testament begins to set a pattern for the way God calls persons to leadership:

1. Each person is specifically chosen and called by God. There are no calls issued at random. God called Noah, Abraham, Deborah, Gideon, Moses, Isaiah, David, Esther—each by name and for specific purposes. This pattern is immediately established in the New Testament, as Jesus chose individually, by name, those whom he wished to serve with him (see Mark 3:13-19). Each follower stands alone, deciding how to respond to the call. No one and nothing else shields the person at the moment of the call.[1] Where will the call lead? What decisions or sacrifice will the call ask of me? Bonhoeffer says that in order "to answer this question we all have to go to [Christ], for only he knows the answer. Only Jesus Christ, who bids us to follow him, knows the journey's end. But we do know that it will be a road of boundless mercy."[2]

2. An anointing accompanies the call. God equips those whom God calls. This anointing is described through the use of various metaphors throughout the Old and New Testaments. In the Old Testament the anointing with *oil* is often used, but the oil means different things in different situations. For example, it is an anointing of gladness (Ps. 45:7); of divine provision (Ps. 23:5); and of consecration for service (Gen. 30:30; Isa. 61:1ff).

Similarly, in the New Testament *grace* is given to those who answer the call: for example, the grace of joy (John 15:11; Gal. 5:22); the grace of suffering (Mark 8:31; Rom. 8:17); and the grace of power (Eph. 3:20). Hard as it is to understand, the sufferings and joys of ministry are inseparably related. Joy is the fruit of suffering in and for one's ministry (Heb. 12:2).

3. *God asks all that we have—nothing more, nothing less.* The Old Testament early establishes the principle of surrendering everything to God. For Abraham, it was the costly sacrifice of his son Isaac (Gen. 22:1-19).[3] The widow who cared for Elijah had but a measure of flour and a bottle of oil; nonetheless, the prophet asked for it, no more, and no less (I Kings 17:8-16).

The same principle is established early in the New Testament. For example, at the feeding of the 5,000, the disciples complained that they did not have nearly enough for the task. Jesus asked them what they had—and accented this by saying, "Go, look." After finding only five barley loaves and two fish, their mournful response was, "But what are they among so many people?" (John 6:9). Undissuaded, Jesus asked for the five loaves and two fish. He asked for everything they had, no more and no less.

So extreme is Jesus' teachings on this principle that his words are nothing less than jarring to a sensitive person. Are we who respond to the call, in fact, to embrace a poverty greater than the creatures of the wild? Should we not take time to bury our dead or say good-bye to our families? What is required in each follower's life is that he or she "rely on Christ's word, and cling to it as offering greater security than all the securities in the world. The forces which tried to interpose themselves between the word of Jesus and the response to obedience were as formidable then as they are today."[4] We might write Christ's teachings off as the Rabbi's hyperbole, but this yet leaves us with Jesus' insistence that "no one who puts a hand to the plow and looks back is fit for the kingdom of God" (Luke 9:62). This is a hard saying; who can hear it?

4. *Ministry is a cross to bear.* Something of us must be given, and broken, before our ministry will bear fruit. The five loaves and two fish proved sufficient for the task—after Christ had "broken" them,

and given them back to the disciples. The cross is a costly burden to carry, says Macrina Wiederkehr, because the source of salvation requires "us to make a choice. Do we have the courage to accept it? It is costly, yet it brings life. The cross is always costly. It costs us our lives. The dust of our Lenten ashes turns before our very eyes into Easter glory. Our frailty fades into splendor. Our life given becomes life received and renewed."[5]

The cross is there from the beginning. One need not look for a cross, or for suffering, for each follower has a cross, some say destined or appointed by God. There are "some [whom] God deems worthy of the highest form of suffering, and gives them the grace of martyrdom, while others [God] does not allow to be tempted above that they are able to bear."[6] Enduring the cross is not necessarily tragic; rather it is good news, indeed, for it means that out of one's deepest failures and pain arise the possibilities for the most effective ministry. This is, in fact, a universal truism. (For example, alcoholics are the most effective in ministering to alcoholics.) Out of one's brokenness dawns a more effective ministry.

5. *Face-to-face conversation with God about one's ministry is to be a regular part of each day.* Thus the Old Testament describes amazingly frank conversations between God and those whom God called for service. Accordingly it is recorded that "the LORD spoke to Moses face to face, as one speaks to a friend" (Exod. 33:11); God instructed Jonah to go to Ninevah, and Jonah fled from the call (Jon. 1:2-3); God asked Elijah, "What are you doing here, Elijah?" And Elijah felt free to complain (I Kings 19:9-10).

Likewise, the relationship between Jesus and his disciples was characterized by tenderness and intimacy, forthrightness and honesty. They complained to him that his lessons were too long (Mark 6:34-36); they asked deep and painful questions (John 21-25); and they disagreed with his plans, to a degree that even tempers flared (Mark 8:31-33). This same intimacy between God and God's servants today is attested to in the (almost shocking) words of Nikos Kazantzakis, as he describes the effects of the call upon his life and relationship with God:

My prayer is not the whimpering of a beggar nor a confession of love. Nor is it the trivial reckoning of a small tradesman: Give me and I shall give you. My prayer is the report of a soldier to his general: This is what I did today, this is how I fought to save the entire battle in my own sector, these are the obstacles I found, this is how I plan to fight tomorrow. My God and I are horsemen galloping in the burning sun or under drizzling rain. Pale, starving, but unsubdued, we ride and converse. "Leader!" I cry. He turns his face towards me, and I shudder to confront his anguish. Our love for each other is rough and ready, we sit at the same table, we drink the same wine in this low tavern of life.[7]

The Testing of the Call

The "call" of leaders is filled with paradox. Perhaps the greatest paradox is that the One who issues the call is the same One who tests it; sometimes most severely. The examples of testing in Scripture illustrate that the most severe tests come to those who are the most faithful. One thing is certain, however, the testing is not meant as punishment for ineffectiveness or for faithlessness. No, indeed, the testing is meant as a *graduation* to even greater faithfulness and effectiveness. It is meant as a seal of God's approval upon the work already done. Does this sound like idle conjecture?

The testing story of Abraham is probably the most ascetic and well-known in the Old Testament. We shudder at its severity: "After these things God tested Abraham. . . . [God] said, 'Take your son, your only son Isaac, whom you love, and . . . offer him there as a burnt offering'" (Gen. 22:1-2). In like manner Joseph, the one of highest fidelity, was sent to prison. The list could on and on, but these two are enough to give us a graduate-level education in the testing of one's ministry. Were Abraham and Joseph tested because of lackadaisical efforts for God? Hardly! These two had already demonstrated a faith in God and a concern for others that was above reproach. Now God had chosen them to assume even greater responsibilities; one to become the father of a great nation, the other to protect the seed of Abraham from extinction. But before each graduated to new possibilities—*God tested them.*

This same theme of testing, as a hinge event upon which swings the future ministry of the tested one, carries over into the New Testament. Upon Jesus' baptism, the Spirit immediately drove him into the wilderness, where for forty days he was tested. Was this testing to correct some flaw in his character? Was God somehow displeased with him? No! He was tested because he had been faithful, and now an entirely new opportunity was opening up to him, the ministry to the Galileans, and therefore testing must come (Luke 4:1-14).

Strange that God should choose to manage God's personnel this way. Actually, when you think about it, it seems that those who failed the test in the first place were better cared for by God than were the faithful. Consider Jonah. His response to the call within him was to run in the opposite direction, looking for a place to hide—and so God graciously provided him a hiding place. No hiding place for Abraham or Joseph or Jesus—but for Jonah, a hiding place. You see, he had already failed the test; there was no need to test him further. The results were already in.

The Resistance and Acceptance of the Call

Not only must faithful ministry be tested, but it must also be resisted. Without resistance there can be no acceptance of the ostentatious and unbelievable promises that God makes to the called one. The promises of God are seldom resisted because they are too small or undesired—but because God's promises are too good to be true. A good example of this is Zechariah resisting the promise of a son—though he had prayed for a son for many years. Yet when the promise came, Zechariah resisted. It seemed too good to be true (see Luke 1).

This theme of resistance and acceptance, and the plot that without resistance there can be no acceptance, comprise the story line of the entire Gospel of Luke.

Having stated the principle of resistance to the call in chapter 1, Luke then proceeds to demonstrate the essential relationship between resistance and acceptance in the lives of every person he introduces in his book. For each and every one of them, without resistance, there is no acceptance. Sometimes the resistance is within, at other times the resistance is raised by the onlookers—the crowd of observers who resist the promises Christ makes to the people he meets along the way.

The same is true for our calling and our ministry. Without resistance, no acceptance. As is true in most things in the life of the leader, our *internal resistance* is often more belligerent than the *external resistance* to our ministry. But both are important, because without resistance our ministry remains weak, diffuse, and unsure. So the leader must learn to embrace the resistance to his or her ministry, whether internal or external. For these, too, are numbered among the gifts God gives to those whom God calls.

This is not to say that we should surrender to and nurture our resistance. Far from it. It is to say, however, that "all things work together for good for those who love God, who are called according to [God's] purpose" (Rom. 8:28). Nonetheless, when John the Baptist, the son of resistance, had accomplished his purpose for the ministry of Jesus, he was set aside, and in a dramatic manner. The symbol of resistance could no longer further the work of the symbol of acceptance. This is a hard saying, but John understood it, and said without a whimper, "He must increase, but I must decrease" (John 3:30). Small wonder that someone should observe that God's thoughts are not our thoughts, nor are our ways God's ways, for God's ways are higher than our ways, and God's thoughts higher than our thoughts (see Isa. 55:8-9).

Yet it doesn't hurt to ask, "Why the resistance?" The answer is made plain in God's plan for all God's creation; that which is not made strong by resistance cannot survive in a harsh and unforgiving environment. So virtually all forms of water creatures must swim against the currents, because this is the only way their muscles will develop, and the fowls of the air must exert their strength against the winds and the pressure of the air or else their wings will be too weak to endure the tests of transcontinental migratory flights. Everywhere in God's creation the principle holds: Without resistance creatures will not long survive.

The leader's *resistance* to the promises of God help make the leader's *acceptances* strong—so long as the leader does not forever give in to the resistance. And the resistance people exert against the leader can make ministry strong, to face even greater resistance in the future. And why would there not be resistance to such a vocation, which demands self-sacrifice, long hours, minimal financial security, and unselfish concern for others? Martin Luther admitted: "Had I known about it before hand, he would have had to take more pains to get me in. Be that as it may, now that I have begun, I intend to perform the duties of the office with his help. On account of the exceeding great and heavy cares and worries connected with it, I would not take the whole world to enter upon this work now. On the other hand, when I regard him who called me, I would not take the whole world not to have begun it."[8]

The Madness of the Call

No matter how the call comes, it ascends to occupy the primacy of all of one's desires and goals. For those who hear the call, there is no other alternative. So compelling is the call that it has sent marching across the centuries an endless pilgrimage of those who—leaving family, fame or fortune—surrender everything to the call and the Caller. Those who do not understand may think this vocation is nice or comfortable or a waste of good talent, but for those who have heard the call it is the Pearl of Great Price, for which one joyfully sells everything. Is this a madness? Yes! There is a madness in the gospel that has to be lived with—when God calls. But for those mad ones who hear and accept the call, there could be no finer adventure.

Many believe God must have been mad to have called *us*. There are times when we believe we must have been mad to accept. The madness of the call is that it most often takes us along paths we do not prefer, and assigns duties for which we feel most ill-equipped. Gideon felt he was the weakest family member in the weakest tribe; Paul wanted to be a young Jewish scholar, not an apostle; Augustine did not want to be an overworked and overworried bishop; Xavier wanted only to be with his beloved guide, Ignatius, yet at a moment's notice he was sent to India and never returned to Ignatius again; Henry Martin sacrificed the intellectual life of which he was fitted for the missionary life to which he was called.[9]

There is more than madness in the call; there is also paradox. Why must the call, so faithfully embraced, be so excruciatingly tested? Why isn't one yes enough? Does God, like a lover, yearn to hear our acceptance of his proposal over and over again? Or are the tests for our sake? Are not all the trials and doubts that dog the trail of the called one—and the coming out of them—but a sure and certain sign that God is with us? And is not new vision born out of the ashes of our disappointments? Is not, says James E. Dittes, "durable, vital ministry, recalled out of the debris of ministry"?[10]

The call to a vocation of ministry encompasses all that we have and all that we are. It is more than performance and activity, however noble and grand our accomplishments may be. It is a call to utter obedience, which "can be a total, unconditional, joyous abandonment to our one King and Master: or it can be a school for cowardice and an *a priori* rejection of the thing that costs a [person] dearest: personal responsibility. . . . Nothing else matters any more and we ought to burn all our boats behind us. There is no going back."[11]

The call beckons. No matter how tough the situation, no matter what is done or said, no matter how intense the trial—one must obey. It is one thing to *begin* well. It is quite another to *finish* well. Only the one who has learned to obey and follow Christ—in all things and to the very end—will finish well.

Ultimately, the greatest bewilderment of the call prevails for the leader who remains faithful, who gives himself or herself to the demands of the call without reserve, only to realize that all along the way it is not our *work* that God desires, but *us.* Somewhere along the way the faithful leader hears God saying, "Well done, good and faithful servant. Now, I don't want your activity anymore; *I want you.*"

The call is once and forever. But our commitment to it is often tested. Perhaps no one can give oneself completely to God in one grand moment. We give ourselves to God little by little—as we come to discover our deepest longings and temptations. We may be always thoroughly committed, but only to the extent that we know ourselves *at that moment.* As leaders, we are formed and reformed over a lifetime. All along the way; through our successes and our failures, our victories and defeats, our saintliness and sinfulness, our acceptance and resistance, God is at work to make us what we are, but not yet.

Our call to leadership is a formation process, through which God uses all of life's experiences to sharpen and expand our leadership capabilities. Far from condemning our failures and temptations, God uses them as grist for the mill in the formation process. In the mystery of God, our resistance and failures are essential to our formation. Thus Julian of Norwich asserts sin as honor and necessity, not impeding God's goodness; for the pain of our sin stabs us awake to our to weakness and our need to rely even more on God's love and grace.[12]

Chapter Five

The Leader's Vision and Ensuing Mission

Then . . .
I will pour out my spirit on all flesh;
your sons and your daughters shall prophesy,
your old men shall dream dreams,
and your young men shall see visions.
Even on the male and female slaves,
in those days, I will pour out my spirit.
(Joel 2:28-29; see also Acts 2:17-18)

The passage above acknowledges an important quality in the nature and the source of religious vision. Vision is a mystical happening (a dream) dreamed in the hearts of God's servants by the Spirit. This movement suggests at least two important emphases in our call to ministry. First, vision cannot be planned. All the planning tools in our kits cannot bring us to vision. Second, the vision is God's vision, shared with us. As such, vision always comes from beyond us and outside of our context, and it is always larger than life.

The vision is foremost an insight into God's splendor, beauty, and power. And, second, the vision is a clearer recognition of our frailties, fears, and fallibility. Then, and only then, are we in any position to gain a clearer vision of the source and possibilities of our calling and our work.

The entire process of seeing God and ourselves is a spiritual endeavor. Our spirituality is the nourishment for vision; it is in one's inner self where the conditions are set right to see God, oneself, and the possibilities God desires to pack into one's ministry. Any discussion of vision, then, must begin with our spirituality, and not our work. Unless we are captured by a vision of God's greatness and our little-

69

ness, we can never have a full and complete vision of our work. And where there is no vision, the people perish; where there is no vision, ministry perishes.

The Three Dimensions of Vision

We have already described a two-dimensional perspective in each vision that characterizes the leader's call to ministry. There are, however, not two but three dimensions of a vision for ministry. The vision gives (1) new insight into the glory and grandeur of God—an "upward" view of God—and (2) new insight into the severe limitations of oneself—an "inward" view of the self. The perspective becomes three dimensional if the vision gives (3) new insight into how things might be—an "outward" view of circumstances—as our ministries might influence them.

A three-dimensional vision is the "impossible dream," in which God is dreaming God's dream in the heart of those who are called to lead. Such "vision" requires a particular "eyesight" that does not match the seeing of those who are not thus "sighted." So they tend to label the one with vision as crazy or dangerous or harmless but "blind" to reality.[1]

An "Upward" View Toward God

When Moses turned aside from the routine of his daily task to gaze upon the burning bush, he soon discovered that he had entered holy ground. Thereupon began the first of many intimate conversations between God and Moses. The very first word God spoke to Moses was his name—Moses, Moses! This was not to be a conversation between strangers; God knew who Moses was. Neither was it to be a conversation for whomever might care to join in. This was a personal and private conversation, toward a particular purpose.

Then God said: " 'Come no closer! Remove the sandals from your feet, for the place on which you are standing is holy ground. . . . I am the God of your father, the God of Abraham, the God of Isaac, and the God of Jacob.' And Moses hid his face, for he was afraid'" (Exod. 3:5-6). Quivering in his fear, barefooted Moses gained a totally new view of God's everlasting greatness and an honest recognition of his own littleness. This was his vision—one that would alter the course and destiny of his life and work forever.

Then God shared with Moses God's dream for the liberation of the oppressed slaves. God dreamed this dream in Moses. God's dream became Moses' dream—and this is vision, also. Moses' vision is all of these: new insight into the glory and power of God, new recognition of his own incapacity, and a dream of what God's greatness might accomplish through his littleness, if only he dared to "put it all on the line."

To dream an "impossible dream" for one's ministry without a clear estimation of our frail and meager resources would be dangerous, indeed. For we would likely go trooping off to slay Goliath with our broken sling and lop-sided stones, only to find that our blustering arrogance was not enough to produce effective ministry. On the other hand, to recognize our utter inability to perform the impossible tasks of ministry without an energizing view of God's greatness and generosity would only drive us into depression or despair.

So everything depends on a prior insight into the ability of God to accomplish whatever God dreams through us. This insight can neither be planned nor arrived at through analysis. It comes from outside of us, and it is carried into us by God's Spirit. Vision begins with one's internal spirituality. Apart from this, vision will always be limited, or self-centered.

An Inward View of Oneself

Many of us readily identify with Moses' response to God's vision. "Who am I to go to Pharaoh and bring the Israelites out of Egypt? . . . What shall I say? . . . They won't believe me. . . . I'm not eloquent. . . . Please send someone else." With the realization of God's majesty comes a concomitant realization of who we are. We have noble motives and aspirations, but we feel so limited and helpless in the enormity of the task. Moses teaches us how effective one can be in accomplishing God's purpose—after only forty years of preparation in the wilderness. (And we think that three years of seminary is difficult enough.)

In the biblical narrative, Moses is not the only one who must journey far through the wilderness before coming to a clear vision of God and God's capabilities. Indeed, the Scriptures are a chronicle of men and women who were initially immobilized by a puny view of God's greatness, and an exaggerated view of their own limitations. Gideon felt that he was the most ill-equipped to break the embargo against the Israelites; Elijah fled at the words of one woman; Peter described himself as a "sinful man," not fit to be in Jesus' company. Zechariah thought he and his wife were too old for God's promise to come true in them.

In each of these examples, God's dream for these persons was resisted, not because it was too small or beside the point, but because they thought it was too good to be true. They did not believe it was impossible for God to accomplish such things; they simply believed God could not accomplish these things *through them.* (In the vernacular, it blew their minds.)

They thought they were dreaming, not realizing that they were in company with One who could accomplish through them "more than they could ever ask, or think." These great heroes of Scripture, according to the author of Hebrews, teach us an unexpected and often doubted lesson regarding vision: It is more important to pursue one's vision than to achieve it.

All of these [witnesses] died in faith without having received the promises, but from a distance they saw and greeted them. They confessed that they were strangers and foreigners on the earth, for people who speak in this way make it clear that they are seeking a homeland. If they had been thinking of the land that they left behind, they would have had opportunity to return. But as it is, they desire a better country . . . indeed, [God] has prepared a city for them. (Heb. 11:13-16)

An Outward View of the Circumstances

Vision never comes in a vacuum; it comes in response to a real call and is germane to a specific time and place. Responding to vision is risky business. No one in his or her right mind would have undertaken the task set before Gideon with such meager provisions. But, once captured by vision, it made little difference to Gideon, because he could do nothing else. A vision aligns one's thinking and feeling and doing into one common volition, in which one would rather die than not try (see Judg. 6:22-27; 7:2-22).

This quality of vision is beautifully painted into the story of the twelve spies whom Moses sent into the promised land to spy out its conditions. They all went with open eyes and ears, and they all gazed upon the same scene; but two of them saw an entirely different reality from the other ten. Who was painting a true picture through their report? They all were. However, their respective views of God, the congregation, and the formidable task caused them to envision very different realities and outcomes. The two spies had caught Moses' vision. They were captured by a vision of what could be; the others saw only what was predictable.

The lesson in the story of the twelve spies is quite clear: As you think, so you are; as you view things, so conditions will become. The Old Testament writer wrote long ago: "For as he thinketh in his heart, so is he" (Proverbs 23:7, KJV).

Mission: Turning Visions into Reality

Out of vision arises a clear and compelling understanding of what the mission of our ministry is to be. Mission is the bridge that connects vision to reality. If vision is God's dream dreamed in us, then mission is the waking dream, embodied in the life of the leaders and the congregation.

Vision cannot be planned; mission, however, is the grand plan, the achievement of which will likely require many lesser plans, strategies, and activities.

> Personal mission is a new and compelling realization about who we are to be—and what we are to do.

The vision stories in Scripture demonstrate that the leader's mission begins to clarify in the Divine encounter, in which the vision is imparted. No vision, no clear sense of mission. The vision that Moses received from God suddenly clarified the answer for which he had sought forty years: his role in setting God's people free and how he was to go about the task. His mission, once clear, would continue to unfold for forty more years as he slugged it out with the problems, pitfalls, and resistance of leading a reluctant congregation from slavery to freedom.

This same principle is demonstrated in the encounter of the virgin Mary with the divine messenger. Her *vision* is exquisitely stated in the Magnificat, the magnificent song of Mary. But when she said, "Tell God that I am at his service. Let God do to me whatever God wishes," she had *mission* on her mind. Her vision was God's dream, to be dreamed through her. Her mission was her own intensely personal and practical role in birthing the vision into reality.[2]

The vision is God's; it cannot be planned. The mission is ours, and its accomplishment must be planned and executed. Both require that we give ourselves without reservation to each realization.

The prayer of St. Ignatius is an example of the abject commitment that must be given to one's mission:

I am moved by your grace to offer myself to you and your work. I deeply desire to be with you in accepting all wrongs and all abuse and all poverty, both actual and spiritual—and I deliberately choose this, if it is for your greater service and praise. If you, my Lord and King, would so call and choose me, then take and receive me into such a way of life.[3]

We always project onto the external world the inner thoughts, feelings, and attitudes that preoccupy us. You can see the world differently by changing your mind about what you see. If in my ministry I see myself as a pawn in the hands of the bishop or district superintendent, never getting a good appointment or call, I will experience failure and depression throughout my ministry. What other outcome could be predicted? If this tragic attitude is my vision, then I will work to make it so.

How important it is, then, that we choose our thoughts more carefully. God can hardly implant a vision of expansive ministry and noble achievement into a heart preoccupied with petty, fearful, base desires. As we think, so we are. As we are, so will our ministry be.

The vision is God's first, then to be shared with those who dare to believe against all odds. Vision is not stupid or capricious action. Vision is a total giving of oneself to God for the ministry, until God is pleased to share God's dream with us. Vision is fragile; it must be tended carefully. Vision can be blurred, and even lost.

Vision is seeing in and for others what they cannot see for themselves. One very often has to die for one's vision in order for it to become fully real. This is the principle of death and resurrection—the cross and Easter. It is hard to imagine that a pastor can have a vision for a congregation, and then leave it after a very few years in search of a more appealing appointment, or at the first sign of resistance.

The encounter with God means coming to an interior attitude of complete openness to whatever God may wish to give of God's self to us. Such encounters with God change our perception of realities—our rules and regulations about what can be done and how it can be done. And then we are ready to plan our mission—to hear what we are to do.

AN UPDATED "PILGRIM'S PRAYER"

> O Lord, I am not weary of your pace,
> Nor weary of my own patience.
> I provoke you not with a prayer,
> Not with a wish,
> Not with a hope
> To more haste than consists with your purpose,
> Nor do I prefer that any other thing
> should enter your purpose
> but your glory.
> to hear your steps coming towards me
> is the same comfort
> as to see your face present with me.
> whether you do the work of a thousand years in a day,
> or extend the work of a day
> to a thousand years,
> as long as you work
> it is light and comfort.
> (based on "Pilgrim's Prayer," by John Donne)[4]

Chapter Six

Managing Your Own Effectiveness[1]

Things which matter most must never be at the mercy of things which matter least.   Goethe

One of the tragedies of human existence is that many men and women live their whole lives without ever really attracting their own attention. As a result, they get far less out of living than they should—and contribute much less to the world than they could.[2]
                                             Robert R. Updegraff

Our goal in this chapter is to induce you to become more reflective about your work and the results of your efforts to become more *reflective.* It seems peculiar to encourage religious leaders to be more reflective, for the very nature of their calling is one of repose, meditation, and prayer. Yet the common testimony among religious leaders is that they have no time for quiet reflection. However, the one who hopes to be an effective leader must become more reflective. Why? There are at least three answers to this question.

First, we live and work in a turbulent environment. The environment in which the leader works is changing, rapidly and radically. The time-worn paradigms for religious leadership are crumbling. Gone are the old handholds. Misleading are the tidbits of conventional wisdom. Change is the order of the day. Dramatic change always brings uncertainty, ambiguity, and fear. And in the throes of radical change all organizations tend toward ineffectiveness. Only a leader with the capacity to be reflective can guide the congregation through turbulent times.

Second, the priorities are changing, as are the means for achieving them. Peter Drucker aptly teaches that whatever is being done today in all likelihood will be a candidate for abandonment in a few years.

We are not suggesting that the timeless truths and values of the Christian community be abandoned. But the tangible programs, the intermediary goals, structures, and strategies by which the church seeks to embody its core values must change and change again—or else the church will soon be little more than a religious museum, dead in the waters of irrelevancy.

Third, the church's successes of yesterday are killing us today. Machiavelli's words to the prince hold true; more kingdoms have collapsed through success than through failure. In times of great success, leaders feel little need to be reflective. Rather, the impetus is to go, go, go. But to go, go, go when the congregation is headed in the wrong direction will only get it there faster.

The church needs leaders who do not take *themselves* seriously but will take *their job and calling* seriously. That religious leaders should take their job more seriously is one of the church's greatest problems. That you take your job more seriously should be among your greatest concerns. The one thing that will not—cannot—be forgiven is to not take one's calling and responsibilities seriously. Incompetence may be forgiven—but not this flippant sort of apathy.

The Influence of the Leader's Example

A major complaint of leaders today is that they have little influence in their congregations or in the larger community. There is, however, an influence no one can take from you—the influence of your own example. You lead primarily by example, not by precept. There are tools and concepts, but they are nothing compared to the influence of your example (see I Peter 5:3).

The church is a human organization, and it tends to take on the personality of its leader. If you have been at your present charge any reasonable length of time, then your congregation is largely a mirror reflection of you. When others look at your congregation they see you—written out in large script. You are setting the example *of what* and *for what.* If you do not like what you see when you look at your congregation—then change it, by changing yourself. Take all the time necessary to reflect in leisure about the example you are setting in public and in private. Then make the public and private changes necessary to align your example with your desires for the congregation.

The secret for effective leadership is to manage yourself well. Four crucial steps are required for managing one's own effectiveness:

1. How to keep your heart for God, alone, and the passion of your call burning in your belly;
2. How to keep yourself out of the activity trap;
3. How to continue life-long learning; and
4. How to influence all persons who serve in paid or volunteer positions to perform.

These four leadership concerns are influenced mostly by the leader's own example. It does the leader well to ask: If my congregation were exactly like me, would I be satisfied with it? If the response is negative, then the result of one's leadership is anticipated in an ancient proverb: If we do not change our direction, we are likely to end up where we are headed.

Keep Your Heart for God and Your Calling Secure

Keeping one's heart for God is the fundamental concern of the effective leader. This is the only way to avoid spiritual boredom. So important is this that we have already devoted discussion to it in terms of spirituality (chap. 3) and call (chap. 4).

Congregations perpetuate a great myth. When recruiting a new pastor, personnel committees are somehow all programmed to say, "What we want is a leader," which being interpreted means, "What we want is a shopkeeper. Keep the old machine going, don't be too entrepreneurial, don't rock the boat." Then having selected a new leader, the entire system sets about to domesticate the pastor before he or she can do any damage to the status quo.

Accept the fact that you do not have too many hours that are your own. Every day you are greeted with a host of activities and expectations of someone else's doing. You must swim for your life, if ever you are to avoid the rapids of the activity trap. You can be more effective by thinking through to the few things you might do that would make a fundamental difference in the entire organization, and then giving yourself to these only.

Taking Responsibility for Your Own Effectiveness

In manging your own effectiveness, you must consider three questions.

The first question is, **What do I do well?** Notice the question is not What do I like to do? Most leaders start with this question. Focusing on what you do well will often make your efforts second best, for it isn't necessarily true that what you like to do is the thing that you do well, or that what you dislike you will therefore do poorly. There is scant proven correlation between what one likes to do and what one does best.

The quest here is to discover the most important gift God has given you, your charism—and to project this onto all that you do. Then you will be leading from your strength, thus making your weaknesses more irrelevant. Coming to clarity regarding one's charism is often not an easy search. But there is help.[3]

The second question is, **What does this organization need most —and how can I get it done?** Think through this question: What is the one thing that could now bring a new dimension to this church, and all its entities, *that only I can do?* Along the way you will discover many things that might bring new dimensions to the church—*that someone else could do.* Give all of these into the responsibility of others. "We will have to learn to build organizations in such a manner" says Peter Drucker, "that any [person] who has strength in one important area is capable of putting it to work."[4]

The third question is, **How can I project what I do well on that which needs most to be done?**

When you have determined what is the one thing that only you can do, concentrate your time and energies on it, and then you will have broken out of the activity trap. Your work will no longer be shopkeeping or maintenance. Your efforts will make a fundamental difference in the life and future of the congregation. Then you will grow—and so will your effectiveness.

To do this will push you back to the fundamental priorities for your effectiveness in this place. Now you will know what is the arena of your fundamental leadership contributions to the congregation. So concentrate on that one thing—certainly not more than two things, because you can do only one or two things well at the same time. But don't be too hasty about deciding to concentrate on two things, and never concentrate on more. The Lord creates very few, if any, universal geniuses. It is far better to be brilliant in one thing than to be mediocre in several.[5]

The Golden Thread

Often leaders must identify and implement a single intervention that is crucial to the effectiveness of their organization. Searching for the one thing that only you can do or represent is akin to the quest described in many stories in literature in which one searches for the "golden vial," the "golden coin," and the like. The leader who figures out how to do this will often be perceived as a strong leader, and perhaps even described as a hero. To find the "golden thread" is to identify the one thing that will make the greatest fundamental difference in the organization. Often the "golden thread" is a small, almost subtle, change in relationships, or in the programs and ministries of the church.

In every organization there is hidden one golden thread. But taking hold of it is often mingled with risk. There is always a risk in giving oneself to one thing alone, for one may become dominated by it in unholy ways.

Though there is a risk in concentrating on one thing, there is far greater risk in not concentrating. The leadership dilemma here is over which risk to take: the one that may fundamentally change the congregation for the better, or the one that will likely ensure mediocrity throughout the entire system in the congregation.

The leader who believes that there are more than one or two golden threads has not sufficiently thought through the fundamental priorities of the congregation. In chapter 18 of this book you will read the story of WhaJa Hwang, a Korean laywoman who has discovered the secret of finding the golden thread as well as anyone we know.

The Silver Threads

While there is only one golden thread, there may be two or three silver threads—those things that may bring a new dimension to some part of the organization, but are not so likely to cause systemic change throughout. What does the leader do with these silver threads? First, if you cannot find the golden thread, then choose a silver thread and concentrate on it. Second, the silver threads are usually those things of great importance *that someone else can do.* So give each silver thread to one of the best performers in your congregation, asking him or her to concentrate on this alone.

Finally, the third question for prioritizing the few things that can make a difference in your organization is *How can I apply the one thing that I do well to the fundamental needs of the organization?* Having discovered what you do well—your charism—and having decided the one thing that would bring a new dimension to the entire organization, the next step is to project your charism onto the one thing that would bring fundamental change to the entire organization. If the congregation absolutely won't let you do that, then get out of that position. For pastors, this is perhaps the only compelling reason to leave a parish.

Deciding how to project what you do well upon your priority is more an art than a science. Altogether too often the congregation will resist what the pastor does well and will resist his or her giving major attention to the priority, because to do so will certainly require a shift in the way one uses personal time and energy. Many persons and groups are in the congregation who prefer priorities that are not those of the leader, and they have decided already how the pastor should spend his or her time and energy.

A few principles can be listed to help a leader do what he or she does best.

First, *pay the rent.* James Glasse, in *Putting It Together in the Parish,* observes that in every congregation there is a unique set of things a pastor *must do.*[6] When the pastor pays attention to these things, then the congregation will allow him or her to pursue the priorities. By doing these few things, Glasse says, the pastor is paying the rent, and when the rent is paid the congregation will go along with, and even support, the pastor's use of his or her remaining time.

Many of our consultations are timed during pastoral transitions. In one situation the pastor was radically different from his predecessor, at least in the eyes of the previous pastor's faithful followers. Not shaking hands before and after worship, not using the King James version, and not reading from I Corinthians 11 at every communion service were only a few of their complaints. The new pastor had to learn what it meant to "pay the rent," at least until a segment of the congregation had successfully worked its way through the pastoral transition.

We might wish the situation were different, that the pastor did not have to pay the rent. Nonetheless, the leader must accept the fact that he or she is a prisoner of the organization; there are not many hours that one can call one's own. Pay the rent, and then get on with your priorities.

Second, *write out your priorities for future review.* When you have decided your fundamental priorities, state them in writing, along with what you expect to achieve in each of them. Next, write out a brief statement of how you plan to achieve them. The entire plan should not occupy more than half a page. Finally, set aside a day every three months to review what you have written, to see what you have accomplished, and to plan your strategies for the next three months. The simplicity of this principle belies its influence on the accomplishment of your fundamental priorities.

The very act of becoming clear about and committed to your priorities will influence your conversation in private and in public meetings. It will direct the way you view and think about everything else that is going on in the organization, the themes and content of your sermons, and the way you spend your time and energies. What you become clear about and committed to is what you will accomplish.

Amid the trivia of the daily routine, it is easy to forget our commitments and our plans. Writing them down and reviewing them regularly will keep them fresh in your mind and will act like a beacon guiding the use of your time and energies.

Prioritizing those few things that will make a difference in the congregation will help you to keep out of the activity trap. But this alone is not enough. *You must also communicate those priorities to others in the congregation.*

Communicate Your Priorities to the People in Your Organization

Make sure that the people understand you—and that you understand the people. The congregation cannot support your priorities if the people do not know what they are. Tell the people what you are thinking and doing. Organizations are tolerant, but they generate misunderstandings, which are the basic problem in any organization and the barriers to organizational effectiveness. All misunderstandings include problems of communication. So communicate! The guiding principle here is: Do not surprise your people by keeping your priorities secret.

Write out your priorities and send a copy to everyone who needs to know and to everyone upon whose support you must depend to achieve them.

Your written communication should include:
1. This is what I am going to concentrate on.
2. How would this affect you and your interests or responsibilities?
3. What are your priorities? Please tell me!

Prioritizing what will make a difference in your congregation, communicating those priorities to others, and reviewing their responses will give you the criteria by which you can manage your effectiveness.

Manage Your Time in the Light of Your Priorities

Ineffective church leaders are plagued by two extremes in their ability to manage themselves: compulsion and procrastination. The obsessive-compulsive leader—the overworking pastor—will never be truly effective. Rather, he or she will be driven by the urgent and trivial matters of ministry. This malady has been obvious throughout the twentieth century, according to Lloyd Douglas:

> You will do well to avoid contracting this silly business of chattering about how busy you are. Beware of beginning it; for it is as dangerous as a drug addiction. Once you get your little piece down pat, and find yourself repeating it, on all occasions—too busy to eat, too busy to sleep, too busy to study, too busy to do much but talk about how busy you are— you'll never get over it! It becomes an obsession, a mania, a psycho-neurosis! If you've begun it, stop it, while it is yet day![7]

Those who are driven to get more done may actually accomplish less, for the temptation is to get lost in the obsession of urgent things that may not be worth the time and energy. Working *harder* does not necessarily mean working *smarter*. Church leadership is prone to this, in part, because it is difficult to measure one's effectiveness in ministry.

The church leader who procrastinates, the underworking pastor, is also a slave to ineffectiveness. The procrastinator is undisciplined, always waiting until the next day to start a task or to make the necessary changes. Waiting until it's too late, getting work done late, or working frantically at the last minute are all signs of the procrastinator. Some pastors, in their vulnerable moments, have confessed to having habits of watching television forty to fifty hours a week, including Saturday nights, still not having adequately prepared for Sunday morning. If your pattern of time management comes close to this, for the sake of your call and ministry, change it!

There is a lot of talk about managing time—as if one's time isn't managed already. Your time is always managed, never worry. If you don't manage it, someone else surely will. In fact, this is one of the leader's ongoing conundrums—how to wrest the use of one's time away from others. Drucker states that time is the leader's scarcest resource. There are more people and more capital, but time is fixed.[8]

An 80/20 rule comes into play here. We achieve 80 percent of our results in about 20 percent of our time. Learn where your time goes. One of the best tools for managing time is to keep a time log for thirty days, twice a year. However, keeping a time log and not assiduously reviewing it is also a waste of time. This review should be a part of the days you set aside to review your written priorities and plans.

In the review, ask yourself these questions: (1) Which of these activities are not adding to my fundamental priorities? (2) Which of these can be done by someone else? (3) How do I enlist someone else to do them? Remember, getting this done is often more of an artform than a science. According to Drucker, prioritizing large blocks of "discretionary time" is necessary for the leader to work on the important tasks that will make a meaningful contribution to the organization.[9]

Also, get rid of all the time wasters that clutter your own calendar. For example, in the congregation there are likely persons who are members of the local Rotary Club, the Lions, the Jaycees, the Kiwanis Club—everyone of whom wants the pastor to be a member of his or her club. To attend any one of these may consume two to three hours a week. To attend two or three of these will require the equivalent of one day a week. One must ask whether attending these clubs adds to the accomplishment of one's fundamental priorities. If the answer is no, then you must develop the art of saying no gracefully, in such a way that the members will respect you for it.

More insidious than the blatant time wasters are those that tickle one's own fancy, such as making speeches, praying over the meal at a function attended by important people, or offering the prayer at a graduation.

> We know a preacher who spent two days, and a lot of energy, flying to Sweden and back, simply to speak at a high school graduation.

These things may be fun, they may be heady, but if they do not add to the accomplishment of your fundamental priorities, they are time wasters and should be avoided like a plague. Let those who have no clear sense of their priorities waste their time.

Stephen R. Covey, in his best-selling book *The 7 Habits of Highly Effective People,* has identified two attitudes that define a leadership activity: *urgent* and *important.*[10] Urgent activities require immediate attention—NOW! They act upon us and implore us to respond. It is difficult to ignore a ringing telephone. Whether the voice on the other end signals a crisis or a simple request, the urgency compels us to stop what we are doing and react. Urgent matters make for *reactive* leaders.

Important activities, on the other hand, have to do with results— those activities that contribute to the organizational mission, values, or goals. While we react to the urgent, we must save time to pursue the important matters, because the important matters require us to be intentional about our effectiveness. Important matters require us to be *interactive.* A time-management matrix in Figure 6.1 can help assess the difference between the urgent and important things in a pastor's life and ministry.[11]

Church leaders who spend most of their time with urgent and important matters (Quadrant I) address important organizational concerns that need immediate attention. If a leader stays in this quadrant very long, the only alternative he or she takes to the beating of constant pressure is to deal with concerns that are not important or urgent (Quadrant IV). This alternative provides some relief. Thus leaders who lead by crisis tend to spend most of their time in these two quadrants.

Figure 6.1

Urgent	Not Urgent
Quadrant I Crises Deadlines, problems Serious misunderstanding among lay leaders	**Quadrant II** Building relationships among pastoral staff, lay leaders Planning, time off for reflection Continuing education Sabbath
Quadrant III Some telephone calls, mail, reports, meetings and interruptions, etc.	**Quadrant IV** Busy work, trivia work, some telephone calls, reports, meetings, time wasters, etc.

(left axis: Important) (right axis: Unimportant)

Some church leaders spend most of their time on urgent and unimportant matters (Quadrant III). While such leaders *think* they are in Quadrant I, the felt urgency may actually be the expectations of others. Church leaders who spend most of their time in Quadrants III and IV, for the most part, lead irresponsible lives, unable to manage themselves effectively. Urgent or not, these concerns are not important.

The heart of managing your own effectiveness is in Quadrant II. Here the church leader is dealing with important concerns that are not urgent. By concentrating on priorities in Quadrant II (the nonurgent but important), Quadrant I (the urgent and important) concerns are slowly reduced. Quadrant II is vital to managing your own effectiveness, because the priorities in this quadrant deal with building vital relationships, taking time out for personal reflection, thinking important issues through, taking care of oneself, and spending time with God.

For those leaders who spend most of their time in Quadrants I and III, it may seem unrealistic to be in Quadrant II (not urgent but important). Nouwen tells of his own experience when the demands of teaching pressed in on him. While he was taking a prayer sabbatical at a Trappist monastery, some students dropped in on the second day. After struggling to spend time with them in sacrifice of his own time alone, he wrote: "The question, you see, is not to prepare but to live in a state of ongoing preparedness so that, when someone who is drowning in the world comes into your world, you are ready to reach out and help . . . let them be part of your life in God."[12] This is an example of Quadrant II in action.

Build Continual, Life-long Learning into Your Life and Work

The leader's greatest challenge is how to keep one's brain awake, and how to keep hatching new ideas. So learn about learning continuously.

Structure the Organization to Give Continual Feedback

Most things are learned by feedback on experience and by reflecting on the methods and results of one's work. It is imperative, therefore, that the leader ask for feedback—in useful form. Since people do not all learn in the same way, it is important that you teach those around you how to give useful feedback.

In addition, there are more comprehensive forms of feedback. For example, the *examen of consciousness* is a method of continual feedback, carried out between you and God without the involvement of other persons. Whatever form of feedback is best suited to the individual, all feedback is most useful when it is immediate; that is, as near to the experience or event as possible. For example, Bill Hybels, pastor of Willow Creek Church in Barrington, Illinois, meets with a group of staff and elders immediately following the Sunday morning celebration to enlist their feedback on every part of the service.

In addition to these more formal methods of gaining feedback, there is an almost limitless number of ways to elicit feedback, limited only by the extent of one's imagination. For example, the proverbial suggestion box may be used to gain a continual flow of feedback and new ideas. Then there is the use of occasional "consumer" groups, focus groups, written questionnaires, and the like. Continual feedback, of course, is only one way of continuing one's life-long learning to keep one's brain awake and to hatch new ideas. In addition, there are informal, one-time learning experiences and the more formal, long-range learning experiences.

Study the Masters

Read books. Publishers' studies indicate that the average pastor buys only between six and twelve books of any kind during the year and reads only three to six of those books, according to two studies: Evangelical Publisher's Association, and Hartford's survey of 1,500 top church leaders. We are not suggesting that the leader become a bookworm, though that would be preferable to becoming a TV addict, or one who must read the daily newspaper from masthead through the want ads.

But we do suggest that, in order to be effective, one must learn to read according to one's fundamental priorities and learning needs. Find the books that are written by those who are masters at the craft that matches your own priorities. Then do not merely read them; devour them. Further, when you find a book that speaks to you in an out-of-the-ordinary way, devour everything the author has written. Allow the author to become your companion-in-absentia. Always keep a few books on hand that are yet unread, so that they are available when the time comes for you to read one of them. Twenty books read at random will do less good for keeping one's brain awake, and hatching new ideas, than will the thorough digestion of five books written by the masters in one's learning area.

Formal, Long-range Learning Experiences

Whatever else one does for continual learning, there is no substitute for the discipline of long-range learning experiences, where the person is under obligation to study, apply, and reflect on the practical application of one's learning. For most people, these programs provide more structure for continual learning than they are able to fashion for themselves.

This is the era of adult learning. More adults are back in school, and participating in other learning experiences, than ever before. As a result, there is a plethora of guided learning opportunities. In response to this, religious institutions now provide learning opportunities to fit almost every leader's learning interests.

Utilize the Influence of Your Own Example

The influence of your own example is the most powerful motivation you have on the congregation's attitude and performance. For good or ill, your example motivates persons whether you want it to or not. Therefore, your example is a powerful tool for managing your own effectiveness. It is also your most powerful tool to mold the performance and effectiveness of others.

First, *do the things you want others to do.* Remain involved in the ministries of the church. For example, if you want persons in the congregation to visit newcomers or those in the hospital, be a visitor yourself. Then recruit and train others to make effective visits. Think through what an effective hospital visit looks like—then go with the hospital visitors and model an effective visit for them. Hundreds of pastors have tried to avoid visiting by recruiting others to be visitors. It never works because the essential ingredient is missing: the influence of the leader's example. And it isn't enough to set the example once, because people have persistently short memories.

A prime example of the influence of the leader's example, and the need to remain involved in the doing of the ministry, is the role model that President Jimmy Carter sets in Habitat for Humanity. Habitat for Humanity was a little-known ministry until Jimmy Carter quietly picked up a hammer and went to work. No speeches, no large financial contribution, just putting on overalls and working alongside others. This is what captured the imagination of others, who soon found themselves giving their time and effort to building homes for the poor. Would Jimmy Carter have captured the attention of the press by giving speeches on the need for housing for the poor? Would he have succeeded in getting the message of Habitat for Humanity on literally dozens of prime-time news segments? We think not. The speeches of former presidents are hardly exemplary. Every American knows that Jimmy Carter is a wealthy person. For him to have given a few thousand dollars to any particular cause would have found most people saying, "So what? He probably did it for a tax break." But for a former president to join the rank and file, to dirty his own hands—this is newsworthy. Who would argue that his example is far more persuasive than whatever speeches or money he might have given for Habitat for Humanity?

What is also so compelling about his example is that *he continues to do it.* He remains involved; we suspect because he feels called of God to this ministry, and because he knows that if he wants the program to flourish he has to set the example, again and again.

Second, *be tough on yourself.* Set your own standards of performance high. Then demand excellence from others. Be as tough on them as you are on yourself. People tend to rise to the level of expectations a trusted leader holds for them. If you set low expectations for yourself, this is what you will achieve. Likewise, if you set low expectations for others, this is what they will achieve. Here, again, the influence of your own example comes into play. No one rises above the level of his or her own self-expectations, and few workers rise above the example set by the leader.

Third, *create procedures for practicing and rewarding work well done.* Peter Drucker, in *The Temptation to Do Good,* observes that the religious leader has great difficulty in differentiating his or her role as a priest from his or her role as the leader of the organization. In conceding the temptation to protect intentionally incompetent workers, or reward mediocre ministry, the pastor will eventually bring the entire operation to ruin. The most potent influence on the quality of the ministry is that of the leader's example.

A legend sums up this chapter. One of great wisdom was asked by a young leader, "What is the greatest gift in the world?" Without hesitation the one of great wisdom replied, "That, my student, would be all the time you need. . . . But such a measure of time can be given to no one. Each person must help himself or herself to a portion and learn to use it wisely, else many of the blessings of this most precious of all gifts will be denied."

Time carries with it no guarantee that it will serve us—it is only made available to us. We are responsible to learn how to get the most out of the passing hours, days, months, and years. Perhaps the rewarding, and even successful, life is not so much a matter of carrying out the large projects as it is mastering the daily routine of living.[13]

The next chapter revisits the leader's journey inward. When the interior life is not examined, when earlier issues of one's life are not dealt with, or should the pressures of duty and time become too intense, the leader can soon be headed for disaster and, sadly, take the organization down as well.

Chapter Seven

The Dark Side of Leadership

The leader whose mission and task is to care for others . . . must not be a slave to one's own unexamined passions. Otherwise the souls entrusted to one's care may be subject to manipulation by the supposed carer, whose passions are projected on to the relationship.[1]
Thomas Oden

Ambition is attended by some grave dangers. Keep your ambition preserved in a solution of humility. Remember that the most eminent preacher who ever lived humbled Himself and became of no reputation. If it comes to pass that by industry, application, and the proper use of your talents, you should become a ranking member of your profession, known far and wide . . . so be it. If that never comes to pass, and you spend your ministry merely going about doing good, your name unknown except to those whose hearts you have touched by personal contact, you may find satisfaction in remembering that "many there be who have no memorial; who perished as though they had never been; but their righteousness hath not been forgotten, and the honor of their deeds cannot be blotted out."[2]   Lloyd C. Douglas

In the preceding chapters, we have considered the strong role the leader's vision plays in interpreting and shaping reality, for both the leader and the congregation. We can hardly overemphasize the importance of the leader's compelling vision for his or her ministry. For some pastors and other religious leaders, however, the vision that compels them is not from God. George Aschenbrenner delineates two very different sources of vision to which we might give ourselves:

Welling up in the consciousness and experience of each of us are two spontaneities, one good and for God, another evil and not for God.

These two types of spontaneous urges and movements happen to all of us. . . . For one eager to love God with his or her whole being, the challenge is not simply to let the spontaneous happen but rather to be able to sift out these various spontaneous urges and give full existential ratification to those spontaneous feelings that are from and for God. We do this by allowing the truly Spirited-spontaneity to happen in our daily lives. But we must learn the feel of this true Spirited-spontaneity.[3]

It is sobering to consider that the various urges, compulsions, and motivations that compel our leadership may spring from dark sources as well as from God. How essential, then, that the faithful leader nurture a growing sensitivity to the intimate ways God comes to us—and reveals to us, at God's own pace, the mystery of God's design for our ministry.

Virtually every story of "call" in Scripture gives witness that inherent in the call is a vision for one's ministry. Aschenbrenner asserts, however, that there is another witness being made. And for many the motivating forces that drive decisions and actions spring from spirits other than God's Spirit. Jesus told his disciples that "nothing outside a person that by going in can defile, but the things that come out are what defile. . . . For it is from within, from the human heart, that evil intentions come" (Mark 7:15, 21a).

Testing the Spirits

The ancient church was aware that visions, and prophetic messages and actions, may emanate from sources other than God. Jesus, himself, told them: "On that day many will say to me, 'Lord, Lord, did we not prophesy in your name, and cast out demons in your name, and do many deeds of power in your name?' Then I will declare to them, 'I never knew you; go away from me, you evildoers' " (Matt. 7:22-23).

For this reason, the ancient congregation "tested the spirits" to see whether they were of God. This process of testing the authenticity of a vision or action soon came to be called "discernment," or "discerning of spirits." The idea that the spirits must be tested for authenticity remains to this day. For example, the Friends employ a simple method in which anyone may "sound the call," but the community must test it before it is accepted as God's word to the congregation.[4]

The Unexamined Life Is Not Worth Living

Quite apart from the work of the congregation, the leader must regularly examine his or her own consciousness to know the sources of the spirits that influence his or her desires and actions. The dangers and temptations that daily confront the pastor are insidious and powerful. On the one hand, there is the constant adulation and respect shown to one who is "called of God to be our leader." This is heady stuff. On the other hand are the secrets and intimacies that are a normal part of the pastor's work. This is often sensual stuff. Out of these come attitudes and actions that may not be of God, but which the leader may excuse or risk, believing that while others should not succumb it is all right for him or her to do so.

History is replete with the sagas of religious leaders, both famous and obscure, who have fallen prey to their unexamined passions. In her profoundly instructive book *Is Nothing Sacred?* Marie Fortune gives an account of six women in a congregation who were sexually abused by their pastor, who fell in battle against the darksome spirits that affronted him.[5] Paxton Hibben quotes a nineteenth-century preacher who ironically described his own condition before his fall:

> Excuses for moral delinquency are, therefore, usually processes of self-deception. At first they may not be; but at length a man who tries to deceive himself comes into that state in which he can do nothing else but deceive himself. A man can put out his eyes, inwardly, so that at last he will not see that a lie is a lie, and a truth a truth. Deceit may be known to be so at first. It then becomes less and less noticeable and finally the mind is falsified and lives without frankness, openness, truth or purity. And nothing is more common than that men may be in that state, and with a certain kind of exterior morality, making them noticeably good in exterior matters while they have actually lost power of moral discrimination in respect to their own inward habits.[6]

In recent years, organizational literature recognizes that the interior life of the leader, when ignored, can lead to disaster for the leader and the organization alike. This area of study is establishing that the unexamined interior life of a leader represents the dark side of leadership—an "internal theater" that strongly influences the character and quality of the leader's leadership.

The pastor's interior life, left unexamined, takes on a dark side that will be projected upon the congregation. Paul instructed a congregation to "test everything; hold fast to what is good; abstain from every form of evil . . . and may your spirit and soul and body be kept sound and blameless" (I Thess. 5:21-23). When self-deception is operating in the life of a leader, a certain degree of devastation is inevitable. C. Welton Gaddy writes: "The human destruction of deception has divine motivation. Exploding myths and facing facts is holy work (and, not surprisingly, the labor of human beings desirous of good health)."[7]

Expressions of Neurotic Leadership

Leadership behavior tends always to become habitual. Therefore, the leader must continually reflect upon the behaviors and the results of his or her leadership. Further, this assessment must be unflinchingly honest. Apart from this your leadership behavior will become a matter of habit. And this habit may blind you to behaviors and results you would deplore in another person. The bad habits or temptations of the religious profession, when left unexamined, open the door to powerful, entrenched emotions, influencing the leader's subconscious to the effect that wrong looks right, or at least acceptable. Sooner or later an unexamined religious leadership will erode into neurotic dysfunctionality—which both the leader and the congregation exhibit.

Manfred F. R. Kets de Vries and Danny Miller explore the effects of a leader's personality and motivations upon an entire organization. More specifically, they emphasize the dysfunctionality and neurosis of the leader rather than "normal" behavior and relationships.[8] Understanding leadership requires one to go beyond the surface level and probe the leader's inner world, which is called the theater:

> Thus, core themes in a leader's "inner theater" cause him or her to choose certain courses of action, and these themes hold the key to success or failure as a leader. Similarly, the key to a leader's relationship with his or her followers is the psychological forces at play between them. Such forces exist at the intrapsychic, interpersonal, group, and organizational levels. . . leaders can become prisoners of their internal psychic theater so that their actions become self-defeating.[9]

Not all dysfunctional or troubled organizations can be explained by neurotic motivations and behaviors on the part of the leader. However, in studying their sample of dysfunctional organizations Kets de Vries and Miller have concluded that, "the symptoms will be thematically related. They will collectively form a gestalt, or configuration of signs, all of which seem to be direct manifestations of one particular neurotic style."[10]

These five dysfunctional, neurotic styles of leadership are reflected in the organizations led by such leaders. The five styles are the dramatic, suspicious, detached, depressive, and compulsive leadership dispositions.[11] (See Figure 7-1). Each style or personality of leadership, along with a brief description of the structure (authority, procedures, rules, information systems), corporate culture (leadership norms, goals, perceptions, emotions, and fantasies), and strategy (market strategy and innovation) is described below.

The Dramatic Organization

Leadership Style: Dramatic leaders are unconventional risk takers who—bored with bureaucracy and structure—need action, excitement, and stimulation. The dramatic style combines two psychological orientations: the histrionic (theatrical, seductive, and showy) and the narcissistic (egotistical and grandiose).[12] With an exaggerated view of themselves, dramatic leaders sometimes act as self-appointed messiahs who are preoccupied with their own needs while taking others for granted. This leader is unable to connect with the emotional needs of followers, and may even possess a derisive disregard for others. This person takes others for granted within the organization and believes in his or her own entitlement to things—what really matters is the self. "The search for personal glory and power, coupled with vindictive action, is an ageless phenomenon, and has often been regarded as the 'disease' of kings, dictators, and prophets."[13]

Again, it is a matter of degree—healthy narcissism and self-concept are necessary for everyone, including leaders. The charismatic leader, with self-confidence and willingness to resist group pressure, may be the constructive catalyst necessary to "do the right thing" to save an organization that may already be in or near great peril.

Organizational Structure: The dramatic leader's neuroses, projected upon the organization, set in motion the dynamics that cause the entire institution to exhibit the same neurotic dramatic behavior.

Figure 7.1
The Characteristics of "Neurotic" Organizations

Type	Organization	Executive
Dramatic	Too primitive for its many products and broad market; over-centralization obstructs the development of effective information systems; second-tier executives retain too little influence in policy-making	Needs attention, excitement, activity, and stimulation; feels a sense of entitlement; has a tendency toward extremes
Suspicious	Elaborate information-processing; abundant analysis of external trends; centralization of power	Vigilantly prepared to counter any and all attacks and personal threats; hypersensitive; cold and lacks emotional expression; suspicious, distrustful, and insists on loyalty; overinvolved in rules and details to secure complete control; craves information; sometimes vindictive
Detached	Internal focus, insufficient scanning of external environment, self-imposed barriers to free flow of information	Withdrawn and not involved; lacks interest in present or future; sometimes indifferent to praise or criticism
Depressive	Ritualistic; bureaucratic; inflexible; hierarchical; poor internal communications; resistant to change; impersonal	Lacks self-confidence, self-esteem, or initiative; fears success and tolerates mediocrity or failure; depends on messiahs
Compulsive	Rigid formal codes; elaborate information systems; ritualized evaluation procedures; thoroughness, exactness; a hierarchy in which individual managers' status derives directly from specific positions	Tends to dominate organization from top to bottom; insists that others conform to tightly prescribed procedures and rules; dogmatic or obstinate personality; perfectionist or is obsessed with detail, routine, rituals, efficiency, and lockstep organization

Culture	Strategy	Guiding theme
Dependency needs of subordinates complement "strong leader" tendencies of chief executive; leader is idealized by "mirroring" subordinates; leader is catalyst for subordinates' initiative and morale	Hyperactive, impulsive, venturesome, dangerously uninhibited; executive prerogative to initiate bold ventures; diversifications and growth rarely consistent or integrated; action for action's sake; non-participative decision-making	Grandiosity: "I want to get attention from and impress the people who count in my life"
"Fight-or-flight" culture, including dependency, fear of attack, emphasis on the power of information, intimidation, uniformity, lack of trust	Reactive, conservative; overly analytical; diversified; secretive	"Some menacing force is out to get me; I had better be on my guard. I cannot really trust anybody"
Lack of warmth or emotions; conflicts, jockeying for power; insecurity	Vacillating, indecisive, inconsistent; the product or narrow, parochial perspectives	"Reality does not offer satisfaction; interactions with others will fail; it is safer to remain distant"
Lack of initiative; passivity; negativity; lack of motivation; ignorance of markets; leadership vacuum	"Decidiphobia"; attention focused inward; lack of vigilance over changing market conditions; drifting with no sense of direction; confinement to antiquated "mature" markets	"It is hopeless to change the course of events; I am just not good enough"
Rigid, inward directed, insular; subordinates are submissive, uncreative, insecure	Tightly calculated and focused, exhaustive evaluation; slow, unadaptive; reliance on a narrow established theme; obsession with a single aspect of strategy, e.g., cost-cutting or quality, the exclusion of other factors	"I don't want to be at the mercy of events: I have to master and control all the things affecting me"

Dramatic organizations tend to grow at a rapid pace; therefore, the organizational structure tends to lag behind the growth. After the initial rapid growth, the organization will finally fall into patterns of deep decline. Dramatic leaders keep meddling in the routine matters of the organization, with a preference toward intuitive, informal leadership. The chief executive may have too much power, while the managers with the greatest expertise may have the least authority.

Organizational Culture: Dramatic leaders attract followers with dependency needs, followers who idealize their leader by exaggerating his or her strengths and downplaying his or her weaknesses. With the world revolving around the leader as a "hero," the followers subordinate their own individual needs to the leader, who often controls the subordinates through manipulative behavior.

The Strategy: The strategy within a dramatic organization is lived out in the hunches and quick impressions of the leader. The leader is impulsive and venturesome, leaving little or no room for participatory decision making. The real needs and interests of those whom the organization is attempting to serve are often ignored in favor of the dramatic leader's intuition.

The Suspicious Organization

Leadership Style: Leaders who have a suspicious disposition are defensive, cold, vindictive, and hypersensitive. Lacking emotional sensitivity, suspicious leaders insist on the loyalty of followers, and they control others by their incessant involvement in organizational details. Highly secretive and suspicious of others, they cannot get enough information to protect themselves, and they insist on knowing what all others are doing in the organization. With the leader's attention to minutia, the "big picture" is often overlooked. Blind to their own shortcomings, they are quarrelsome and often blame others. Clear categories are often seen in separating the loyal friends from critical enemies—and there is no in-between.

Organizational Structure: Information is power, and the suspicious organization desires to hoard power at the top. Thus vital information for making good decisions at other organizational levels is not shared. Reactive strategies are more common than proactive, since there is never enough good information available for making good decisions. The quest for details becomes a compelling compassion for everyone, as a means of defending oneself against the continual threat of others.

Organizational Culture: Suspicion is everywhere. Reality is categorized into "good" and "bad" and "us" versus "them." The organization is characterized by hostility and insecurity. Problems are distorted and magnified. Since suspicious leaders are extreme controllers, those who are hired and promoted will usually reflect and promote the leader's own views. Within such a climate of distrust, the atmosphere is often depressive. Persons are more concerned about pleasing the boss than doing their job.

The Strategy: With such a preoccupation for details and distrust in monitoring the environment, it takes a long time to make a decision. There is always more data to gather and to analyze. When fear predominates, it is difficult to make decisions that are creative and carry a certain amount of risk. With the emphasis on the leader's external perceptions, strategies are fragmented with little integrating mission or purpose.

The Detached Organization

Leadership Style: Detached leaders demonstrate emotional aloofness toward others. Desiring to be alone and private, they find it difficult to establish close relationships. Detached leaders avoid and repress their own feelings while feeling alienated from others. Given their low self-esteem, it is hard for them to be themselves. In interpersonal relationships, detached leaders sometimes act like they are not in the present—they also seem indifferent to praise, criticism, or the feelings of others. Effective leaders know how to take care of the emotional needs of others; detached leaders don't know how to do this. It is difficult for subordinates to work for detached leadership because they do not know what is expected of them and do not receive specific feedback about their performance.

Organizational Structure: Because of the detached leadership, a leadership vacuum is created at the next level, where "second-tier" leaders see an opportunity to pursue their own interests, since the leader is not available. Sometimes the organization may function well as long as the second-tier leaders provide the necessary warmth and energy needed to provide vision and emotional support for those in the organization. The organizational structure is thus fragmented.

Organizational Culture: There is an emotional vacuum in detached organizations with the political infighting of the second tier managers who attempt to advance their own projects and influence the chief executive officer. The detached organization's climate is insecure and full of conflict, easily becoming a political battlefield.

The Strategy: Decisions in the detached organization are made by only a few trusted members of an inner group. As the detached leader vacillates among the different proposals of his or her subordinates, no clear sense of direction emerges. Ambiguity prevails. If there is a strategy, it is the strongest of individual goals and political maneuvers at the second-tier level of management. Therefore, strategy is splintered as competing forces promote their own causes with no coherent, holistic game plan.

The Depressive Organization

Leadership Style: The depressive leader and organization are worn out, lacking initiative and confidence. Such leaders are extremely passive with a capacity for mediocrity and even failure. With a sense of powerlessness and lack of self-confidence, depressive leaders may also be passive-aggressive in their interpersonal relationships. Feeling that things are hopeless, they are apprehensive about the need for change. Often, depressed leaders will wait for a "messiah" from the outside to make key decisions and rescue the organization.

Organizational Structure: Stable environments will permit the depressive organizations to almost run themselves, surviving longer than those in environments that are experiencing rapid change. Depressive organizations are usually timeworn bureaucracies who have lost sight of the changing environments. If they survive, it is only because their environment is relatively stable. The mission of the organization has been lost to administrative processes that are routinize, predictable, and hierarchical. Programs are inflexible and outdated. The structure tends to be impersonal with poor internal communication.

Organizational Culture: The culture of a depressive organization is another leadership vacuum and lack of initiative and motivation. What pervades throughout the organization is passive, negative pessimism toward the future and the world. People procrastinate and "pass the buck" for organizational failures.

The Strategy: The lack of initiative and mediocrity makes it difficult for any kind of strategy or intentionality. Decisions are avoided, maybe never taking actions toward solving problems or setting a direction. Procrastination is the norm. The focus is not outward on environmental opportunities or challenges; rather, the focus is inward. The success is in the past; it is assumed that the markets of yesterday are the same today. Much energy is spent on handling routine matters and details, the perfect climate for the "activity trap."

The Compulsive Organization

Leadership Style: Above everything else, compulsive leaders desire to control everything and everyone in their lives. The assumption of the compulsive leader is that the more control he or she has over an organization, the more likely problems will be solved. A fear of losing control drives them to desire a world in which everything is predictable and ordered. Compulsive leaders cannot relax while being serious and formal in their interpersonal relationships.

Organizational Structure: As in the suspicious organization, in the compulsive organization there is an emphasis on formal controls, rules, and regulations. The crucial difference between suspicious and compulsive organizations is that compulsive organizations emphasize scrutiny on internal operations and procedures, while suspicious organizations monitor more closely the external environment. Operations are manualized with attention paid to the smallest details of formal policies, rules, and procedures. The structure is also extremely hierarchical with status given to the position.

Organizational Culture: The compulsive organization is a rigid bureaucracy characterized by ritualized roles, standardized details, rules, and procedures. The emphasis on inward activity and organizational rigidity works well with subordinates who are submissive and insecure.

The Strategy: Every move and step is carefully planned out. As with the depressed organization, the environment of the compulsive organization must be relatively stable in order for it to survive. Surprises are avoided with each carefully planned move. Each detail is planned ahead of time; nothing is left to chance.

The five neurotic expressions of leadership, described above, paint a montage of the dark side of leadership—a vivid reminder of the perils of leadership, when the leader lacks self-discipline, and the leadership behaviors go unexamined.

The negative consequences of neurotic leadership can be prevented, according to Kets de Vries and Miller, when leaders develop their capacity for inner reflection. If leaders "pay far more attention to their own interior processes, their own inner needs, their own capacity for such things as honesty and self-reflection and true empathy," they will learn to avoid "traditional management settings, where rote, uncritical or even hyperactive behavior is more the rule," and they will "not only articulate and enact goals to inspire their followers, they [will] also pay attention to their own inner worlds to retain an attitude of reflection, objectivity, and inquiry."[14]

A TEST FOR ASSESSING ONE'S MOTIVATIONS AND BEHAVIORS

Kenneth Blanchard and Norman Vincent Peale have developed a checklist of ethical questions that they suggest will help the leader to examine the source of his or her motivations:

1. Is it legal? Will I be violating either civil law or [church] policy?
2. Is it balanced? Is it fair to all concerned in the short term as well as the long term? Does it promote win-win relationships?
3. How will it make me feel about myself? Will it make me proud? Would I feel good if my decision was published in the newspaper? Would I feel good if my family knew about it?[15]

To which we would add:

---

4. Is it suitable material for prayer? Is this something I am pleased to discuss with God? Or do I prefer to keep it to myself?

---

5. Does it support my ordination vows? Does it reflect the motivations I perceived when I was ordained? If my actions were publicly announced tomorrow, would it reflect well on my colleagues in professional ministry?

These questions suggest a simple subjective exercise, but they help the leader avoid the rationalizations that follow moral failure. For all religious leaders, we urge, also, the examen of consciousness, discussed at length in chapter 3 and focused more directly in a life of prayerful communion with God.

The Perils of Leadership

Quite apart from the five dysfunctional leadership styles listed above, there are other jeopardies into which the religious leader may fall. Kenneth Prior discusses several of these in a unique study of the many leaders in Scripture who did not finish well. It is true that all leaders are potential victims of these perils. It is also true that no profession is more prone to these realities than is the clergy profession.[16]

According to Prior, religious leaders often battle power and prestige, sexual infidelity, impulsiveness, marital stress, criticism, depression, oversensitivity, and inadequacy. All of these, plus the dysfunctional leadership expressions and more, constitute the "dark side" of religious leadership—darksome forces with which many, if not all, religious leaders must do business.

Certainly not all of these desires or appetites are inherently sinful, nor do all signal a life apart from relationship with God. Some, however, are unambiguously sinful and will, if entertained, cause us to build barriers behind which we hope to escape the searing scrutiny of God's love. How shall we relate to one of our colleagues who has fallen prey to one of the clergy sins? For the most part we shoot our wounded.

In *Spirituality for Ministry*, Urban T. Holmes discusses the "sins of the clergy."

Many of us when we think of the sins of the clergy recall the "fallen priest" in literature, such as the Reverend T. Lawrence Shannon in Tennessee Williams' play, "The Night of the Iguana." He was a boozer, a wencher, and had lost his faith. Yet, such a person is less a sinner than he is a casualty. American religion is obsessed with the "warm sins" such as illicit sex and gluttony. . . . What we fail to realize is that pastor or priest who succumbs to the sins of passion is fallen in the same manner as a fallen soldier. These are demons that threaten anyone who sets out upon the path through chaos. Some will lose.

The sins that should concern us far more deeply are those that prevent the ordained from ever exercising their spiritual vocation. These "cold sins" truly violate the mission of the pastor to be a symbol, symbol-bearer, and hermeneut. They arise not from an excess of passion, but from a fear of passion. They are the product of a calculated apathy, sustained only by the embers of a dying soul.[17]

Holmes identifies the "cold sins" of the clergy as acedia (spiritual boredom), the lust for power, insulation from and evasion of confronting those conditions that sap our energies and cause our own spiritual emptiness, the confusion of means and ends, the fear of failure, and extramarital relationships. With what care we must tend our lives, else we will be numbered among the "fallen soldiers" of our profession.

Also, with what care we should "watch over one another, and care for one another." Ours is a lonely and danger-fraught profession. None of us should attempt it alone—no more than would one lonely soldier go forth to fight a battle and win a war. We need each other. Will we ever learn to remember this? Demands for total competency can become heavy. Divine causes can get very sick. Pure meanness can be perpetrated under a guise of righteousness. Meeting behind a sign that says 'church' does not guarantee the people involved will act like a church. Help from beyond oneself is essential for the maintenance of sanity and strength, not to mention a proper spiritual perspective and healthy personhood. A minister can victimize others. A minister can be victimized by others. Every minister needs a minister."[18]

In our discussion of the leader as a person, we have focused on the interior attitudes, spirituality, call, vision, and mission of the person who responds affirmatively to the call of God to enter into ministry. We have explored the ways a minister can manage his or her own effectiveness. Problems in the church are as much the result of the pastor's forgetting he or she is a person as they are the result of the pastor's forgetting he or she is a pastor.[19] As Calvin suggests, "Without knowledge of self there is no knowledge of God."[20] In considering the dark side of leadership, we have suggested that the examen of consciousness must become a regular discipline in the leader's day. Finally, we have recommended that we live and work out our ministries in "communities bound together by covenant." To be in such a community should be the single greatest goal of every religious leader. Many of us will not finish well without it. We need each other to keep us in touch with our humanness.

We will now turn our attention away from the leader as a private person onto the leader as a public figure. In the chapters that follow, "The Changing Roles of Today's Pastor," we will identify and discuss the unique responsibilities and contributions the pastor brings to the congregation—those few, but crucial, contributions that only the leader(s) can make.

PART TWO

WHAT THE LEADER
BRINGS TO THE CONGREGATION

PART TWO

What the Leader Brings to the Congregation

Introduction

The preceding section of this book focused on the leader's interior life. This is the best starting point for religious leadership, because *the leader's identity* at the core of his or her being has much greater influence on the congregation than what the leader *knows* or *does.* This is not to disparage the important skills and wisdom the leader must bring to ministry. One must, however, establish the leader's identity and integrity as more important than what the leader does.

The inner qualities of the leader are of no small importance in a discussion of religious leadership, because the tone of the congregation's life and ministry, is, to a significant degree, a mirrored reflection of the interior qualities and condition of the leader. The congregation reflects the leader's inner, secret life. If the leader is broken, duplicitous, angry, then the congregation will reflect these qualities. If the leader is collected, complete, at peace, then the congregation will (eventually) reflect these qualities.

As we said earlier, the greatest influence a pastor has on the congregation is the influence of his or her own example.

In Part Two, "What the Leader Brings to the Congregation," we will discuss the unique leadership contributions that the pastor brings to the life and ministry of the congregation. These things the leader must attend to, or else they will not be given their place of importance in the life and work of the congregation. Chapter 8 will consider two recent empirical studies regarding the essential qualities and roles for ministry. These studies can bring much insight and instruction to the pastor who has *eyes to see* and *a heart to care* about the true quality of his or her ministry.

Chapter 9, "The Congregation's Spirituality," addresses what the leader brings to the spiritual formation of a congregation by way of his or her own spiritual journey, and by knowing the seasons of spiritual experiences through which God is leading the congregation. The congregation's spirituality opens the people up to be receptive to God's vision for them. Spiritual formation is, in part, preparing the congregation to allow God to dream God's dream in them.

Chapter 10, "The Leader as Guardian of the Corporate Vision," discusses the leader's role in crafting a corporate vision for the future of the church. Personal vision is one thing; corporate vision is quite another, primarily because it is the blending of the personal motivations and visions of the leaders and the people together with God's vision for the congregation. Chapter 11, "Understanding the Congregational Lifecycle," discusses the specific stages of the lifecycle of a congregation, and chapter 12, "The Leader's Role in Congregational Renewal," explains how the leaders may help to prolong the life of a congregation by launching it into continuous renewal stages. The search for renewal requires the ability to lead through change, and sometimes even as it stands on the brink of death.

Chapter 13, "The Leadership Team of the Congregation," considers how the ruling board functions as a leadership team. The pastor cannot provide effective leadership alone. Being "lonely at the top" for most pastors is of their own making, whether from fear, prideful unwillingness, or the inability to invite others to work alongside them. Christian leadership was never destined to be a solitary act.

Finally, Chapter 14, "Don't Forget to Fly the Plane," considers a systems view of the congregation from the leader's perspective. No one else sees the congregation as a whole or as clearly as the leader. It is this capacity to keep one's eye on the entire organization that will prevent organizational myopia and ineffectiveness in ministry.

Chapter Eight

The Changing Roles of Today's Pastor

A modern heresy is the idea that ministry is primarily a career rather than a calling. . . . Any time ministry becomes just another way of making a living, an occupation, or a profession, then a critical New Testament dimension is missing. What is absent is the sense of being summoned, even commanded, by God into ministry. Since the earliest disciples were "called" by Jesus to drop their work and follow him, the church has asked of its prospective leadership the nature and meaning of their call. . . . Whenever in the history of the church the ministry has become more of a career than a calling, the church's mission has stagnated, and the people have suffered.[1]

Donald E. Messer

Two recent studies illustrate the widespread desire among congregations that their pastors come to their task out of a sense of God's summons, and that they keep their hearts for God alone, asking only for an opportunity to serve the congregation and society.

The Pastor's Priorites for Effectiveness

Perhaps no one understands the large church (1,000+ in attendance at the major weekly service) so well as the Leadership Network.[2] In the late 1980s the Leadership Network conducted a study to determine the ingredients necessary for the continued vitality of a large congregation. Beginning with focus groups, Leadership Network then surveyed pastors and lay leaders in a thousand congregations to determine the characteristics of the pastor that are most crucial to developing a large and vital congregation.

The focus groups dealt with two questions. The first question was What must be happening to keep a large church growing and effective? The following cluster responses were given:

Item #1. The church must live out of a vision, which originates with the senior pastor and leaders, and is announced and advocated by the senior pastor, that keeps the church focused on Christ and generates a pervasive attitude of enthusiasm and defines the uniqueness of that church.

Item #2. Preaching that is biblically based, clear and practical; gives practical handles for everyday situations and motivates persons to put the concepts into practice in their daily lives.

Item #3. Worship must be of superior quality, dynamic, with excellent music appropriate to the age and sub-cultures of the people. It must be motivating and healing.

Item #4. The senior pastor must give strong leadership and enable the staff and lay leaders to also give strong leadership, which gives a clear sense of purpose and direction in ministry and which puts strong emphasis on involving increasing numbers of laypersons in carrying out ministries of service. There must be effective and innovative programming to meet the needs of the congregation and the community.

Item #5. A comprehensive assimilation process that puts major emphasis on an increasing number of small connecting groups which develop strong interpersonal relationships and allows every person to feel known and wanted in a large congregation, and provides for continued spiritual growth.

Item #6. The pastor must continually give himself or herself to the daily disciplines that keeps one living out of a heart for God, releases the Spirit within, and enables one to keep a clear vision and sense of priorities for himself or herself and the church.

The second question asked of the focus groups was What are the things the senior pastor must attend to in order to remain effective in his or her leadership, and to keep the large church growing and effective? The following cluster responses were given:

Item #1. The pastor must adhere to private spiritual disciplines, develop "holy habits," love God with a passion—he or she must live in the Scriptures, pray, love God with fidelity and integrity.

Item #2. The pastor must be possessed by a clear vision for the church, be able to articulate it clearly and with persuasion, and be able to advocate and mobilize for it.

Item #3. The pastor must be a skilled personnel manager of paid and volunteer staff—to recruit, train, supervise, and evaluate team effectiveness.

Item #4. The pastor must be skilled in time management to guard time for his or her own personal, spiritual, and professional growth, and to preserve time for dreaming and planning the future of the church.

Item #5. The pastor must be skilled in organizational management—able to understand the needs and culture of the congregation, to understand the needs of the community, to create and model institutional values and goals, and to organize the church around missional objectives.

Item #6. The pastor must be a role model of family life—give time and attention to meeting family needs.[3]

Because many of us never expect to pastor a congregation of 1,000+ in the major weekly service(s), we might be tempted to dismiss the Leadership Network studies as interesting but irrelevant to our situation. However, a later study determined that by and large the clergy role expectations are similar in small, medium, and large congregations.

The Pastor's Best Preparation for Ministry

McCormick Theological Seminary conducted a large, nationwide, study exploring the expectations of congregations and judicatory executives regarding the role expectations of the pastor in congregations of all sizes.[4] The study, conducted in 1989–90, asked a cross-section of laity, pastors, and denominational executives of Protestant churches of all sizes in several denominations to identify the ministry roles a pastor must fill in the church. Norman Shawchuck directed the research project.

The Better Preparation for Ministry Project also began with focus groups to gather information to assist in developing the plans for a large mailed survey. The survey discussed and ranked twenty-one possible ministry roles. The roles are listed in rank order in figure 8-1.

Figure 8.1

Ministry Roles

Ministry Roles	Rank	Mean (Scale = 1-4)
Personal Integrity	1	3.7670
Preacher	2	3.7339
Care Giver	3	3.6527
Worship Leader/Liturgist	4	3.6186
Sense of Call	5	3.4924
Interpersonal Skills	6	3.4829
Personal Spiritual Renewal	7	3.4828
Wisdom	8	3.4730
Spiritual Guide	9	3.3220
Teacher/Educator	10	3.2915
Manager/Administrator	11	3.2912
Evangelist/Witness	12	3.2453
Personal Witness	13	3.2056
Prophet	14	3.1829
Resident Theologian	15	3.1481
Stewardship Enabler	16	3.0047
Denominational Participant	17	2.7978
Leader for Social Justice	18	2.7785
Public Leader	19	2.5599
Scholar/Learner	20	2.4721
Ecumenist	21	2.4403

The definitions of the ministry roles are in the Better Preparation for Ministry Questionnaire, Appendix I. A significant characteristic of the survey results was that the responses of all the participants, of many denominations and churches of all sizes, were in much agreement regarding their understanding of what the pastor must pay attention to in order to be fully effective.

The responses generally clustered the twenty-one ministry roles into three categories, which center around (1) the pastor's personal qualities, (2) the pastor's ministry to parishioners, and (3) the pastor's service beyond the local church.

The Pastor's Personal Qualities (The Pastor as Person)

The first eight roles desired of the pastor by American Protestants focus on the pastor as a person; they are a combination of personal qualities (personal integrity, sense of call, interpersonal skills, personal spiritual renewal, and wisdom). An analysis of the three remaining qualities in this category (preacher, care giver, worship leader/liturgist) indicates that the respondents feel that these three roles have more to do with the personal integrity of the pastor than with learned skills. For example, in defining the pastor as a care giver, the respondents spoke more of the pastor as a caring person than as one who is able to provide care-giving structures or insightful counseling. Likewise, in referring to the pastor as a preacher or worship leader, the emphasis was placed on the worship service as a healing experience, rather than as a homiletically correct sermon or a liturgically correct ceremony.

The Pastor's Ministry to the Parishioners

Roles #9-16 (spiritual guide, teacher/educator, manager/administrator, evangelist/witness, personal witness, prophet, resident theologian, stewardship enabler) comprise the second category and generally have to do with the pastor's ministry to parishioners; the ministry to persons through the pastor's services offered to the congregation and the community.

These ministry activities were ranked as second in importance to the personal qualities listed above. The respondents did not say that these ministry roles were unimportant. Rather, they said that they were important, but not enough. The study did not point to an either-or split. Instead it found that who the pastor is as a person greatly affects the pastor's ability to minister to the congregation and community.

The Pastor's Service Beyond the Local Church

Occupying the lowest rankings are five items that cluster to make a third category of roles the pastor performs beyond the local church. It is interesting to observe that while these roles (denominational participant, leader for social justice, public leader, scholar/learner, ecumenist) are those least regarded by laity and judicatory executives, they are generally the roles often most highly regarded as priorities by theological training institutions.

It is helpful to remember that seminaries and other types of educational institutions are best equipped to train the student in matters of scholarship and ideas so that pastors become better listeners and careful thinkers. Seminaries could be doing a better job in helping to develop the student's sense of personal discipline and personal wholeness, by emphasizing and requiring rigorous study habits, and by providing an environment in which daily spiritual and physical disciplines are offered and participation is expected. Seminaries cannot manufacture winsome students who exhibit a caring persona and an obvious sense of integrity. Many of these qualities are shaped early in life and are honed during the daily grind. But seminary instructors can become examples of integrity who unabashedly discuss their sense of personal call to ministry and who exhibit a deepening evidence of wisdom in matters of faith and life.

The evidence presents a clear and compelling picture of what comprises effective pastoral leadership in the congregation. As consultants to congregations, we are not surprised by these conclusions, because this is what we hear as we visit with the members of congregations, and it is what we are told by the judicatory personnel responsible for the placement of pastors. The church yearns for pastors who are persons of integrity—whose private life and public ministry reflect health and wholeness, and whose leadership brings health, healing, and direction to brokenness and estrangement.

Chapter Nine

The Congregation's Spirituality

"My superiors are more concerned about my holiness than with my work. . . . And that's no small thing for a congregation."
                                                                Carlo Carretto

The literature lists countless different definitions of *spirituality*. Our working definition of *spirituality* for the congregation is the same as for the individual.

Spirituality is the means by which we develop an awareness of the presence of the loving Lord in our lives, and the processes by which we keep that awareness alive and vital, to the end that we become formed in the Spirit of Christ.

For the individual and congregation, there are important dimensions that keep spirituality at a holistic and integrative level. First, it is important that spirituality include the sum of human experience. Every season of experience is indispensable in integrating God's story with the story of the individual and congregation. Second, spirituality is born and grows out of a gifted relationship with the living Lord of all life. Third, spiritual discernment is possible when the person's life is being guided by the Spirit, when his or her thoughts and motives are being transformed by the Scriptures, and when he or she is being nurtured within a community of faith.

The Western Model Versus the Scriptural Model of Spirituality

Spirituality is the means by which persons may be related to the Spirit who is God; it is the joining of a person's spirit with God's Spirit. The Western model, according to Richard J. Hauser, is inconsistent with the spirituality demonstrated in Scripture, which is diagramed in figure 9.1.[1]

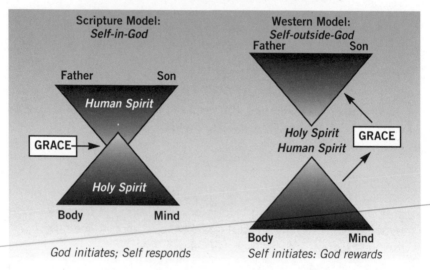

Figure 9.1

Western Model of Spirituality versus
Scriptural (Neo-Western) Model of Spirituality

According to the Western model of spirituality, external behaviors are more important than internal motivations. Because the Spirit is outside the person, the motivation comes from one's own natural capacities. The self is the initiator of good deeds, and God rewards the person by grace outside the person. The focus is on a reward for oneself, now or in heaven.

In the scriptural model, there is an inner power flowing from the presence of the Spirit of Christ within the person. Grace is extended to the total person who is transformed into the likeness of Christ by the freely given gift of the Holy Spirit. The focus is on the love of God and others here and now, not at some later time or event. Such an emphasis is on *inner attitudes and consciousness of the internal movements of the Spirit.*[2] As such, Christian spirituality includes the capacity to develop a discerning heart among the many voices and motivations within, and to determine which aspirations are "seeded" there by God.

The Western model of spirituality has prevailed in the American Protestant Church since the "spiritual awakening" in the late 1800s until the present. The emerging trend in several segments of the Protestant church might be categorized as a neo-Western model, which in many respects resembles more closely the scriptural model of spirituality but set in the context of the Western world. It is fair to assume that this paradigm shift will continue and spread into larger segments of the church.

Spirituality is being formed in the nature of Christ and patterning one's life after the example of Christ. The incarnation reminds us that "Christ is willing to take form amongst us here and today."[3] Many people would never think of missing the Sunday services, and yet many of these persons are not being formed in the nature of Christ. And others who work (often overwork) at their jobs in the church do not follow the example of Christ.

Dietrich Bonhoeffer speaks of formation in Christ's likeness, not achieved by our "spiritual" efforts to become like Christ, but taking place when the forms of Christ—Incarnate, Crucified, and Risen One—"form" in us.[4] To be formed with the One Incarnate means "no more pretense, no more hypocrisy or self-violence, no more compulsion to be something other, better and more ideal than what one is."[5] God loves each person; God became a person. To be formed in the likeness of the One Crucified means a call to suffering, pain, and death. This is the radical nature of the leader's spiritual life, to bear all the suffering imposed upon him or her in ministry as a "fellowship of suffering" with Christ. Such suffering eventually produces endurance, character, and even hope (see Rom. 5:3-5). To be formed with the Risen One is to experience Christ's life in the midst of death, to become a new creation,[6] to become a new leader before God.

Many church leaders fall into the trap of equating ministry with spirituality. Ministry and spirituality are related, but they are not the same. Ministry *consumes* energy. Spirituality *restores* energy. Ministry not supported by an appropriate spirituality is ultimately doomed to boredom, stagnation, disappointment, infirmity.[7]

Spirituality is paying attention to the life of the Spirit within. It is bearing the Spirit's fruit: love, joy, peace, patience, kindness, generosity, faithfulness, gentleness, and self-control (see Gal. 5:22-23); and a mature spirituality cultivates a discerning heart. These fruit stand in stark contrast to the fruit born in a congregation whose spirituality is "nonformed": fornication, impurity, licentiousness, idolatry, sorcery, enmities, strife, jealousy, anger, quarrels, dissensions, factions, envy, drunkenness, carousing, and things like these (see Gal. 5:19-21); not to mention quarreling, jealousy, anger, selfishness, slander, gossip, conceit, and disorder (see II Cor. 12:20).

Espoused Spirituality Versus Lived Spirituality

We have worked as interventionists and conflict arbitrators in congregations of many denominations, and as clergy seminar trainers for twenty years. In our work with congregations and pastors, we are left with an abiding impression: A vast gulf sometimes exists between the spirituality espoused by a congregation and the spirituality lived out by the members.

A group may find itself in serious conflict and yet demonstrate the fruit of the Spirit, or a group may disagree and quickly move to enmities, factions, quarreling, slander, gossip and disorder—while all the time claiming to be deeply spiritual people. These folk would never think of missing church on Sunday morning, but they worship a shadowy God and practice a darksome spirituality. The results are far removed from the fruit of the Spirit that Paul encourages for the congregation. There are various spiritualites, but to espouse a particular spirituality does not necessarily make one a spiritual person.

For example, there is a pentecostal spirituality, demonstrated by such phenomena as glossolalia, prophecies, and healings. However, after having worked with many pentecostal churches in severely damaging conflicts, we observe that not everyone who espouses a pentecostal spirituality is being formed in the nature and example of Christ. As a matter of fact, some of these folk can be surprisingly unlike Christ when they do not get their way in the congregation. Yet, when told this, they respond by saying, "If you were more spiritual, then you would know that God is leading us (and not you)." The same can also

> be said for persons espousing other spiritualites, whether con-
> fessional, activistic, charismatic, Wesleyan, reformed, or
> Catholic. How can this be? Because many congregations are
> taught the corpus or form of their spirituality without ever being
> formed by it, and many individuals handle the elements of a
> spirituality without allowing themselves to be formed by them.

The life of the Spirit within the congregation needs tending, otherwise it will not bear the fruit and ministrations of the Spirit. It is perhaps especially important for liberal social activists and conservative
evangelicals to hear that what the church lacks today is not work,
activity, projects, or a commitment to save the lost or the suffering.
What is missing, or at least very scarce, are the elements of prayer,
meditation, self-giving, intimacy with God, fidelity to the Holy Spirit,
and the conviction that Christ, and not we ourselves, is the architect
and builder of the kingdom. While action is needed and necessary, the
pastor and leaders must be very careful that the many ministries and
activities of the congregation do not smother the more delicate and
important elements of prayer and submission to the pruning activity
of the Spirit. "If action is missing and there is prayer," says Carlo
Caretto,

> the Church lives on and keeps on breathing, but if prayer is missing and
> there is only action, the Church withers and dies. . . . I am convinced
> that if [the church] gave half its energies to prayer, it would achieve
> much better results. . . . I, too, was one of these crazy people, working
> away and not praying sufficiently.[8]

If preaching and liturgy were sufficient to form the congregation in
the nature and example of Christ, then every congregation would
have been so formed long ago. If social action were enough to form
the church in the Spirit of Christ, then the congregations would have
been formed in the nature of Christ within the past thirty years. All of
these—preaching, liturgy, social action, pastoral care, evangelism—
are important, but they are not enough. Lacking in our time is a confession that one may espouse a particular spirituality without ever
becoming a spiritual person. Indeed, the congregation's leaders must

see it as a major responsibility to tend the spirituality of the congregation so that its espoused spirituality becomes its lived spirituality.

The idea that the spiritual formation of the congregation may require something more than the Sunday services; the Wednesday night program, Bible study, or prayer meeting as well as social action; or evangelistic fervor may come as a surprise to some readers. But we suggest that many church leaders have never seriously considered spirituality as something different from worship or study or programmed ministry.

The second reason why many church leaders do not place priority on spirituality and spiritual formation is that the denominational agencies responsible for the selection and oversight of clergy are largely disinterested in the topic, whether for the clergy or for the congregations. Indeed, many judicatory agencies are far more concerned about the ministerial candidate's Meyers-Briggs scores than they are about his or her spirituality. This has left the clergy quite alone to search for their own spirituality, even as they carry the burden for the spiritual formation of the congregations.

Further, while the rhetoric may be otherwise, pastors in almost every denomination quickly discover that such basic pastoral acts as prayer, searching the Scriptures, or offering spiritual direction and companionship are hardly noticed or rewarded by those responsible for clergy placement. Highly rewarded are numbers and activities, the increase in church attendance or membership, the increase in moneys given to denominational administration or missions, or service on a denominational board. We pastors know this and, regretfully, many of us drift into playing the game that leads to greater success—as viewed by the Western church paradigm for successful ministry.

Though it may lead to poverty or lack of recognition in the eyes of other leaders, pastors must take seriously the challenge of forming congregations in an authentic Christian spirituality. In assuming this responsibility, there are certain roles the pastor must fulfill.

The Leader's Experience and Example

The most important thing a pastor brings to the spirituality of the congregation is his or her own experience and example. Spirituality is more *caught* than *taught*. There is much that can and should be taught about spirituality; nonetheless the congregation will never understand or desire the spiritual journey proffered by the Spirit until they see and feel it in the experience and example of their pastors. Jesus knew this, so when persons asked him the way into a deeper spirituality he would usually invite them to follow along with him and learn from his example. *Example,* as we are using it here, means more than what the leader does; it also means what he or she represents by way of personal experience. In matters of the Spirit, it does the congregation little good if the pastor attempts to represent something he or she has not accepted as normative for his or her own life. Perhaps in all the world Mother Teresa represents best the attracting power of the influence of a leader's example in living the Christian life. "Just allow people to see Jesus in you; to see how you pray, to see how you lead a pure life, to see how you deal with your family, to see how much peace there is in your family. Then you can look straight into their eyes and say, 'This is the way.' You speak from life, you speak by experience."[9]

It is easier to tell people that *they* should nurture the spiritual life or how *they* should practice the spiritual disciplines than it is to *do so ourselves.* The fundamental requirement for the spiritual formation of the congregation is the experience and example of the pastor. In matters of spiritual formation, a picture is truly worth a thousand words. In formation, the guide must know the way from personal experience and accompany the sojourner along the way. Merely pointing in the general direction will never do.

The Pastor as Spiritual Companion

Each of us can recall the times when we wished we could just talk to someone "spiritually older and wiser," to be with one whom we could share with regarding our future dreams or our present suffering; one who would listen to us in our present confusion, or just be there for us. How deeply we yearn for someone to be our spiritual companion and guide-along-the-way. Some of us have those spiritual companions.

There are two kinds of guides or directors. One type is represented by the traffic cop, directing traffic from his position in the middle of the intersection. When one is lost, one may venture to ask the cop for directions, but no one ever expects the cop to actually accompany them to their destination. The cop may give a map or point in a certain direction or say, "Go three blocks north and two west," or yell, "Get out of the intersection; you're blocking traffic!" Whatever happens, it is highly unlikely that the traffic cop will leave the intersection to accompany the lost person to the desired destination.

The other type of guide is represented by the host in a fine restaurant. As soon as the guest arrives the host steps forward and asks, "May I help you?" "Smoking or non-smoking?" "Do you prefer outside or inside?" Upon learning the person's desires, the host always accompanies the guest to a desired table. The host never sends the person off with a floor plan of the restaurant or a wave of the arm in the general direction the hungry guest is supposed to go.

When it comes to forming the congregation in the Spirit of Christ, two things of importance stand out in bold relief: First, the pastor must be on the journey; the pastor cannot lead where he or she has never been. Second, the congregation will not journey beyond the pastor; the congregation will not venture where the pastor is not leading. This is a hard saying. It would be more comfortable to work like the traffic cop—to give a map or a few verbal instructions—but spiritual formation is a case where only those who have eyes to see can lead; the unseeing and unknowing cannot. In forming the congregation's spirituality, the pastor's own companionship is his or her best resource.

The pastor's role as spiritual companion of the congregation should be the central work of the pastor's entire ministry. In filling the pastoral role, "Three pastoral acts are so basic," says Eugene Peterson, "so critical, that they determine the shape of everything else. The acts are praying, reading Scripture, and giving spiritual direction. . . . Besides being basic, these three acts are quiet. They do not call attention to themselves and so are often not attended to. . . . Without these practices there can be no developing substance in pastoral work. Without an adequate 'ascetic' the best of talents and best of intentions cannot prevent a thinning out into a life that becomes mostly impersonation."[10]

When we accept the Western model for spirituality, it sounds incredible that the pastor's greatest work is accomplished when he or she is in prayer or searching the Scriptures or offering spiritual companionship to others. Yet, Peterson's understanding of these basic pastoral acts is not unlike that of the leaders in the ancient church who, when they saw their ministry responsibilities expanding, made some hard choices—in order to give themselves to prayer and the Scriptures, rather than doing the many other urgent things.

These, then, are three basic pastoral acts, and each act begins with the pastor. First, the pastor prays, searches the Scriptures and seeks spiritual companionship and guidance. Then, the pastor teaches the members of the congregation how to pray, how to search the Scriptures, and becomes for them a spiritual companion and guide.

The Pastor as Knower of the Seasons

One of the things the pastor brings to the congregation is an understanding of how the Spirit leads the people in their journey. We have described the congregation and individuals as pilgrims on a spiritual pilgrimage; as sojourners on their way to a Presence that calls them onward. Spirituality is a *way*, much more than a *station*. It is a *journey*, much more than a *destination*. For each congregation, indeed for each individual, the journey takes its own twists and turns, for the Call and the Presence relate to each congregation, and each person, for what they are—unique and special to God. Henri Nouwen calls this journey the Way of the heart.[11]

As unique as each congregation's journey may be, it is not capricious. Indeed, the Scriptures and the records of church history have left a witness that God leads the congregation with intentionality through (again and again) certain experiences, some joyful and bright; others sorrowful and dark—but through it all God leads. The entire Old Testament is a story of the journey that the congregation of Israel took into and out of slavery, through the wilderness wanderings, and finally into the promised land. The story continues into the New Testament, where Jesus the Christ guides persons estranged from God, through resistance, persecution, trial, and torture into and out of the wilderness of death and finally into resurrection and life.

Over the centuries the church recognized that its journey is much like the journey of the Old Testament congregation, and much like that of Jesus. It became clear that Christ's sojourn through life could be understood as one passing through certain seasons of spiritual experience. The church named these seasons Advent, Christmas,

Epiphany, Lent, Easter, Pentecost, and Kingdomtide, (or Harvest Tide, or more recently, Ordinary Time). Along the way the church recognized that, indeed, these seasons describe the experience of every congregation, and so the liturgical calendar was organized around these experiences as a way of reminding, guiding, and comforting every congregation, and individual, as they journey through the seasons in their own lives. Liturgical colors and themes were given to each season as a means of visually and poetically communicating the felt experience in each season. The seasons with their respective colors and themes may be suggested as follows:[12]

Figure 9.2

The Seasons of Spiritual Experience

SEASON	THEMES	COLORS
ADVENT	Preparation, Expectation, Longing, Hope	Purple (royalty)
CHRISTMAS	Surprise, Joy, Celebration, Birth, Gift	White (pure, unsoiled)
EPIPHANY	Light, Manifestation, Call, Mission, Witness, Sowing the Seed	Green (new things growing)
LENT	Introspection, Repentance, Tiredness, Discouragement, Death	Purple & Black (royalty & Death)
EASTER	Resurrection, New Life, Redemption, Triumph	White (pure, unsoiled)
PENTECOST	The Holy Spirit, Power, Dynamite	Red (flames of fire)
HARVEST TIDE (Ordinary Time)	Gathering in, Reaping Fruitfulness	Green (growth & fruitfulness)

The seasons of spiritual experience make up the felt experience that congregations and individuals pass through as they progress in their spiritual journeys. Over the years we have served as spiritual companions with many pilgrims, and we have conducted spiritual life retreats for multiplied hundreds of people from across the denominational spectrum. We find that the seasons of spiritual experience make sense to people; they recognize the experiences as their own and can tell us the season that their church is in.[13] With this conscious awareness they are then able to better understand their responses to God's Word, to prayer, and so on.

Many of our readers will not be familiar with or interested in the seasonal aspects of the liturgical calendar, and that response is quite acceptable. The names given to the seasons are not the point in the process. The fact that God does lead the congregation and each spiritual pilgrim through these seasons of experience is the reality. Further, the pastor must understand this and learn how to discern the season the congregation is in at a particular time and know how to lead most effectively in that season. To lead a congregation that is in Lent (that is in a season of introspection, tiredness, and discouragement) as though it were in a Christmas or Easter season of experience will only drive the people deeper into their sense of unworthiness and abandonment. This is not *leading* the congregation so much as it would be *misleading* the congregation because the pastor has missed the signs of the season into which God has called the congregation. This leading would be going contrary to the people's experience and God's leading. One of the greatest gifts a pastor can bring to the congregation's spiritual journey is to know where the people are in their season of spiritual experience, and then act as a companion to them *where they are*, not where the pastor thinks they ought to be at that time.

Pastors who live out the Western model of spirituality, discussed above, have difficulty when relating to the seasons of spiritual experience, because it is not self-controlling or oriented enough toward work or action. The Western model of spirituality naturally leads to a spirituality of doing; keeping busy, being good, meriting God's favor, earning rewards, escaping judgments. All these things must be done to get God's attention or the attention of the powerful people among us, because God remains outside us.

The scriptural model, however, places the Spirit of God inside us. Thus to be in conscious relationship with God requires that we develop the capacity to be still, to be transparent, and to pay attention to the gentle nudges, imaginations, and insights by which the Spirit guides us ever closer to ourselves and to God. That God speaks with the still, small voice is everywhere apparent in scripture.

The scriptural model of spirituality presents a constant movement between action and passivity, doing and reflection, experience and discernment, solitude and community, silence and conversation. Indeed, all the actions and experiences of one's life, both good and bad, become grist for the mill, used by the Spirit to instruct, change, and form us in Christ's nature. In the scriptural model there can be no Easter without Lent and no Epiphany without the preparation of Advent and the pure gift of Christmas.

To see the spiritual life as a *journey* rather than a *fixed condition* totally rearranges the leader's thinking about how to support the congregation's spiritual growth. Perhaps of greatest importance is that the leader may then gain a new appreciation for the influence of his or her example. If you are not already on the journey, then we beg you to begin today. If you are already on the journey, then we encourage you to continue—to the journey's end. "My exodus does not end," says Carlo Carretto, "when I die in my bed, but when I die on the Cross of Christ. Now [this] is something to fear. And we want to shout, 'No one can go that far!' And we would be right. But we know that the miracle worker is love itself. God is God . . . the God of the impossible."[14]

We will now address certain abilities that the congregation and its individual members must develop in order to progress along the way of spiritual formation. These abilities (or prerequisites) are, for the most part learned, and the leader must make provision for them to be taught to persons who are exhibiting signs of wanting to begin their own spiritual journey.

The Prerequisites for Spiritual Formation

The scriptural model of spiritual formation suggests that the pilgrim must develop dispositions and abilities that enable the person to listen to the Word *from* within. These prerequisites have to do with the ability to act, to experience life, and then to reflect on the experience; to articulate the experience for oneself and to others; and to discern the movements of the Spirit gently and persistently shaping and directing the inner self and outer life as lived day-by-day.

The prerequisites are not necessarily developed in a linear order. Rather, they are touchstones to be visited again and again as one progresses on the spiritual journey, as depicted in figure 9.3:

Figure 9.3
The Prerequisites for Spiritual Formation

Community

Pray with mind and heart; meditate on Scriptures

Discern God's will and direction for our life

Reflect on life's experiences

Tell our story to another whom we trust

Solitude

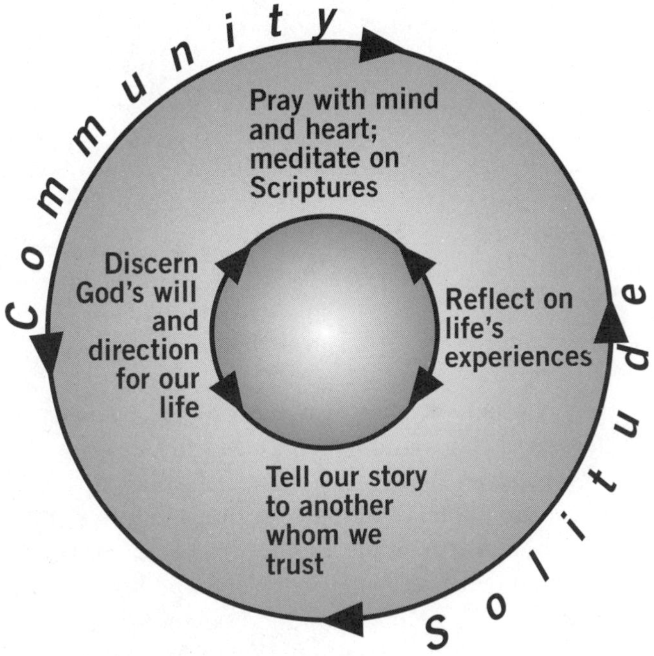

An understanding of these prerequisites for spiritual formation is of great utility to the pastor who chooses to take seriously his or her singular opportunity to form the congregation in Christ's nature. They immediately suggest certain crucial needs both for teaching and for community experience: for example, to teach persons how to pray affectively (praying with mind and heart and body together); to assist busy, noisy people to sustain silence without anxiety, in order to get in touch with the interior movements of the Spirit; to teach people how to reflect on their life experiences in such a way as to discern God's leading in their lives; to create small, trusting communities in which persons may articulate their experiences and hear the voice of God responding through the conversations and relationships with the other members of the group; and finally, to teach people the ways and means of discerning the will of God throughout the totality of life.

The Balance Between Solitude and Community

In the Western model of spirituality we have no difficulty understanding the *individual* and *solitary* aspects of spirituality. Indeed, the model is based on a premise of solitary Christians, each having exceedingly private access to God, and each carrying solitary responsibility for his or her life. Then, these solitary souls gather occasionally for community worship or work. However, our own experience tells us that only the superstar saints make the journey well alone. Maybe a few "saints" and some isolated hermits do. But the rest of us weaklings, whose promises to God always far exceed our practices, whose spirits are emaciated from lack of bread for the journey, and whose trail is marked with the scars of our many failings and fallings—we know that we cannot make this journey alone. Nonetheless we keep trying, because we know no other way.

But there is another way, and it is the way of covenant communities, small groups of spiritual pilgrims journeying together, each sharing the others' burdens, and each holding the other up—in the most intimate and private affairs of life and journey. So we say then that an essential ingredient for forming the congregation in the nature of Christ is the movement between being alone and being together, sustaining solitude and community. Indeed, silence and solitude, and spiritual conversation and community, form the vortex in which the other prerequisites for deepening the congregation's spirituality hold together. So interrelated and interdependent are these two experi-

ences in the formative process that those who best understand the
means by which a congregation can be formed in the nature of Christ
consistently claim both conditions as vital. We recognize, then, with
Dietrich Bonhoeffer, that "One who wants fellowship without solitude
plunges into the void of words and feelings, and one who seeks solitude without fellowship perishes in the abyss of vanity, self-infatuation, and despair. Let him who cannot be alone beware of community.
Let him who is not in community beware of being alone."[15]

Spiritual pilgrims need other pilgrims who will speak God's Word,
especially when Christ's Word in one's own heart is weaker than the
Christ in the word of a fellow pilgrim, when one's own heart is uncertain and the fellow pilgrim's is sure.[16]

Nouwen points to the dangers in being alone on the spiritual journey: "Boredom, resentment and depression are all sentiments of dis-
connectedness. They present life to us as a broken connection. They
give us a sense of not-belonging. . . . We perceive ourselves as isolated
individuals surrounded, perhaps, by many people, but not really part
of any supporting or nurturing community."[17] This has been the experience of Christians from the beginning. In fact, participation in the
ancient church presupposed small groups, characterized by mutual
accountability and care. This was true of the Jerusalem movement
and of Paul's wider missionary work.

The fledgling communities organized by Paul met regularly in private homes, each group with its own network of relationships and
associations. These groups achieved a high level of intimacy among
their respective members while, at the same time, enjoying a strong
identification and bonding with the larger religious movement spread-
ing across the land.[18] The conviction that spiritual nurture and growth
depend on small communities of persons who meet regularly for
mutual guidance and support has survived to this day.

In chapter 3, we discussed the need Jesus felt for himself to have a
small community with whom he could live in covenant and mutual
support. We said that the leader must also live in covenant with a
small community. This is the same thought we are discussing here for
the members of the congregation. In considering small communities
within the congregation whose purpose is to provide the setting in
which persons may articulate their own experience and be assisted to
discern the leading of God for their lives, as well as a place where

mutual face-to-face accountability may be shared, it is important to distinguish these communities or groups from the more familiar church groups—a prayer group, Bible study group, learning group, support group, work group, counseling group, self-help group, or any other group whose focus is not on the spiritual formation of the individual and the group as a whole.

To this point we have emphasized that the spiritual formation of the congregation, and individual members, depends on aloneness and community. Aloneness is something Protestants seem to understand. What the protesters discarded in the Reformation had a great deal to do with the idea of accountability to another person, and the idea that the church was essential to one's salvation, in favor of a belief in the rugged, solitary believer. Some of the more modern protoges of the belief in rugged individualism are Jim Bakker, Jimmy Swaggart, Jim Jones, and the pastor across town who leaves every person to sink or swim on his or her own, save for attending the Sunday services, and serving on some administrative committee. But the Sunday service is hardly a place where intimate community and accountability can happen. If the congregation numbers forty or fifty people, it is too large for this to happen, unless the pastor is a highly skilled group leader and has the courage to radically alter the design and content of the service.

Authentic community is a place where we can be our real selves with God in the presence of another. We are not talking about "pseudocommunity."[19] Bonhoeffer contrasts the fear and loneliness of the pious community with the freedom to be honest:

> The pious fellowship permits no one to be a sinner. So everybody must conceal [his or her] sin from [himself or herself] and from the fellowship. We dare not be sinners. Many Christians are unthinkably horrified when a real sinner is suddenly discovered among the righteous. So we remain alone in our sin, living in lies and hypocrisy. But it is the grace of the Gospel, which is so hard for the pious to understand, that it confronts us with the truth and says: You are a sinner, a great, desperate sinner; now come, as the sinner that you are, to God who loves you. He wants you as you are; He does not want anything from you, a sacrifice, a work; He wants you alone. . . . This message is liberation through truth. . . . He wants to see you as you are, He wants to be gracious to you. . . . you can dare to be a sinner.[20]

Community can be a place where we receive the acceptance from others that we often fail to provide for ourselves, as well as a place where we can embrace the challenge, albeit reluctantly, to move beyond where we are at present. Has the community served the individual well in helping him or her become free, strong, and mature, or is the individual weak and dependent? Has it taken the person by the hand for a while in order that he or she may learn to walk again, or have relationships made the individual feel uneasy and insecure?[21]

Beyond the concepts of solitary endeavor and of covenant community, and the understanding that there are certain crucial prerequisites to spiritual formation, there is also the understanding of *the means of grace* that God provides the community and the individual.

The Means of Grace

The "means of grace" refers to means, not ends, and grace, not merit. The means have no intrinsic value. There is no merit in simply doing them for the sake of doing them. Their value is only in their ability to prepare the Christian to receive; to open up the channels between God and the congregation or individual, to receive the grace that only God can give.

The means of grace were taught and modeled by example in the life of Jesus, as he sought to keep his own spirituality alive and vigorous. The means of grace are prayer, searching the Scriptures, the Lord's Supper, fasting, and spiritual conversation. Added to these "inner" means are the "outward" means: acts of mercy (social ministries), avoiding doing harm to anyone, and attending all the ordinances and services of the church.

The listing of the means of grace as we have them above is more or less as they were taught by the Reformers and the post-Reformation church in Europe. In later years the listing of the means of grace was expanded by certain groups to match their own experience and need. For example, Richard Foster, in his modern classic regarding the means of grace, titled, *The Celebration of Discipline*, writes that "the Disciplines are God's way of getting us into the ground; they put us where [God] can work within us and transform us. By themselves the spiritual Disciplines can do nothing; they can only get us to the place where something can be done."[22] As such the spiritual disciplines are the "door to liberation." In his work Foster listed the spiritual disciplines under three categories, as follows: the Inward Disciplines (meditation, prayer, fasting, and study); the Outward Disciplines (simplicity, solitude, submission, and service); and the Corporate Disciplines (confession, worship, guidance, and celebration).

Dallas Willard sees the spiritual disciplines as daily, "natural" acts that we do to further abilities we would not otherwise have: "When through spiritual disciplines I become able heartily to bless those who curse me, pray without ceasing, to be at peace when not given credit for good deeds I've done, or to master the evil that comes my way, it is because my disciplinary activities have inwardly poised me for more and more interaction with the powers of the living God and [God's] kingdom. Such is the potential we tap into when we use the disciplines."[23]

Willard divides the means of grace into two major categories: Disciplines of Abstinence (solitude, silence, fasting, frugality, chastity, secrecy, and sacrifice); and Disciplines of Engagement (study, worship, celebration, service, prayer, fellowship, confession, and submission).[24] Abstinence is closely related to "asceticism" or training, as in athletic discipline for a sporting event. The disciplines of abstinence are supplemented by the disciplines of engagement, both of which provide the "outbreathing and inbreathing of our spiritual lives, and we require disciplines for both movements. . . . Abstinence, then, makes way for engagement."[25]

A review of the ancient, Reformation, and modern understandings of the means of grace reveals some common threads that run across the centuries—namely, the concept of private and communal disciplines, of inward and outward movements, of activity and passivity, of work and rest, of action and waiting. An understanding of the means of grace is of utmost importance to anyone who desires to become a companion to a congregation or individual on their spiritual journey, for they immediately suggest a myriad of topics, learning and experiential areas, exercises, and structures.

Some of the means of grace are readily understandable to the Western model of spirituality, others are foreign. The more active means make sense (e.g., acts of mercy, attending the church services, Bible study, learning) and immediately catch the attention of the pastor formed in the Western model. However, the more passive means are often overlooked or outright disdained (e.g., fasting, silence, prayer, solitude, the Lord's Supper) and are not common practices in many churches acclimated to the Western model. The pastor who is seriously concerned to provide sufficient bread for the spiritual journey of the congregation, and of individuals, will model and teach all the disciplines, and not pick and choose as fits the initial fancy of the congregation.

In this chapter we have labored to convince the reader that the spirituality of the congregation is something different from the many other areas of the congregation's life and work. All areas of the church's life are interrelated, and there is an exchange of influences. Nonetheless, the total sum of the church's activities does not necessarily correlate to a vigorous spirituality in the scriptural tradition.

If the congregation is to journey toward a deeper and more intimate relationship with the loving Lord, the leaders must set the tone. The greatest resource for this is the example and transparent experience of the pastor. Out of his or her own spiritual journey the pastor is able to offer spiritual companionship to others in the congregation whom the Spirit calls to the spiritual pilgrimage.

The context for spiritual formation includes small communities of persons within the congregation living in covenant with one another regarding their commitments—individual and shared—to God and to the community. The bread for their journey is offered by the Spirit through the means of grace, those spiritual disciplines that serve to keep persons open to the grace God is always seeking to offer the sojourner and the community of faith.

Finally, the journey is different for each congregation, group, and individual. However, God leads all through the seasons of spiritual experience. Again and again, the questing group or individual will visit each of the seasons, not in a strict linear order, but as the Spirit chooses to lead them.

To be the spiritual companion and guide for the congregation is perhaps the pastor's highest calling and privilege. Many pastors, however, have had little training for this privileged responsibility. Once the pastor begins to search in earnest for resources, however, he or she will discover they do exist in rather abundant measure. What matters most is a sincere desire and commitment to serve the congregation in this way. Finding the necessary resources will not be an impossible task.

Out of a spiritual encounter, persons and congregations see God in an entirely new light, as well as seeing themselves and the service opportunities or imperatives to which God is calling them. This clearer insight into God, self, and call is known as *vision*. We will now turn our attention to discussion of the "Leader as the Guardian of the Corporate Vision," and the one who sets individuals free to pursue their own visions, even as they blend their private aspirations and energies with the vision of the larger congregation.

Finally, there is a single resource that thousands of persons and hundreds of congregations are finding immensely helpful in supporting both the "times alone" and the "times together." This resource is now available in two editions: *A Guide to Prayer for Ministers and Other Servants*, and *A Guide to Prayer for All God's People*. Both are authored by Reuben Job and Norman Shawchuck, and are published by the Upper Room.

Chapter Ten

The Leader as Guardian of the Corporate Vision

The bravest are surely those who have the clearest vision of what is before them, glory and danger alike, and yet notwithstanding go out to meet it.   Thucydides

The future announces itself from afar. But most people are not listening. The noisy clatter of the present drowns out the tentative sounds of things to come. The sound of the new does not fit old perceptual patterns and goes unnoticed by most people. And of the few who do perceive something coming, most lack energy, initiative, courage, or will to do anything about it. Leaders who have the wit to perceive and the courage to act will be credited with a gift for prophecy that they do not necessarily have.[1]
                                                    John W. Gardner

Earlier, in chapter 5, we discussed how essential it is that the leader be possessed by God's vision for his or her ministry. This emphasis on the leader's personal vision must be balanced proportionately with the fact that the congregation, in order to reach its highest potential, must be possessed of its own corporate vision. Individual members and subgroups within the congregation can and generally will also have their respective visions of the ministry God is calling them to do, even if a corporate vision is unexpressed.

Vision is not in the leader's private domain. In a healthy congregation, vision will reside in the hearts of many, as the leaders set the people free to discern God's vision for their life and ministry. A congregation is at its best when vision is breaking out everywhere.

The corporate vision is a congregation's image of its God-given possibilities. It is God dreaming God's vision of the Kingdom in the heart of the congregation. It is the congregation's unshakable belief that God is working a purpose through them that is larger than any one of them could imagine. So important is vision that Scripture declares the congregation will perish without it (see Prov. 29:18).

The congregation's vision of its life and ministry must clearly connect with the values and actions of the corporate body and its individuals members. Apart from this, the vision is little more than a pipe dream—words blowing in the wind. Vision is more than an image of the future; it can empower a congregation to make the future image a reality.[2] The congregation's corporate vision becomes a path where there is no pathway; it brings clarity when there is obscurity and provides the impetus to keep going no matter how formidable the roadblocks. Vision transcends; it lifts the entire congregation to new realizations of possibilities; it generates enthusiasm and power; it aligns the thoughts, emotions, and actions of the people in pursuit of a common and compelling purpose.

Corporate vision does not take place apart from a leader, formal or informal. The leader is not the only one in the congregation who may discern God's plan for the congregation, but the leader's participation in the discerning process is essential. Visionary leaders, not preoccupied only with the present, spend time thinking about the future. These leaders, explains John Gardner, "describe the outlines of a possible future that lifts and moves people . . . they actually discern, in the clutter and confusion of the present, the elements that determine what is to come."[3] Such people are not satisfied with the status quo; they desire to make a difference, to make things happen, to change the existing realities, to do something that hasn't been done before. In a study of ninety highly successful leaders, Warren Bennis and Burt Nanus concluded that all of them

> had an agenda, an unparalleled concern with outcome. Leaders are the most results-oriented individuals in the world, and results get attention. Their visions or intentions are compelling and pull people toward them. Intensity coupled with commitment is magnetic. And these intense personalities do not have to coerce people to pay attention; they are so intent on what they are doing that, like a child completely absorbed with creating a sand castle in a sandbox, they draw others in. Vision grabs. Initially it grabs the leader, and management of attention enables others also to get on the bandwagon.[4]

The congregation, as a body, can and must have its own vision. However, individual members and subgroups may also have their visions for the ministry to which God is calling them.

Three Kinds of Churches

In our work as consultants with churches, we have discovered that, when it comes to converting desired images of the future into concrete action and change, congregations sort out into three types: wishing churches, dreaming churches, and visionary churches.[5] And we can quickly get a feel regarding which category a church falls into by conversing with the leadership team and individual members, and reviewing a few official documents.

The "Wishing" Congregation

A vision of the future can be a powerful motivation for the congregation. Sometimes, however, an image of the future makes no difference on the present realities—things don't change; they stay the way they are and always have been. This describes a wishing congregation.

While a wish is a desired condition, no one really expects it to come true. Because of this, there is no shouldering of responsibility, expended effort, or positive results. A wish means very little because, while a leader or congregation would like to see the wish come true, they believe that the reality is beyond anything possible. The future desired condition will never become a present reality. Further, a group may absolve itself from any responsibility to convert their wishes into realities by wishing for totally impossible things. Rather, they get their kicks out of *talking* of lofty wishes, and then excuse themselves from any responsibility to change a single jot or tittle. People who are wishing a desired future condition spend much time talking (usually complaining) to one another—and that's about all.

The "Dreaming" Congregation

A dream, like a wish, is another way by which many congregations express their hopes of the future. One distinction between the wish and the dream, however, is that dreams are attached to the persons' emotions. A dream is a wish accompanied by emotional responses. However, while much emotional energy is attached to corporate dreams, congregations will not invest the resources necessary to turn a dream into reality. In fact, they spend all their energies pining over their dreams and have no energy left to put the dream to work.

A pastor may be very enthusiastic about ideas received from attending a graduate class or seminar at another church. And the excitement may last for a time. However, it is emotion without commitment. Thus it remains only an emotional dream of the congregation. Some congregations dream the future by dwelling on the past. With much emotional energy, these congregations play "if only" games about the past, and, like those who wish, do precious little to search for a fresh vision of the future. They may express their dreams with tears, pain, or enthusiasm. But then they wake up to reality and slither away to take up the task of safe guarding the status quo.

The difference between a wish and a dream is that wishes are wished and then lightly discarded. But dreams cling to the emotions and paralyze the congregation because they know it is too good to be true—for them. The conversations of a wishing congregation are dull, boring, and stupefying. The conversations of dreaming congregations are enthusiastic, emotional, and paralyzing.

In a charismatic or pentecostal congregation that yet practices the gifts of tongues and interpretation or prophecy, when a person stands to announce, "Thus says the Lord . . . " and nothing changes in the life and work of that congregation, one may suspect that this is a dream, and not a prophetic vision for the congregation.

The "Visionary" Congregation

Congregations possessed by a vision from God are distinctively different from wishers or dreamers. A vision, while also a desired future reality, is more than an idea or an emotion—it is a *desire that captures* the heart and mind and coalesces the resources of the group toward whatever action is necessary to cause the vision to become a concrete reality. Expressed another way, "Vision is a waking dream."[6] Persons who have vision make great sacrifice, even to the point of death, to see that the vision becomes a reality. Vision is larger than life. A group *has* its wish or dream, but vision has the group. Wishers and dreamers *attempt to shape the future* through much conversation, while a vision *shapes persons* through conviction that leads to action. Leaders and members of visionary congregations will see their dreams become realities.

Corporate "Visioning" Is a Process

Vision cannot become a reality if it is not shared. A vision is shared when individual members of the congregation hold a similar image, and aspire together to achieve the future suggested by the image. Corporate visioning is a process that: (1) begins in the spirituality of the leader and congregation through an encounter with God; (2) develops in and through the church leaders who communicate the vision to the congregation; and (3) involves the church leaders who empower the congregation in such a way that they, together, enact the vision. Vision can arise from many sources within a congregation. And the leader can facilitate or hinder this from happening. The vision belongs to God, and God dreams it in the life of the congregation.

The visioning process in "closure" cultures takes place in a linear, logical process that usually begins with the leader and is "sold" to the followers. It is goal-conscious and time-oriented. This process usually starts with the vision or statement of mission, and out of the vision or mission flow goals, objectives, and action plans. The chain of command and the organizational chart are highly valued—the focus is on efficiency and completion. Anything else seems chaotic and cumbersome.

In "non-closure" cultures, participants operate out of contextual logic. The vision emerges out of interaction and relationships that bring persons to dream the future together. As such, "visioning" is an open-ended process. What is important are

harmonious relationships. People rely on their relationships
with people whom they can trust. Leaders earn their leadership
through the quality of relationships they establish with others.[7]

The Spirituality of the Congregation

Episcopal priest Terry Fullam defines vision as "the product of God
working in us. [God] creates the vision, and we receive it; it becomes
a rallying point, a goal toward which we move as [God's] people."[8]
Fullam describes his own experience in receiving a vision from God:
"In my own case, the Lord spent most of a summer working on me to
prepare me for this church, first through Scripture and then through
a rather strange experience that is, I suppose, unique to me. . . . I
didn't hear God audibly, but his word to me was so clear that, had I
heard him out loud, it [an audible hearing] would have added nothing. It gave me the courage to step into an unfamiliar role. It has provided stability for me ever since."[9]

The congregation in the Old Testament and the ancient church
of the New Testament proved to contain ordinary people who
accomplished extraordinary deeds out of their encounter with God.
Without exception the "call" stories in Scripture demonstrate that
the call was accompanied by a vision of new possibilities, and an
anointing of the presence of the Holy Spirit, who works alongside
the persons to make the impossible possible. Abraham, for example, responded to the call of God to "set out for a place that he was
to receive as an inheritance; and he set out, not knowing where he
was going" (Heb. 11:8). This same experience of call can happen at
a corporate level.

Upon closer look, one sees that the persons in Scripture who experienced a vision in their encounter with God were busy people who
possessed the ability to reflect on the value of their results. Moses was
tending the flock of his father-in-law, Jethro. Gideon was beating out
wheat in the wine press. Saul was "breathing threats and murder
against the disciples of the Lord."

On a corporate level, the disciples of Jesus caught glimpses of Jesus'
vision while following him around. However, the vision had not as yet
"caught" them. It was only after they had time to reflect on their

experiences and relationship with Jesus, and to experience an encounter of the Holy Spirit, that they gave themselves fully to the vision Jesus consistently held up before them. Then they passed on their vision or wrote about it for their congregations. Whether of an individual or a community, Scripture consistently holds forth the truth that vision comes only to people who are already doing something and who have developed the capacity to reflect upon their actions and results.

In order to be possessed of a vision, the congregation must develop a "clear eye" toward their own situation and a "big ear" toward God. God does not speak to people out of a vacuum, but out of their concrete realities. And God tends to speak softly—in nudges and hunches, in a gentle turning of one's will toward God's desires. In a frenzied and noisy world such as ours, many people never develop the capacity to sustain the silence and openness necessary to transparently assess their situation and its potentialities or to enter into the silence where God's still, small voice may be heard.

So far we have said that in order for a congregation to move through wishing or dreaming into vision, the leaders must (1) lead the congregation into a deeper, more vital spirituality, (2) teach them how to listen for God's call, (3) support them to sustain the interior silence out of which God speaks, (4) develop discernment within the hearts of the people, and finally (5) help persons see how their individual visions fit together with the corporate vision.

Encourage the Call in Individuals and Find Common Ground in a Higher Corporate Vision

The corporate vision only matters to people to the extent it reflects their own personal vision. Therefore, the corporate vision moves closer to reality when it includes the hopes of the followers, enabling them to blend their own personal vision with the corporate vision. Senge uses the metaphor of a hologram, a three-dimensional image, to illustrate how personal visions relate to shared visions:

> If you cut a *photograph* in half, each part shows only part of the whole image. But if you divide a *hologram*, each part shows the whole image intact. Similarly, as you continue to divide up the hologram, no

matter how small the divisions, each piece still shows the whole image. Likewise, when a group of people come to share a vision for an organization, each person sees his [or her] own picture of the organization at its best. Each shares responsibility for the whole, not just for his [or her] piece. But the component "pieces" are not identical. Each represents the whole image from a different point of view. It's as if you were to look through holes poked in a window shade; each hole would offer a unique angle for viewing the whole image. So, too, is each individual's vision of the whole unique. We each have our own way of seeing the larger vision. When you add up the pieces of a hologram, the image of the whole does not change fundamentally. After all, it was there in each piece. Rather the image becomes more intense, more lifelike. When more people come to share a common vision, the vision may not change fundamentally. But it becomes more alive, more real in the sense of a mental reality that people can truly imagine achieving. They now have partners, "cocreators"; the vision no longer rests on their shoulders alone. Early on, when they are nurturing an individual vision, people may say it is "my vision." But as the shared vision develops, it becomes both "my vision" and "our vision."[10]

Terry Fullam suggests that "vision arises out of a burden to know the will of God, to become whatever God wants us to become . . . we believe the Lord will speak to us corporately, not individually. [The Lord] never seems to give the whole vision to any one of us. We're constantly putting a jigsaw puzzle together."[11] In larger churches, more often than not, the vision is shared through the pastoral staff and volunteer leaders; in smaller churches, the vision is shared through the members.[12]

Traditionally, in most congregations, the pastor comes up with the compelling vision that captures the imagination and energy of the constituency. This process works well and serves the common good for many congregations. But there is another type of leader who, "rather than creating a single vision and then selling it to others, has the ability to listen to others and help them articulate a shared vision which reflects their deeply-held values."[13] Leaders who are committed to a shared vision constantly encourage persons to listen for their own call and develop a personal vision that aligns itself with the corporate vision.

Terry Fullam asked every communicant in the church to take stock of his or her life and write him a letter. He describes his instructions: "Look at the stewardship of your life—your natural abilities and your opportunities—and tell me in letter form about yourself. What obedience is the Lord calling you to do? What thing is he commending? What are your dreams for your life, for this body, and for the interplay between the two?

"I told them I would put their letters in order according to the parish list and then share their dreams, praying for each of them. I announced that on Christmas Eve I would bring all the letters to the altar, offering their gifts to the Lord. And then at this time next year, I will mail the letters back for review.

"There's a great reservoir of commitment in this church and a desire to find God's will. In this way, I hope to help people focus on vision."[14]

Gordon Cosby describes how persons in his congregation respond to a personal call to a specific mission.

Our procedure now is to start with one person or a small nucleus of persons who have heard a call for a specific mission. Then others gather around that call; they gather initially around "call" incarnated in a person or persons. A new group begins with a clearly understood outward journey as well as a commitment to the inward journey. . . . The person upon whom the Word of God has come sounds the call in a variety of ways. Often in personal conversations within the community he or she discovers another to share the call. The fire of God kindled within his or her own spirit inflames another. . . . The person's call may be shared with the Sunday morning worshiping congregation or with any segment of the community. A number of people may respond or none. If no one responds, the person waits, nurturing his or her own life in Christ and praying for those who can hear. He pursues his call individually, waiting for the moment others can share it with him. If others respond, they share their life together, evoking one anther's gifts, and

> praying for clarity in hearing God's will as to their mission. If the new group lives and senses God in its midst, it may share its call within the church council to see if it is confirmed by the representatives of the existing mission groups. This serious testing of the call is extremely important.[15]

Persons will not follow a leader, no matter how noble his or her vision, if they do not see how it enables them to realize their understanding of the gospel and God's purposes through them. Since no organization will exactly mirror an individual's expectations, the difference becomes a leading edge for growth in both the organization and the individual. "The incongruence between the individual and the organization," writes Chris Argyris, "can provide the basis for a continued challenge which, as it is fulfilled, will tend to help persons to enhance [their] own growth and to develop organizations that will tend to be viable and effective. The incongruence between the individual and the organization can be the foundation for increasing the degree of effectiveness of both."[16]

These are important, but they are not enough. An additional ingredient is the leaders' ability to communicate the vision in a clear and compelling manner.

Communicating the Vision

The skill that distinguishes visionary leaders from other leaders, says Henry Mintzberg, is "their profound ability with language, often in symbolic form, as metaphor. It is not just that they 'see' things from a new perspective but that they get others to see them."[17] The essence of leadership is the ability to influence others to volunteer their separate energies and resources to a common pursuit. The ability to do this rests on the leader's capability to communicate the vision in a clear and convincing manner. People cannot respond to a signal if the signal is unclear, and they will not respond if the signal is dull, flat, or boring.

The "I Have a Dream" speech by Martin Luther King, Jr., delivered before 250,000 people on August 28, 1963, and the influence of his commitment to that vision, is perhaps modern history's best example of how a leader can communicate a vision to the people. That this was Dr. King's vision and not merely an idle wish or frivolous dream was attested by his willingness not only to live for it but to die for it. So clear and compelling was the signal that the words convinced his friends and converted a host of his enemies.[18]

In a corporate community, convincing the people to commit their individual consent and action to the vision finally comes to rest on the leaders' ability to communicate in a manner that excites not only persons' intellects, but also their imagination and passion.[19] By using metaphors, congregational stories, histories,[20] examples, anecdotes, slogans, symbols, and word pictures, visionary leaders are effective in expressing a vision that bands people together. Robert K. Greenleaf asserts, "Someone in the church must paint the dream. . . . The growing edge church will be a painter of dreams for all of its people, something to lift their sights above the ordinary and give them a great goal to strive for."[21]

We recommend following these important steps when communicating a corporate vision.[22]

1. *Identify the constituents in your congregation.* Make a list of the individuals and groups whose honest response, input, and support you wish to elicit toward the congregation's vision. In a larger congregation, you may work through key individuals and programs in the ministry structures; in smaller congregations, you may primarily work through key individuals.

2. *Find the common ground in the needs, aspirations, and dreams of your congregation.* In knowing and understanding the aspirations of the followers, leaders can reflect with them, "This is what I heard you say. This is how your personal dreams can blend into a common vision for all of us." While it may be conscious or unconscious, people desire to see their leader symbolize their hopes and dreams. As Westley and Mintzberg conclude, "By wedding perception with symbols the visionary leader creates a vision, and the vision, by evoking an emotional response, forms a bridge between leader and follower as well as between idea and action."[23]

Visionary leaders are those who have the ability to capture the imagination of followers and motivate them to realize their goals for the church and for themselves. Visionary leaders sense the hidden potential that others can bring to the corporate vision, inviting their involvement in the spiritual enterprise of the church. This requires spending time as a loving, personal shepherd among the flock, listening and feeling with their pain and hurts, as well as their desires and aspirations. Among the plethora of research techniques aimed at discovering persons' perceptions, there is no substitute for relationships.

3. *Articulate the vision in concrete and positive terms.* A vision of the future must be made concrete in order for others to understand and support that vision. Being prepared to verbalize the corporate vision to different constituents on the spot can invite them to be aware of and participate in the vision. It is helpful for leaders and members of the congregation to be able to tell the essence of the corporate vision in three to five minutes, using metaphors, images, stories, analogies, and examples. If a vision can be expressed in a few words, it has a better chance of being understood and accepted.

The vision should also be stated in positive terms, such as "We will . . ." versus "We will try. . . ." While the roadblocks of achieving the vision may be noted, the difficulties should not be the major focus.[24] The visionary leader believes in the epiphany of the vision and will encourage others to stay in the process of praying for and working toward its appearance. Visions are not to be covered up; they are shining lights for any organization.

4. *Model the vision in your own behavior and be genuine.* If you, the leader, are not excited about the vision, if you don't really believe in it, then it will be most difficult to convince anyone else. If you are not excited about future realities, how will you convince others to be? Persons who are not authentic in what they say and do are readily discovered, and they will attract few followers. Without passion and genuineness, the vision will never get off the ground. It remains a wish or a dream.

Empowering People to Enact the Vision

A corporate vision happens when the personal visions of the leaders and individual members are cohesively aligned together in a synergetic relationship with God's desires. As such, the vision comes from outside the congregation: It comes from God.[25] Leaders know that vision cannot be accomplished alone; it requires the best efforts of a partnership, working together to accomplish the vision. The degree of individual commitment to an organizational vision is not either-or. In reality there are varying degrees of how people feel about vision. Peter Senge describes the difference between compliance and commitment toward vision, including the several levels of personal compliance.

POSSIBLE ATTITUDES TOWARD A VISION

Commitment: Wants it. Will make it happen. Creates whatever "laws" (structures) are needed.

Enrollment: Wants it. Will do whatever can be done within the "spirit of the law."

Genuine compliance: Sees the benefits of the vision. Does everything expected and more. Follows the "letter of the law." "Good soldiers."

Formal compliance: On the whole, sees the benefits of the vision. Does what's expected and no more. "Pretty good soldier."

Grudging compliance: Does not see the benefits of the vision. But, also, does not want to lose job (or status). Does enough of what's expected because he [or she] has to, but also lets it be known that he [or she] is not really on board.

Noncompliance: Does not see benefits of vision and will not do what's expected. "I won't do it; you can't make me."

Apathy: Neither for nor against vision. No interest. No energy. "Is it five o'clock yet?"[26]

In our experience with congregations, most of what passes for commitment to vision is really a form of compliance. Often we hear pastors express their desire for the congregation to "buy into" their vision. Enrollment and commitment imply free choice; "being sold" may not imply free choice. Commitment is a free choice. As such, efforts to manipulate commitment can only mean some level of compliance. Having commitment toward a corporate vision includes a personal responsibility for implementing the vision, for making it really happen.[27]

The attitudes of the pastoral staff and volunteer workers at every level of the ministry structure are important in implementing a corporate vision. In fact, Warren Bennis describes the corporate vision on three distinct levels in the organization: the strategic level of vision is the overriding philosophy (and theology) of the organization; the tactical level of vision is that philosophy in action; and the personal level of vision is the philosophy which is demonstrated in the behavior of each individual in the organization.[28] All three levels are crucial for a corporate vision. For example, if the Sunday school teacher, nursery worker, or greeter is rude, helpless, or incompetent, probably the pastors and lay leadership are either inept or lack a coherent, corporate vision for that congregation.

Vision Incubates in a Climate of Support, Trust, and Open Communication

The realization of a vision has human and relational elements to it. While spiritual energy is important for a congregation, the elements of support, trust, and open communication provide emotional and psychological energy for the entire enterprise.[29] Though everything else may be in place, a vision may not become reality because of a lack of support, trust, and open communication—which keeps the people apart, not trusting one another. Trust in an organization is like an "Emotional Bank Account."[30] Without trust, people tend to be defensive, and there is little opportunity for open, honest communication. When the "Emotional Bank Account" is full of trust with sufficient deposits, there is the potential for creativity and energy necessary for "visionary daydreaming" and implementation.

According to Greenleaf, nothing will happen until there is trust: "Trust is first. . . . A serious error of an earlier generation was to put administration first. Administration is important, but it is largely a skill, and skills are secondary."[31] The elements of support, trust, and open communication are interactive with each other—that is, true support and trust are characterized by open communication, and vice-versa. Mutual trust among persons within a congregation means mutual influence and interdependence.

When the trust level is low, communication may easily become distorted. Feelings may be disguised and information falsified in order to protect oneself from perceived threat. This distortion can go both ways. For example, the leaders may not be open in financial reports for fear the congregation may not support such spending. Or staff members may communicate to the pastor and ruling board what they think they want to hear. Temporarily serious problems are avoided or ignored. In all such situations of low trust and poor communication, vision breaks down and dissipates.

Leaders who do not demonstrate a genuine trust for colleagues and followers are, themselves, perceived by others as less deserving of trust. While trust may not be necessary in routine situations, Kouzes and Posner believe that "trust is almost always needed when leaders are accomplishing extraordinary things in organizations."[32]

Everyone in the congregation plays a part in building trust. Trust is a reciprocal process between persons or among groups, and it fundamentally relies on personal integrity. On one level, trust requires self-disclosure; being willing to disclose what you desire, what you value, and what you stand for. But it also requires being sensitive to others, listening to their wants, values, needs, and viewpoints. Greenleaf observes that "servant leaders may stand alone, largely without the support of their culture, as a saving remnant of those who care for both persons and institutions, and who are determined to make their caring count—wherever they are involved. This brings them, as individuals, constantly to examine the assumptions they live by. Thus, their leadership by example sustains trust."[33]

Trust is needed when an extraordinary vision is hoped for in the congregation. There is no substitute for trust.

Why Visions Do Not Succeed

Why do visions succeed, and how do they fail or die prematurely, even though they may possess intrinsic worth? "Visions spread because of a reinforcing process of increasing clarity, enthusiasm, communication and commitment. As people talk, the vision grows clearer. As it gets clearer, enthusiasm for its benefits builds. . . . Enthusiasm can also be reinforced by early successes in pursuing the vision."[34] If these reinforcing elements in the process continue to function, increasing numbers of people will commit themselves to the vision.

However, a number of factors can interrupt the process, slow it down, and even destroy the vision. Peter Senge identifies four major conditions that can slow down or perhaps completely thwart the cycle of commitment toward a vision.

1. "The visioning process can wither if, as more people get involved, the diversity of views dissipates focus and generates unmanageable conflicts."[35] If persons feel that the emerging vision can no longer be influenced by their input, or if they feel that their own visions do not matter, then enthusiasm for the corporate vision will dissipate. A vision, in order to become a reality, needs the strong support of many people. Leaders who are willing to empower the visions of individuals and groups in the congregation further the possibility for a larger corporate vision to evolve, and the sum of the whole will be larger than the many disparate visions that reside among the people. If, however, the visioning activity becomes an advocacy process for the desires of a special interest group (even if it's the leadership team) or some individual (even if it's the leader), it will result either in compliance or conflict, and not commitment.

2. "Visions can also die because people become discouraged by the apparent difficulty in bringing the vision into reality."[36] By definition there is a gap between a vision and current reality. Organizational discouragement can happen when people are not able to hold the gap between vision and current reality in creative tension. Personal mastery is necessary to overcome this discouragement and avoid organizational paralysis in the light of a vision that seems too good to be true. Many visions often take years before they can be brought into reality. (The vision that compelled Moses to bring the slaves out of Egypt into the promised land took forty years to accomplish. In the biblical metaphor, the number forty generally means "a very long time" or "a lifetime.") However, most individuals and congregations cannot live and work for long periods of time without seeing some small gains and having opportunities to celebrate at least some small successes. For this reason leaders must plan the work and ministry in such a way that there may be a series of small successes, which are highly celebrated, in order to keep the larger vision clear and to keep the people from being overwhelmed by the long haul.

3. "Emerging visions can also die because people get overwhelmed by the demands of current reality and lose their focus on the vision."[37] Time and energy are needed for the long haul—the sweat and sacri-

fice needed to accomplish any worthwhile corporate vision. When energy is drained on current crises and simply dealing with current day-to-day realities that consume the group's time and energy, it becomes very easy for the vision to be forgotten until another day. For this reason the congregation's vision must be ever and always held up as the top priority. Vision that is not given priority will never be more than an idle wish or a nostalgic dream.

4. "Lastly, a vision can die if people forget their connection to one another."[38] An important motivation toward accomplishing a corporate vision is the desire for people to be connected to each other and to a larger purpose. How quickly the spirit of a vision can be blunted when people lose respect for each other. When the group is divided into "us" and "them," into those who are loyal and those who are not, the relationships no longer contribute to genuine enthusiasm. People must have time and skill to reflect on their own visions, and be able to share their hopes and dreams for the congregation with one another or the corporate vision will soon die.[39]

Vision is the fusion of the passion, desires, and energies of the congregation into a compelling volition that gathers up the past, the present, and the future of the congregation into one God-given and God-led pilgrimage.

Whatever vision is for you and your congregation, it is meant to bring an indescribable sense of a better future in the will of God—the only thing worth dying for.

Chapter Eleven

Understanding the Congregation's Life Cycle

You can't step twice into the same river, for other waters are continually flowing on. Heraclitus circa 500 B.C.E.

L ike machinery, organizations tend to wear out, decline in effectiveness, and cease to be. Will Rogers once said: "Last year we said things can't go on like this, and they didn't. They got worse."[1] Organizations consume energy; a condition known as atrophy.[2] All organisms, organizations, and processes tend toward atrophy. Left to themselves, things get worse; they degenerate or become irrelevant—because they fail to adapt to the changes in their environment.

Nowhere in human organizations is this more certainly so than in North American religious organizations. Over the past fifty years the changes in the North American socioreligious scene have been tremendous, taking a heavy toll on religious institutions. As recently as forty years ago, the main attraction in evangelical outreach in every major city was the revival center, or a large church known as the city's "soul saving station," always located in or near the downtown area and drawing crowds from all around. Today the revival centers are no more. All of these were highly successful religious institutions in their time, but the times changed.

As recently as fifty years ago, a congregation on the edge of a city, numbering two hundred members, was considered a large church. Fifty years ago the pastoral staff generally was a solo operation. Today, there are in the suburbs surrounding every major city at least one congregation numbering several thousands of members, and some smaller congregations numbering several hundreds of members. These large congregations are often staffed by ministry teams of a dozen or more pastors.

Fifty years ago it was assumed that a congregation would thrive, or at least survive, indefinitely. Few persons, if any, foresaw a day when a congregation of 200 members may very well disappear—and some quickly. The next fifty years will likely witness the decline and/or demise of many churches and religious institutions that today are going about their affairs as though there were no end to their tomorrows. But unless they succeed in adapting to the changes rushing toward them, they will not survive.

Congregations, like all human organizations, have a life cycle. In passing through their life cycle, some congregations learn to renew themselves and thus extend their life cycles from one cycle to another. Other congregations do not learn. They remain blind to the changes, or choose to ignore them, claiming that their theology or ecclesiology is right for all time. These churches are candidates for stagnation and demise. When a congregation is no longer able to interpret reality, that congregation is headed for serious trouble.

Robert Greenleaf describes institutions that survive over a period of time as those who have an appropriate instinct that includes the ability to chart a successful course, regardless of the unpredictable environment that is rushing toward it. Greenleaf describes a boyhood experience of dog sled racing.

The setting was a cold January morning in a little town in Wisconsin, where I then was, on the southern shore of Lake Superior. It happened to be a Saturday when they had their annual dog sled derby on the ice. A one-mile course had been staked out by sticking little fir trees on the ice. . . .

It was a youngsters' meet and the contenders ranged all the way from large boys with several dogs and big sleds to one little fellow who didn't seem over five with a little sled and one small dog. They took off at the signal and the little fellow with his one dog was quickly outdistanced—he was hardly in the race. All went well with the rest until, about halfway around, the team that was second started to pass the team then in the lead. They came too close and the dogs got in a fight. And as each team came up the dogs joined the fight. None seemed to be able to steer clear of it. Soon, from our position about a half mile away, there was just one big black seething mass of kids and sleds and dogs—all but the little fellow with his one little dog who gave this imbroglio a wide berth, the only one that managed it, and the only one to finish the race.

As I reflect on the many vexing problems and the stresses of our times that complicate their solutions, this simple scene from long ago comes vividly to mind. And I draw the obvious moral: No matter how difficult the challenge or how impossible or hopeless the task may seem, if you are reasonably sure of your course, just keep on going![3]

Like the boy with the one dog sled, who looked far enough ahead to change his course from the rest of the pack, congregations will need to chart their course and stick to it, while at the same time making the necessary changes to accommodate the unpredictable and uncontrollable influences that are rushing upon it. However, most congregations are oblivious to this because they are entirely focused on their day-to-day routine. They see only the "sled" and the "ice" immediately in front of them.

The leaders of congregations that will continue to thrive (regardless of size) must learn to look farther ahead and anticipate the future.

Life Cycle Theory of Organizations

Organizations are born, grow, age, and die. At each stage of development, from inception to maturity, certain challenges must be overcome if the congregation is to survive. First, the challenges stem from the fact that the congregation itself is changing. There is a continual march of internal changes to which the congregation must adapt. Second, the challenges stem from the fact that the congregation's environment is continually changing. If the church does not learn to adapt to these internal and external changes, it will not survive. Finally, however, the congregation will grow old and die. A simple sketch of the life cycle of most organizations may be drawn to depict the major organizational life cycle stages: inception, growth, maturity, and decline.[4]

The Second Presbyterian Church of Evanston, Illinois, serves as an example of a congregation that progressed through the life cycle, from birth to death.

The Second Presbyterian Church of Evanston is a magnificent edifice built in 1926 in southeast Evanston, at a time when south Evanston was synonymous with wealth and gracious living. After a slow start, membership started to grow rapidly, and the eventually 1,300 adult voices gave life to the sanctuary. Eventually the character of south Evanston began to change. The moneyed social classes were dying or leaving for southern climes, to be replaced by less affluent, younger people who either were not interested in joining a Presbyterian church or who were likely to move a bit farther north, where two other Presbyterian churches were closer. In the mid-1960s, the church's Reverend David H. Pottie was attacked by minority groups as being anti-Semitic and bigoted, and sidewalk demonstrations by human rights groups took place. Pottie resigned in 1967, and the church dropped almost five hundred members in the next year. Shortages of funds led to the cutting of youth programs, and, as a result, young families never came for a second visit. Finally, in 1977, the church was down to a membership of two hundred, with a regular Sunday attendance of only sixty to eighty persons in a sanctuary built for 1,300. The church finally closed its doors in 1978, a victim of a changing neighborhood and social environment.[5]

Figure 11.1
The Life Cycle of a Congregation

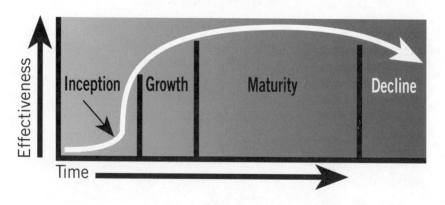

The Second Presbyterian Church of Evanston is not alone in its journey from inception to death. Every year hundreds of congregations close their doors in America. However, hundreds of other congregations succeed in extending their life from one cycle to another, and thus forestall their demise. The life cycle of such congregations may be illustrated as follows:

Figure 11.2

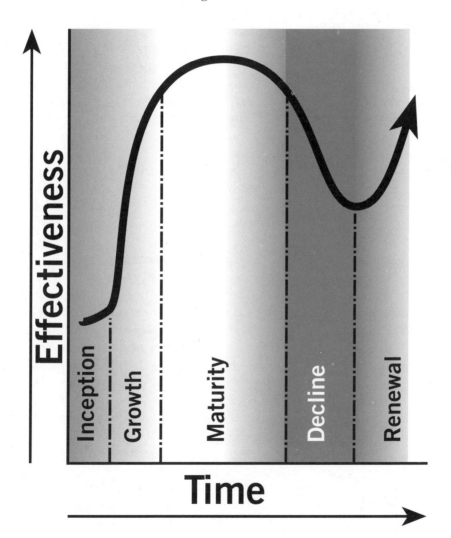

The life cycle pattern diagram illustrates a congregation that has succeeded in stemming its decline by renewing itself through successful adaption to its changing environment. This is never easy, but it can be done. To do so, however, requires that the congregation find a new will and reason to live, supported by innovative and courageous leadership, for the congregation must act decisively, envisioning a new future that at first can only be seen by faith.

> The United Methodist Church in McGrawsville, Indiana, ministers in a set of unique circumstances, not the least of which is that over the years the town has declined to only twenty houses and a grain elevator. The congregation declined along with its community, until in the late 1970s attendance at the Sunday services numbered about sixty-five. The congregation could no longer afford a full-time pastor. The future of the congregation looked bleak, indeed. There was talk about disbanding the congregation. But with the dawning of the 1980s, the congregation decided to commit itself to an all-out missions effort in which every member would do what he or she could to serve the community. This commitment breathed new life into the tiny congregation, and by 1985 the congregation had grown sufficiently to hire its first full-time pastor. This bold decision resulted in an even deeper commitment on the part of its members to serve the community. Over the decade of the 1980s, the members launched several new and ambitious ministries. Soon the congregation decided to build a new complex to accommodate its expanding community based programs and the increasing numbers of new people attending the Sunday services. Presently the attendance at the Sunday services averages 250 worshipers. Recently the church was recognized by the North Indiana Conference as one of the churches showing the highest percentage of growth in the Conference.

Like all organizations, congregations are born, grow, age, and die— but not all. Some die even before completing their initial life cycle, and others prolong their lives through several cycles. In order to prolong its life beyond its initial life cycle, a congregation must learn to adapt to the continual flow of internal and external changes that it experiences. However, there comes a time when the congregation will grow old and die.

As with all theories, there are limitations and possible exceptions to what has here been stated. However, there seems to be an *ebb and flow* to congregational life; congregations are birthed or may be aborted; they grow at different paces, experience crises, sometimes become stagnant, sometimes revitalize, and, at other times, pass from the scene, having lived their day. As the poet Alfred, Lord Tennyson, wrote:

> Our little systems have their day;
> They have their day and cease to be;
> They are but broken light of thee,
> And thou, O Lord, art more than they.
> (from "Strong Son of God, Immortal Love")

While it is important for leaders to understand the various stages in the life cycle of their congregation, it is even more consequential to be able to do something about it, especially in the declining phase. Specifically, what can church leaders do to help bring a cycle of renewal and vitality into a declining phase? Our next chapter addresses these concerns.

Chapter Twelve

The Leader's Role in Congregational Renewal

God is always calling us to be more than we have been.
Loren B. Mead[1]

Bringing about change in an organization embedded in rigidity and inertia is likened to teaching an elephant to dance, according to James Belasco. Beyond the image of a dancing elephant is a lesson about being "bound to the past." When trainers shackle a young elephant to a stake in the ground, the elephant learns to stay in place, giving up any attempt to pull up the stakes. After a while, all that is required to keep the elephant in its place is a small metal bracelet around one of its feet, even when it is not attached to any stake at all. Having once gotten the idea the bracelet is chained to a stake, the elephant will stay—all because of an inconsequential bracelet. Congregations, like elephants, are often bound by restraints, however insignificant they may be. Belasco drives the point home: " 'We've always done it this way' is as limiting to an organization's progress as the unattached chain around the elephant's foot. Success ties you to the past."[2]

The Pitfalls and Opportunities of Change

Change has the ability to thrust even the strongest organizations into decline. But this need not happen. The decline is not due to change but to the organization's *response to it*. On the other hand, change creates fresh opportunities for new enterprise (consider the closing of the last typewriter factory because of the advent of the personal computer and its related industries). Indeed, change is a mixture of bane and blessing; at the same time it challenges our survival and presents new doorways to the future.

165

Changes in American society regarding faith, spirituality, worship preferences, feelings about religious institutions, and so on over the past three decades have proven a bane for many churches. At the same time, however, these changes have proven a blessing for the so-called megachurches, the large pastoral churches and the great number of congregations who have freely, quickly, and effectively responded to the changes in American religious preferences.

Did the changes of the past decades mandate that mainline congregations and denominations should suffer such stagnation and decline? No, indeed, for the same changes that spawned the growth of other churches presented the same opportunities to the mainline institutions. However, they failed to make the necessary innovations to capitalize on the new opportunities brought about by the changes in society. Retiring bishops of one large denomination were asked why their church was losing large numbers of members and what could be done about it. One bishop responded that "more and more churches are involved in maintenance efforts, and our people are being called to express their commitment by engaging in busy work. Many of our worship services are dull, our mission efforts poorly conceived and planned, and there is a chasm between the connectional church and the local church that we seem unable to bridge. [To reverse membership loss] there must be a total re-emphasis on empowering the laity."[3]

Busy work. Dull worship services. No good plans for achieving the mission. The congregations and the national agencies each blame the other. Have these conditions come about because the church has changed? No, they have come about because the church has *not* changed—while the needs and interests in the North American populace, as well as throughout the entire Western world, have changed.

Exactly opposite conditions of those listed above by the bishop are prevailing and attracting tens of thousands of Americans to the megachurches, the large pastoral churches, and to small churches that have realized there is no chain holding them in yesterday's place. These congregations (1) urge and support every one of their people to be engaged in a meaningful ministry, and in doing so play down the notion that serving on a church committee is doing ministry; (2) have a variety of worship services tailored to meet the preferences and needs of specific groups; (3) emphasize the leadership and ministry of the laity; (4) are constantly seeking innovative ways to make the services and ministries of the church filled with excellence and tailored to the modern mind; and (5) avoid those relationships that would constrict the congregation in bureaucratic and out-dated structures.

We may be tempted to blame the denomination's polity, culture, and structures for our problems—and fail to recognize that the resistance to change is our condition as well as that of the agencies guiding the church. Our resistance to change has far more effect on the congregation than does theirs.

If laypersons are engaged in busy work, and not meaningful ministry, who made their assignments? If lay boards spend all their time dealing with maintenance instead of expansive ministries, who meets with them month after month, who sets the tone for the meetings and the agenda? If the worship services are dull and boring, who plans and leads the worship services? If the laity are languid and passive, who meets with them over coffee, who trains them, who sets the tone for the corporate body?

Think about it. Who is resisting change? Who is falling into its pitfalls? Who can actually lead a congregation to grasp the new and fresh opportunities that will come rushing toward it in the next twenty years? The bishop or the pastor who lives every day with the congregation?

The Necessary Abilities for Leading the Congregation Through Change

The only congregations that will thrive in the coming decades will be those whose leaders have learned to *respond* to change, not *resist* or *ignore* it. Joel Barker has identified "three keys" (or abilities) that open the door "to the future of any organization, profit or nonprofit, that wants to participate fully in the twenty-first century. They are: Anticipation, Innovation, and Excellence. When I ask my audiences if they agree with the importance of three 'keys,' they always do. It is hard to argue with them. And yet many organizations think one or two of the three are enough. All three are necessary."[4]

In truth, many large and small organizations in North America are learning Barker's lesson. Unfortunately, however, many are learning the lesson too late to turn a declining stage into a cycle of renewal and

hope. The future has already passed them by. This is perhaps especially so for many congregations, where concepts like *innovation* and
excellence are about as far out of the pale of their thinking as going to
X-rated movies—and for many other congregations where *anticipation* means wondering whether there will be enough money to balance last year's budget.

Anticipation

*Anticipation is the ability to view the congregation through its sea-
sons of spiritual experience.* It is getting an edge on the future; reading the signs of new interests, trends, and opportunities. Many church
leaders have great ideas—too late. Anticipation is hatching new ideas
before their time has arrived. In earlier times the person who possessed anticipation was called a seer or a prophet. Anticipation was
seen as a sort of mystical gift. Today, however, it is understood that
persons can learn to anticipate, and groups within the church can
build anticipation into their work. Anticipation is watching the future.

In chapter 9, "The Congregation's Spirituality," we described the
pastor as the Knower of the Seasons of the congregation's spiritual
journey. This skill could be repeated here, with additional considera-
tions. Not all change pressing in upon the congregation is capricious.
God leads God's people with intentionality and design through changing seasons of experience. It is the leaders' privilege and responsibility
to discern when the congregation is on its journey, in order to lead in
keeping with the Spirit's leading. When the pastor and leaders rightly
discern God's leading, and lead in concert with this, then the congregation is journeying with God and working with God, and not contrary
to God's desires for the congregation and its ministries. Failing to discern the season of God's leading causes the congregation to swim
against the tides of God's desires for the congregation.

The most important skill here is not a skill at all. It is a condition—
to develop within oneself, and the congregation, *a discerning heart.*
The leader of the congregation must lead from the heart *and* the
head, and the precondition for this is a life resting on the Means of
Grace, sustained by much silence and reflection.

*Anticipation is the ability to employ discernment as a major process
in decision making.* Akin to the discerning heart, discussed above, is

the faith-full decision-making method known as discernment, or listening into the mind of God.[5] Discernment is a faith-full means of anticipating the seasons and the changes and the right direction for the congregation.

If the leader desires to open the congregation up to the leading of God, then he or she must learn certain simple rules. First, if the matter at hand is important to the life and future of the congregation, don't vote. Whatever the rhetoric, voting on crucial issues is divisive, and debate is more a test of one's wit and quickness against an opponent. Under such conditions we displace with tension and distrust the quietness and playfulness that is needed to listen by faith in God's desired future for the congregation.

Second, leaders must build time and space between formulating a problem and deciding how to solve it. Allow time out for mental digestion. The serious frame of mind, and the processes used for formulating a problem are different from the sense of freedom and creativity, the quick imagination and the processes used for deciding how to solve the problem, once it has been formulated. The two processes are so different that most people cannot make the shift in the same meeting. Rather, they approach decision making and problem solving with the same sense of gloom and doom they felt while they were trying to figure what the problem was, and its causes.

It is far better to do problem formulation in one meeting and problem solving or decision making in a later meeting. This allows persons the necessary time out for mental and prayerful digestion, before deciding what to do about serious problems or decisions.

We have discovered that often only ten minutes between problem identification and decision making can be helpful. In such instances, we encourage the decision makers to be silent, and go into themselves to listen for an answer or idea from within. On the other hand, we occasionally lead a group into thirty days of "silence," a period in which the decision makers will not discuss the matter among themselves, or with anyone else. We provide the people with a daily guided prayer, reading, meditation, and journaling method, which all agree to follow during the prayerful listening (discernment) period. In virtually every instance we notice the group comes to consensus without any thought of a vote. Then when consensus is reached, they sometimes do vote in order to "make it legal."

Anticipation is reading and conducting futures studies and applying them to the congregation's specific situation. Every pastor who sincerely wishes for his or her church to have a future will become a student of futures materials, and a teacher of it to the leaders of the congregation. Much of this material can be directly applied to your church and community.

In addition, the pastor will move beyond the demographics of his or her community to the socio- and cultural demographics of the community. These demographics can be of tremendous assistance in anticipating future ministry opportunities, and in assessing the ministries that are currently being offered.[6]

Anticipating the future of a local congregation and its community might mean looking into the future for a span of three to five years. Perhaps for major capital projects one must anticipate the future ten to twenty years. But in a turbulent environment such as ours, planning three years ahead is about as far as we may safely predict and plan.

Innovation[7]

Innovation is making change work for the good of the congregation, searching for change, and then exploiting it to fuel new ideas for new ministries. Innovation is doing better with what you have; making something new out of existing resources, programs, and structures. Innovation is the ability to let past successes die after they have lived their day, in order to make room for and release energies to grasp a new and better future.

Innovation is a continual searching for the unexpected, whether good or bad, and using the new situation to leap ahead in exploiting the present and the future. Innovation springs from a number of sources, which may be summarized as follows:

* The unexpected—the unexpected successes, failures, and outside events;
* The incongruity—between reality as it actually is and reality as it is assumed to be or as it "ought to be";
* Changes in society or community that catch everyone unaware; i.e., massive layoffs, housing boom, etc.;

° Changes in community demographics, changes in perceptions and moods, etc.

Innovation is the principle of death and resurrection. God has created all living things in such a manner that life comes forth out of death. For this reason Easter is always preceded by Lent. No Lent, no Easter. This holds true for the congregation as well. Yet a great many congregations and denominations forestall the programs or ministries that promise new life, while they try to resuscitate programs and rites that exhibit every sign of readiness to die.

The ability to utilize the innovative principle of death and resurrection requires the leader to keep his or her eyes open, watching for programs that are trying to die, and then helping them die with dignity. After revamping and retrying a floundering ministry once or twice, help it celebrate its good past, and die. On the other hand, keep your eyes open, watch for ideas and ministries that are trying to be born—and when you discover one, mid-wife it. Help it to be born. This is innovation. It is seizing the unexpected and exploiting its potential.

Leaders who participate in the birth of the new to which God is leading, and who allow the dying of programs whose day has come and gone, participate in the ebb and flow of God's leading. In the congregation, something may need to die in order for something new to be born.

Many leaders have no vision of what God wishes to birth through the congregation, because they spend all their time and energy nursing things that want to die. This survival effort, according to Peter Drucker, is exhausting. " 'Nothing requires more heroic efforts than to keep a corpse from stinking, and yet nothing is quite so futile' is an old medical proverb. In almost any organization I have come across, the best people are engaged in this futile effort; yet all they can hope to accomplish is to delay acceptance of the inevitable a little longer and at great cost."[8]

It is important to ask, "Knowing what we know now, would we start this program or group or ministry today?" A strong reason for continued atrophy in many congregations and denominations is that vital resources and energies continue to be spent on maintaining life-support systems for comatose programs, agencies, markets, and rituals.

Innovation is the "bubble up" principle. Concomitant to the principle of death and resurrection is the bubble up principle. It is disarmingly simple. The leaders simply learn to *listen in order to discover* what is bubbling up throughout the congregation. As you move about among the members of the congregation and the participants in the congregation's programs, *listen.* Listen for new ministry and program ideas. Make note of who makes which suggestions. When you hear the same idea three times, gather those persons together and get them talking about their idea. You will soon know whether this is an idea whose time has come by the quality of their discussions and their degree of commitment to their own idea.

We have come across congregations who utilize this bubble up method to discover and launch many of their ministries. The leaders regularly announce to the members of the congregation, and others, that if three or more persons have a vision for a new ministry, and if they have a plan, the congregation will support them in their ministry endeavor with resources (e.g., consultation, space, money).

In addition to the rather informal bubble up means described above, you may wish to utilize more intentional means to hear what's bubbling up in the congregation (e.g., suggestion boxes, focus groups, consumer panels, town hall meetings, post card surveys).

Consider Charles Simeon, who used the bubble up principle to bring his congregation back from the brink of death. In the latter part of the 1700s Charles Simeon was appointed vicar of the old Holy Trinity Church, whose congregation had dwindled to a handful of very unwilling parishioners. Simeon began his ministry by going from door to door throughout his parish, repeating at every door these words, "My name is Simeon. I have called to inquire if I can do anything for your welfare." The poor and despised living in the bounds of his parish freely offered suggestions, which Simeon gathered together into innovative ministries. Soon the poor and despised began to attend his church in ever-increasing numbers, and this caused the few rich members of the church to hate them even more. They protested to the bishop to get rid of this man who was ruining their church. But the bishop refused to remove Simeon, saying that a little life was better than death.[9]

Innovation is capturing the opportunities that are present at the brink of death. Have you ever felt in your heart the words of Ezekiel as he gazed upon the congregation and pondered, "Can these dry bones live and breathe again?" More than one of our readers will find himself or herself leading a church that stands at the brink of death. Whatever else might be said about serving as the leader of a dying church, there is something very freeing about the situation. When conditions are so bad that whatever you do can hardly make matters worse, you have arrived at the state of pure and unadulterated freedom. However, in order to lay claim to this freedom, one must first name it. Candidly accept the situation for what it is.

Many pastors and congregations, however, either deny the truth or ignore the conditions, going along as if every indicator were pointing onward and upward. Such souls are never free. By not allowing themselves to feel the pain of perceived failure, they deny themselves the freedom to succeed greatly. If your church is dying, name it for what it is, and then set about with abandon to see whether you might find the Golden Thread that holds promise of immediately breathing new life into the gasping body. It can be done—maybe not always, but you will never know the odds if you don't try.

When the congregation is dying, it is no time for business as usual. Doing business as usual is a sure way of driving the last nail into the coffin. When the congregation is dying, something must be done, and it must be qualitatively different from what has gone on before. The Golden Thread never is to be found in the bin marked "business as usual."

There is probably no time when a congregation is more open to innovation and entrepreneurial leadership than when it stands at the brink of death. Over the past four years we have interviewed many small congregations, at the brink of death—that have moved into a new renewal cycle by deciding to utilize the principles of innovation.

We recently came across a small congregation in the rural hill country of east Ohio that found itself at the brink of death. The members decided it was time to call it quits, and they called in the denominational officials to announce their intentions.

The wise judicatory representatives suggested they make a diligent search to discover whether there was anything they could still do to be of service to their neighbors (this is innovation). The weary congregation decided to give it a try, but how were they to discover whether there was a way they might serve the community? After much discussion, the people decided to have a potluck dinner, invite everyone in the community, and ask them whether they saw any way for the church to serve them. They invited everyone, and just about everyone came. After the meal, they put the matter before their neighbors, asking whether there was any way the congregation might serve the community. The neighbors put their heads together, and after much lively discussion said, "Yes! have more potlucks. This is the first time we have all been together since the community school closed. The school used to bring us together. Now we have no reason or place to get together. Just have more potlucks."

The congregation decided that this was reason enough to carry on. They would serve community potlucks four times a year. By doing so this little congregation captured the attention and interest of the community. Persons who never did so before began to attend the Sunday services. The congregation is growing steadily. The church is alive and well. Their innovative approach to search for the Golden Thread worked.

This congregation discovered what many others discovered: Opportunities often abound at the brink of death, and no one opposes innovation when there is absolutely nothing to be lost by trying.

Innovation can happen at "Old First Church." Not only can a small, rural church discover life at the brink of death, but "Old First Church" can also. Raymond J. Bakke and Samuel K. Roberts organized a national consultation to study the phenomenon of Old First church. They concluded that there is hope and a future for Old First. One way is to connect the present opportunities with the vision of the church's founders, to be the incarnational presence of Christ by squarely facing the challenges, not being afraid to modify their internal structures, and by securing the trust of the public.[10] More specifically, Bakke and Roberts assert a viable future for Old First if the following conditions prevail:

1. If there is quality lay and professional leadership within the ranks of Old First.
2. If a sound theological perspective is developed on biblical mission, values, goals, context, and community and put into place at Old First.
3. If a functional history of Old First can be recovered; if Old First can redeem its usable past.
4. If a mission that is genuinely contextualized can be developed that shows how Old First can adjust to new dynamics and new opportunities.
5. If bulky and worn-out structures can be streamlined and refocused.
6. If programs can be ranked to reflect the conscious mobilization and empowerment of church members and the stewardship of their unique gifts for ministry.[11]

Excellence

Excellence is an all-out commitment to quality—doing it right the first time. Continuous improvement is the quest to get a little bit better at your ministry every time you do it. Following the Golden Rule, do your work for others with the same care you would want them to work for you. The buzz words for excellence today are "quality control" and "total quality." But a commitment to total quality is not so new as one might think. Paul suggested it to the congregation at Colossae about 2,000 years ago: "Whatever your task, put yourselves into it, as done for the Lord and not for your masters" (Col. 3:23).

Excellence is found in paying attention to the important things over and against the trivial, or the urgent matters that are always clamoring for attention. It is to be found in concentrating on the vision that establishes the direction; mobilizing the people to achieve the vision; and paying attention to the morale and the motivation of those who do the work of the ministry.

Excellence causes systemic change throughout the entire congregation, not the least of which is that *excellence changes people* fully as much as it changes their work. With excellence comes great enthusiasm and commitment among the persons who do the ministry and an increased sense of satisfaction and support among those for whom the ministry is carried on. Excellence is the acid proof of caring. Without caring there can be no commitment to quality.

If the choir director does not deeply care for the pain and loneliness and the deep-felt worship needs of those who come to find a word of comfort and direction, then she or he will not be committed to excellence in directing and will settle for a mediocre performance. Then the singers will sing without spirit, for they know they are not valued by their leader.

Ayn Rand says that the quickest way to kill the human spirit is to ask someone to do mediocre work.[12] Excellence causes change to come not only at the point of one's ministry, but *in one's spirit* as well. A commitment to quality will signal a return of the spirit to the Sunday school rooms, to the church offices, to the sanctuary, and wherever ministry is performed. Quality, or goodness, is a part of the nature of God. The two words *good* and *God* are very closely related. Excellence brings a great many benefits to the congregation, not the least of which is that it restores spirit and enthusiasm to ministry. And quality with enthusiasm can launch the most dispirited congregation into a new stage of renewal.[13]

Excellence is the ability to keep yourself out of the activity trap. When the congregation is in a growth phase (as depicted in the life cycle, in chap. 11) there is an expansive vision of reaching out, of making a difference in the community and the world. As the congregation passes through maturity and into a declining phase, discussions and energies shift toward self-preservation; there is less sensitivity to the needs within the community and a blindness to the new opportunities for renewal that abound all around them. This closing in upon oneself marks the beginning of the activity trap.[14] This insidious condition will ensnare the wisest and most experienced persons in the church, because "the Activity Trap is the abysmal situation people find themselves in when they start out toward an important and clear objective but, in an amazingly short time, become so enmeshed in the activity of getting there that they forget where they are going. . . . Once-clear goals may evolve into something else, while the activity remains the same—and becomes an end in itself. In other words, the activity persists, but toward a false goal."[15]

Caught in the activity trap, leaders and members believe that the preservation of the congregation's existence is the guiding principle for all decisions and effort. There is no desire to see beyond the congregation's survival; thus the focus is almost exclusively turned inward upon themselves, with little attention paid to the needs of others. Opportunities go completely unnoticed. The members of a church in which leaders are caught in the activity trap tend to be passive observers. They are languid and lethargic. This combination, a hyperactive leader and a lethargic congregation, spells the disappointing last chapter of a congregation or religious institution.

The leader caught in the activity trap is totally unable to see these approaching realities, though they stand at the doorstep. He or she is unable to anticipate the future or to plan and carry out the necessary innovations to capture the future, as compared to being blind-sided by it. Likewise, mediocrity has driven all spirit and enthusiasm out of the place. The fears of the people become a self-fulfilling prophecy; they fear things will get worse, and they do. Entrapment into activties is a terminal disease, easily contracted and almost impossible to cure. The best remedy: Don't get caught in it.

Excellence is a total commitment to quality in every small and large contact with the congregation and the community. Excellence begins in the mind and spirit of the pastor and the leaders. If the leaders excuse less than total quality in their own work, and if they condone mediocre work in any area of the church's ministry, that is exactly what they will get—mediocre ministry. Mediocre ministry is highly contagious, and once caught it may be incurable. There are exceptions, but generally when only one group is allowed to do poor work, nearly all the other groups are likewise uncommitted. The reverse is generally also true. And so we say that excellence is a total commitment to quality in every small and large contact with the congregation and the community.

Must excellence always meet an absolute standard? Is excellence ever measured by a relative standard? These questions do not lend themselves to an easy answer. If the workers' total quality is to be measured on a relative scale, the question becomes: Relative to what? Shall we measure excellence relative to the volunteer's physical and mental capacities? This sounds logical until we observe the physically challenged volunteer minister, and discover that he or she has already set quality standards for his or her work that far exceed the standards the other volunteers tend to set for themselves, though they have no physical challenges. So true is this that many claim there are no physically disabled persons. There are only persons who differ from others in certain ways.

The leaders who genuinely care for all workers and who are committed to excellence in every large and small area of the church's ministry will care enough to place workers in ministries where each one has the capacity to do total quality work.

Excellence is taking discipleship seriously. The ultimate test of a disciple-maker is the quality of his or her disciples. Regrettably much of what goes on under the rubric of discipleship training is, in fact, not training at all, but teaching. The pastor gathers a small group together and spends several months teaching them how to be disciples. At some point they graduate from the course and then each one gathers his or her own small group and teaches them how to be disciples, and so on.

In such pyramids, however, few realize that *teaching and learning are not the same.* There can be much teaching, good teaching, and yet be absolutely no learning at all. The tools for teaching in the classroom or the pastor's study are not the tools for learning. Teachers lecture, but learners learn very little from lectures. Teachers give quizzes or hand out workbooks to fill in the blanks. Learners learn just about nothing from taking a test, and not much more by filling in the blanks.

Teachers who teach discipleship may take their teaching seriously, but they do not take the student's learning seriously. Learning happens by mentoring, modeling, hands-on experience, and reflection on the experience.

Perhaps we have overplayed the matter. But one thing is certain: Enthusiasm for doing quality ministry (whether typing a letter, making a hospital visit, or volunteering in Habitat for Humanity) is *caught* more than it is taught. It is caught by observing the example of the pastor and other persons whom the disciple has decided to emulate as a model. Excellence is first *observed* in the work of others, and then *decided* as a standard for one's own ministry, and then *modeled* by someone who can demonstrate excellence in that area of ministry.

Jesus knew all of this—and so his method of discipleship training was not to sit in his study and talk about it. Rather his call to discipleship was "follow me." Then, after the disciples had observed him sufficiently, he sent them out to try it on their own, always to return to him to talk it over—to reflect on their own experiences and to observe him some more. And thus they learned to be disciples and apostles.

A fundamental key to discipleship is to demonstrate a commitment to total quality and to do one's own work with excellence—and then to call for total quality in the disciples' efforts.

If a volunteer hospital visitor is having difficulty "getting the visit right," it may do some good to sit in the pastor's office discussing it. It will do far more good if the pastor goes with the volunteer on several visits and demonstrates what a quality hospital visit actually looks like. Then the pastor may observe the volunteer's efforts, followed by candid assessment of his or her performance in every aspect of the visit. Then the pastor might say, "Now keep doing it with excellence. For a while I really don't care how many visits you make in a day. I care only that you make each visit an excellent experience for the person you are visiting. If you can do only one quality visit a day, that's fine. One quality visit will do more good for the patients and will be more reflective of the care God wants to show to those who are ill than ten visits done short of quality. When you feel you are doing one visit a day with quality, then move up to two visits a day, and then to three."

The process presupposes that the pastor is himself or herself totally committed to excellence in hospital visitation, and that he or she knows what a total quality hospital visit would comprise.

Is this being too hard on the simple volunteer who has so graciously consented to do hospital visitation? We think not. The only satisfaction the volunteer gets from volunteer work is the satisfaction that someone cares enough about his or her work to care that it is done well. There is no enthusiasm or satisfaction to be gained from the volunteer doing mediocre work. Money is not the reward. The satisfaction for the disciples is the sense that they are doing their work excellently—in the spirit of Christ—who will one day visit them and say, "Well done, good and faithful servant. Your work has been a joy to me. Come on in. Let's celebrate a job well done."

Excellence is continuous improvement through ministry evaluation and feedback, and more informal compliments and/or suggestions for improvement. Continuous improvement requires continual, rigorous evaluation and feedback to the ministry units. There must be established bench marks so that persons can measure their improvement. Evaluation need not be complicated. As a rule the more simple and natural the evaluation can be, the better.

The staff and lay ministry teams at Willow Creek Community Church, South Barrington, Illinois, are methodical and tough in evaluating every aspect of the church's ministry. Bill Hybels, the senior pastor, models this need for continuous evaluation by his own example. For example, every Tuesday, immediately following the weekend services, a group of participants and staff sit down to evaluate every part of the weekend experience, to see how it might have been done more effectively. Everything is evaluated, from the parking lot procedures, to the sermon, to the final word. Participating in this evaluation are those persons who lead the services and activities. By this means the pastors, worship leaders, and workers get immediate feedback on their efforts that Sunday.

The leaders of Willow Creek Community Church have found a simple, yet highly effective, way to evaluate the Sunday service activities and experience. All leaders who care about quality in ministry must find their own methods for measuring quality, and improving it.

In this chapter we have discussed the stages of development a congregation goes through as it progresses from its inception to its final demise. We suggested that wise leadership can prolong the life cycle of the congregation by leading it through stages of renewal. The three keys to renewal are anticipation, innovation, and excellence. These three conditions are essential for leading a congregation to capture the opportunities that are fostered by the internal and external changes that confront the congregation.

The leader sets the tone for and helps to create the conditions in which the congregation is equipped and encouraged to study its future with anticipation, to encourage and support innovative ministries, and to aspire to excellence in all the large and small ministries of the church. This is what it means to manage change, rather than to be managed by it.

Chapter Thirteen

The Leadership Team of the Congregation[1]

You depend upon the board, and therefore you can be more effective with a strong board, a committed board, an energetic board, than with a rubber stamp. The rubber stamp will, in the end, not stamp at all when you most need it.[2]

Peter F. Drucker

The trustee role advocated here goes far beyond [a] limited view and implies a dynamic obligation, an insistent motivating force originating with trustees that obliges the institution to move toward distinction as a servant.[3]   Robert K. Greenleaf

According to Jerome, "There can be no church community without a leader or team of leaders."[4] At the inception of the ancient church, the fledgling congregations had no guidelines for defining their leadership positions or patterns.[5] While different leadership patterns were tested, there were in every place those persons who stood forth as local leaders in the midst of the community ("those who labor among you, lead you and admonish you").[6] Now, after two millennia of schisms, growth, and experimentation there still is no set pattern for governance in the local congregation. However, two distinct leadership groups have emerged: the pastoral staff and the governing board.[7]

Conceptual Problems Confronting the Church Board

Peter Drucker says that all boards have one thing in common: *They do not function.*[8] This adds to the frustration of pastors and board members alike. There are a number of common problems or conditions that erode the church board's ability to function effectively. And when the board does not function, the effectiveness of the ministry team is bound to suffer.

Boards are often either too passive or too controlling. The dysfunction of church boards usually fluctuates between these two dangerous extremes; either they give up all responsibility and authority to the senior pastor and become a rubber stamp of his or her program, or they fight for control, rebelling against the pastor's program and, perhaps, even working to get rid of the pastor.

To be worth the time and energy it consumes, the board must lead, and not merely *rubber stamp* the pastor's wishes (or spend its time trying to stamp out the pastor). Rubber stamping may seem comfortable when things are going well. However, when crisis develops or serious conflicts erupt between board, pastor, or congregation, then the pain is far greater than whatever might be involved to achieve a more appropriate structure and process for the church board.

Many church boards are too passive and never figure out what they are supposed to do. These boards give the pastor unilateral decision-making authority—until the church is threatened by conflict or some other crisis. Then, in the face of threat they hold the pastor entirely responsible for the problem and bend every effort to get rid of him or her. And, in getting rid of the pastor, many boards believe they have finally rid the church of all its maladies.

There are many other problems with a board that abdicates all decision making to the pastor, not the least of which is that the board members never sufficiently understand the church's goals and ministry programs to provide the pastor and ministry units any strengthening suggestions or critical evaluation. Nor do they sufficiently "own" the ministries to effectively advocate for them when the pastor or workers come under fire by critical members of the congregation.

On the other hand, there are church boards who are very active but seldom if ever direct their energies toward any worthwhile effort. Rather, they struggle against the pastor for control of every minute decision, giving the pastor no freedom to plan and carry out the ministry that rightly is his or her responsibility. The predominant issue for such a board is this: Who is going to run the church, the pastor or the board? For such boards the concern is *not* effectiveness, but power. This appetite for power and control often need reside in only one member in order to paralyze the entire board and obstruct the ministry of the church. When the board, or some of its members, grasps for power and control, every interaction between the pastor and the board is treated with suspicion and resistance. In such a milieu, a great deal of time and energy is spent in board meetings—for all the wrong reasons, resulting in all the wrong actions.

However, not all boards are passive or pathologically active; many (but not enough) are healthy and effective. Healthy boards want competent pastors, and healthy pastors want competent boards. This brings our discussion to the most important point to be made in this chapter: *It is the pastor's first responsibility to train the board in how to be effective, and it is the board's first responsibility to train the pastor in how to be an effective pastor.* What is most needed between board and pastor is *interdependence,* each relying on the other for training, support, and guidance.

Members of Boards Are Often Underutilized

According to the best available statistics, ninety million Americans—one out of two—work as "volunteers" on an average of three hours per week in the nonprofit sector. Volunteerism is booming in nonprofit organizations (there are 900,000 nonprofit organizations in the United States, 30,000 having started in 1990). Some authorities believe that within ten years, 120 million people (two thirds of all adults) will work five hours per week as nonprofit volunteers.[9]

Many of these willing volunteers are woefully led and greatly underutilized. Perhaps this is nowhere more true than in religious organizations. Certainly it is true for the majority of church boards, where performance is far below what is reasonable and possible with their available resources, both human and material. Richard T. Ingram has explained the rule of thirds in describing the makeup of most boards.

The first subgroup on the board is the Movers and Shakers. They seldom miss meetings, actively participate, and gladly take on their assignments. The second group, the Semiactivists, usually will

In a conflict consultation, a pastor confided in us regarding his own frustration with the church board. One meeting had an agenda that included forty items, all of them dealing with trivia, including a discussion regarding the correct temperature of the water in the baptismal font. Of course, such important trivia requires time. The meeting adjourned at 2:00 A.M.

A friend recently confided in us that he serves on a para-church board on which the leader sees the board members as a pack of fund raisers. Our friend says he is constantly bombarded with mail carrying frightful descriptions of the dire plight of the agency. He is convinced the agency director's only interest is to frighten or shame him into working harder to keep the place funded. He is looking for a good excuse to get off that board.

Perhaps our favorite story is the time a fifteen-member church board spent two hours on one item until 11:00 P.M., trying to decide how to cut down on photocopying costs. Shortly thereafter, the person telling us of this meeting left the board and the church in search of one that gave its time to more substantial agenda.

respond to a call for help, but often require coaxing and wheedling. They will usually come through when needed, but are not consistently dependable. Ingram identifies the third group as the Phantoms. While their names are seen on the list of board members, they are not seen or heard at the board meetings. They are literally the silent minority on any board.[10] So if two-thirds of board members are not being utilized, what is the problem?

The problem is that most board members simply do not know what they are supposed to do. They have not been trained; they are not fully informed; they feel patronized or unwanted; and sometimes they are treated as the primary leader's pack of fund raisers. In recruiting a person to the board, the responsibilities for being on the board and the expectations of the individual members should be clearly communicated, understood, and accepted. Many boards exhibit a definite mind-set to deal only with trivia, the micro-issues of a congregation's life and ministry. In such a setting, the board member who wants to grow and contribute to more substantial issues quickly becomes bored and checks out of the board process.

How do situations like this come about? We find that boards usually deal with trivia, hour after hour, because that is just exactly what the pastor (or the preceding pastor) wants them to do—consuming all their time and energy with junk agendas, so they will *not have time to lead*, thus leaving the pastor free to go in any direction he or she chooses.

After twenty years as conflict interventionists in local churches, the only times we have worked in situations in which the pastor has literally demanded the loyalty of the rest of the ministerial staff has been in situations where the pastor was serving as chairperson of the board. And, of course, the board is passive. This blindness of pastors and board members to the systemic effects of the "single chief" structure is perhaps fostered by the long-established notion of the absoluteness and self-sufficiency of the pastor, which is perpetuated in the mythology of many Protestant organizations.

Such relationships between the board and the pastor-as-chairperson can go along well for many years, being neither challenged nor critically reviewed until the church finds itself in crisis. But when trust for the pastor begins to erode and there is a need for the board to act decisively and in a positive manner, the board finds itself unable to do so. It falls victim to the accruing result of its past behavior, and being unable to act positively, the board scurries to absolve itself of responsibility by blaming it all on the pastor—or even worse, finds itself in the midst of great crisis, but being among the last to know a crisis exists.

An Incompetent Board Member

The vital interests of the congregation are often ignored in order to protect an incompetent board member. Another conceptual flaw exists in many church boards: Too much of the rhetoric and behavior of the senior pastor and board alike are still devoted to the caring of one individual, and not enough attention is given to caring for the congregation as a whole. There are times when, as difficult and painful as it may be, the concerns and interests of an individual need to be set aside for the sake of the entire board or congregation.

For example, most pastors have experienced the devastating influence of an antagonist, or "bully," on the board. One board bully can paralyze the board's effectiveness and, therefore, seriously wound the ministries of the entire congregation. Likewise, there may also be a pocket of persons in the congregation who have the board bully in their pocket. Any person who comes to board membership "to clean up the church," or to represent the positions of a small group bent upon disruption, must be confronted and asked to change—or leave the board. Yet this almost never happens, because the pastor and the other board members give in to the temptation to do good—to excuse and protect the sullen or belligerent person.[11]

Primus inter pares—First Among Equals

The alternative to the hierarchical, lone chief structure is *primus inter pares*, or "first among equals," which has been an emerging leadership concept.[12] While there is still a "first," a leader, that leader is not the chief. The differences may appear to be subtle; the inner attitudes are radically different. But what is proposed in *primus inter pares* is a top leadership team of equals with a *primus*. The *primus* is one who has conceptual perspective in going out ahead to show the way, and, at the same time, has team-building ability. The *primus* as team builder provides a process by which the team is held together in common purpose in movement toward the institutional goals. It is enabling the team to "do the right things" for the best interests of the congregation.

In the congregation the concept of *primus inter pares* should be carried out on at least two levels. (1) The board and senior pastor should have a peer relationship in deciding the program and staffing needs of the church. (2) The pastor of a large church needs to have around him or her a highly competent ministry management team (associate pastors, lay program directors, etc.), each with specialized expertise that is complimentary to the talents of others on the team.

Finally, while not all of the pastors in a multiple-staff church may sit on the governing board, all the pastors should be a part of the ministry management team, with voice and vote. In the case of large pastoral staffs, having all the pastors attend every board meeting might be a waste of time, and granting all pastors voting rights might constitute an unhealthy voting bloc. Each board and congregation needs to think these matters through in the light of their own situation. (However, we think that if there are fewer than six pastors they should perhaps all be members of the board.)

Obtaining valid and useful information upon which to base good judgments and decisions is a major problem for boards in churches of every size. Having the persons who carry major responsibilities for the church's ministries on the board can go a long way toward correcting these problems. And if they are not on the board they must regularly meet with the board to discuss their ministry, gain feedback, and so forth.

> We are at the time of this writing consulting in a congregation of 900 members, with five pastors. The communication between the pastors and the board could hardly be worse. Yet one pastor told us that during his seven years there as a pastor he has been invited to meet with the board only three times. The board complains that this pastor isn't doing a good job. But how would they know? They have never observed his work firsthand, they have never talked with him about his work, they have never provided him any training in the areas of his suspected weaknesses. So if this pastor is doing a poor job, who is to blame? First, the senior pastor, who doesn't want any other pastors to attend the board sessions, and who has provided his staff no training. Second, the governing board, who has allowed this foolish waste of human ability to go on year after year without calling the senior pastor to accountability.

The Chairperson of the Board

If the board is to function well on behalf of the congregation, it needs an unusual person, a *primus* leader, serving as its chairperson.

First and foremost, the chair of the board should not be a member of the clergy team. When the pastor, as head of the ministry management team, is also positioned as chairperson of the board, there is an unhealthy and potentially dangerous ambiguity in the governance of the church. If there is no *primus* leader on the governing board, it is the responsibility of the pastor to provide the training necessary for the chairperson to grow into a *primus* leader, or to work with the nominating committee to assure a *primus* leader will be brought to this position.

The rule that the pastor must serve as board chairperson is a basic structural flaw that several denominations impose upon their churches. The pastor-as-board-chairperson perpetuates a long out-dated pyramidal structure, at the top of which sits the pastor as the single chief. It should come as no surprise that pastors in these denominations generally do not accept the church board as an important influence, and that the church board has great difficulty in understanding and establishing its appropriate role. According to Greenleaf, the interaction of these two reinforcing elements—the low level participation of board members and the single chief executive—is a clear design for mediocrity.[13]

This arrangement is fundamentally flawed because the pastor is always leading in a situation that suggests a potential conflict of interest. On the one hand, he or she chairs the group that sets the policy which guides the ministry and protects the interests of the membership; while on the other hand, he or she supervises the people and programs that are to carry out the policies established by the board. When someone questions this arrangement, the board members, themselves, often defend it, saying that they want to give their pastor the freedom to be a strong leader. Generally, however, the result is the exact opposite. The preponderance of pastors in such situations are weak in their leadership, resentful of their relationships with the board, and unable to mobilize a coordinated and effective staff.

The chairperson, as *primus* leader of the board and its most public spokesperson to the congregation and staff, should be selected by the board for his or her conceptual leadership, team building skills, dedication to optimum performance, and for the ability to make the board role exciting, creative, and responsible.

The Roles and Responsibilities of the Governing Board

At least six crucial roles and responsibilities must be carried out by the church board.

To Select and Train the Pastor to Be Effective in This Particular Congregation

The fundamental responsibility of the board is to *select* and to train the pastor for effective ministry in their particular church. Each congregation has its own unique history and sentient boundaries. It is the board's responsibility to inform the pastor of these and to run interference for him or her when one of the sentiencies is transgressed.[14] A conventional wisdom among pastors says, Don't follow a long-term pastor, or one who was greatly loved by the congregation. Is long tenure or being loved dangerous to the life of a congregation? Hardly! The problem is neither the tenure nor the relationships, but the fact that over a long tenure many sentiencies are established, which the incoming pastor cannot possibly know. Yet the board takes no time whatsoever to fully acquaint the pastor with unique quirks of his or her new setting. Then when the pastor gets in serious trouble, the board seems paralyzed to protect the pastor from protracted, useless criticism and "trench fighting."

Time after time we are called to work with a congregation in which a small group of members (usually never more than 50 in a congregation of 1,000, or more than 10 in a congregation of 150) have almost immediately set out to destroy the ministry of a new pastor—because he or she has committed some unforgivable infraction, such as standing in the wrong place when offering the benediction, or entering into the baptismal tank with the baptismal candidate. Yet, when we arrive we find the board paralyzed to act, calling no one to accountability for the damage that is inflicted on the pastor and the congregation. The one thing we know in such situations is that the former pastor, regardless of the length of his or her tenure, failed a crucial test: not training the board to be effective.

On the other hand, the main responsibility of the board is to train the pastor and to support the pastor and to call the pastor to accountability for his or her leadership results.

To Provide for an Effective Process for Bringing New Members to the Board and to Work with the Pastor to Train New Candidates

Inarguably, the driving factor behind the incompetence of board members is that they are given no training whatsoever to fill their important role as members of the governing board. The result is that succession on many church boards resembles the blind leading the blind. Earlier we said that training the board was the pastor's responsibility, and so it is. However, the pastor cannot do this alone. The board must set the example and the policies that cause all new candidates to know that they will be required to engage in continual training—so long as they are on the board. Unless the board sets such example and policy, the pastor will almost surely be resisted when attempting to provide training for new board members. The pastor should train them, because the board calls for that training.

To Provide the Appropriate Organizational Structures and Staffing Patterns to Facilitate the Mission and Ministries of the Church

A basic difference between the needs of small, medium, and large churches is that *the large church needs a ministry team.* It is rare for a large church to succeed in finding a senior pastor who is equally competent in all pastoral roles of leader, preacher/teacher, caregiver, and administrator. Even if the large congregation succeeds in finding such a person, he or she does not have the time necessary to give adequate attention to each of these roles. No one person is to be entrusted with the total responsibility and freedom of shaping and administering the ministries of the church, while at the same time carrying primary responsibility for the congregation's pastoral care and priestly needs. Completeness is found only in complementary relationships of persons who relate as equals. In order to ensure the effectiveness of the pastor and ministry team, the board must know the congregation well enough to know what is required in order to offer effective ministry in that place.

In addition to this, it is important for the board to participate in the design of the top administrative structure of the church, including the assignments of those few individuals who are given chief administrative responsibility. The board should not rubber stamp recommendations made by the pastor on these matters. To be proactive with the pastor in deciding the program and staffing needs of the church takes nothing away from the power or authority of the pastor. Rather, it adds to the possibility of the pastor avoiding many land mines, and being more fully effective as leader of the church.

It could be said that the pastor and ministry team should represent something of the highly spirited horse with the bit in its teeth and fire in its eyes, with a driving passion burning in its heart. And the role of the board is to provide the hand on the rein to guide the horse so that efforts are not wasted and the results are consistent with the needs of the congregation and surrounding society.

To Work with the Pastor, Ministry Staff, and Congregation to Develop a Corporate Vision for the Church

The church board is ultimately responsible for the church as an institution and everything that goes on in it. The board must continuously deal with the questions of mission: What business are we in? What are we trying to accomplish? Who will we serve, and what benefits will we offer to society within the context of our own community? To make clear the mission of the congregation is perhaps the most critical job for the board, for upon these decisions lie the ministry and future of the church.

Therefore, the major purpose of the board, along with the pastor, is to be the guardian of the institutional mission. Normally, it is the pastor who facilitates a process for developing a corporate vision for the congregation, because the board does not know how or will not do it. However, it should be the board who leads, or at least works alongside the pastor, to lead the congregation into a sense of corporate vision and a compelling mission. If the board is not involved in this process, it is abdicating one of its primary responsibilities. David Hubbard, former President of Fuller Theological Seminary, makes the point well:

[The board] owns an organization not for its own sake—as a board—but for the sake of the mission which that organization is to perform. Board members don't own it as though they were stockholders voting blocks of stock; they own it because they care. . . . They actually own it in partnership because, in a sense, the organization belongs just as much to others.[15]

To Monitor the Appropriateness of the Church's Mission and to Assess the Performance of the Workers and Program Ministries

Closely related to defining the mission, according to Greenleaf, the board must also "assume a firm obligation to bring their institution to a distinguished level of performance."[16] The board cannot delegate its responsibility for the ultimate results of the church's ministry—not even to the pastor.

Integral to this responsibility is the role that *measures the work of its leaders against the established mission and goals of the church,* and *assesses the quality of interpersonal relationships within the staff and congregation.* Further, the board must assume responsibility for *measuring the satisfaction of the various constituencies* who are being ministered to by the church. Also, it is the board's responsibility to *assess the quality of work and ministry being offered by the staff.* The responsibility of the board is to provide a hand on the rein, to balance the activities and efforts of congregation and staff in such a way that the needs of the entire congregation, and of its surrounding community, are met with more or less equal degrees of attention and effectiveness.

To Create a Continual Climate of Trust

Altogether too often the board does not advocate for the pastor, or the directions the pastor is setting for staff and the congregation. Rather, board members become politely neutral or disavow any involvement in the vision or changes the pastor is advocating. Such behavior on the part of the board throws the congregation into a high state of confusion. Distrust among pastor and board begins to grow. When the congregation is not clear as to who is steering the ship, or when members believe the board and pastor are attempting to steer the ship in opposite directions, distrust and resistance are to be expected.

It is not the pastor's responsibility alone to create a level of trust within the congregation. The board is perhaps the most potent symbol of trust in the entire organization. Board members must not violate the trust placed in them. Likewise, they must work in such a way as to strengthen the trust of the congregation toward the pastor, administrators, and entire ministry team. Apart from doing this, the board is not fulfilling its responsibilities.

When a board is passive, or ill informed, and dedicates a major part of its time to providing a cover of legitimacy for whatever the pastor wants to do—or opposes whatever the pastor wants—there should be no surprise when the congregation does not trust the board. Neither should there be surprise when the pastor adopts certain means of politicking the board so that the pastor may get what he or she wants without critical review. But when this is the relationship between board and pastor, the pastor ends up not trusting them, for he or she knows they are mediocre and that the pastor must relate to them in ways that foster entanglements and favors. The result will be that the longer the pastor serves that congregation the more inappropriate become the intergroup relationships between pastor, staff, and board. In such situations the congregation invariably senses all is not right at the core of the organization, and they begin to distrust all of the leaders.

The Limitations of the Board of Directors

The boards of most churches have set for themselves certain limitations or have capitulated to the limitations placed upon them by the ecclesiastical policies of the denomination.

First, the primary limitation of the board's role in the church is a common assumption held by the board members, themselves, that the pastor and ministry team will see to it that the church performs as it should. They assume that the pastoral staff will see to it that the church operates close to what is reasonable and possible with the church resources.

A second limitation stems from the fact that few persons, regardless of how capable or skilled they are, have the ability to set goals for their own performance and to perform consistently at a high level of excellence. Likewise, few persons are able to judge their own performance objectively. It is not reasonable to expect a pastor and other staff members to do all of these things well simultaneously. Yet the church board often limits itself to affirming goals that are set by the pastor or the clergy staff, while at the same time limiting itself to assessing performance only through the reports and information supplied by the pastor and staff. Boards generally have little independent data available to them except what they gather from the grapevine.

A third limitation is that the board customarily accepts uncritically the information supplied to it by the pastor and other administrators, and it takes no steps to be helpfully critical. Consequently long after problems begin to develop the board still continues to rest comfortably, believing that things are functioning much better than they actually are. This happens because there is no dependable information source that are responsible directly to the board.

Finally, boards in their conventional roles are hampered by the fact that internal constituencies, such as the pastor and the nominating committee, have too much to say about who the board members will be. Altogether too often the pastor and the board members want to select others with whom they will be comfortable. When anyone selects board members based on a comfort level, the result is that those selected are usually mediocre. Pastors need to work with board members who will stretch them, disturb them, and goad them if necessary. But their influence on the nominating process is not likely to support that kind of person.

On the other hand, pastors should not be looked on too critically for their predisposition to select persons based on comfort in relationships, because a cursory examination of most church boards is enough to convince one that there are altogether too many persons who come to the board simply with the view of straightening the pastor out or getting rid of a situation with which they disagree. Such persons invariably paralyze the board, tie up meeting after meeting with redundant and disheartening arguments, and finally lead to the complete frustration of the work of the pastor and of the staff.

The Ambiguity of Power and Authority in the Church

For a church board to recover its legitimate leadership role, it must learn to lead by understanding the ambiguity of power and authority that is always present in a congregation.

The Ambiguity of Power in the Church

The issues of power and authority are always of central concern in any organization, and the church is no exception. The essential definition that might be assigned to the board of a church is that, as a body, it holds all of the ultimate power.

However, the board should not use its power operationally. *The board is to establish policy. It does not manage.* This is a central issue of concern in most churches. There is always confusion between the lines of demarcation separating the power that belongs to the board and the power that belongs to the pastor and other program directors.

Achieving a balance of power is not easy. When the board is reactive, when it does not develop, own, and advocate for the goals and ministries of the church and does not vigorously advocate for the pastor and staff, then the board cannot be trusted with ultimate power. Sooner or later the church will enter into malaise or someone, whether pastor or members of the congregation, will move to take the power from the board. When this happens the entire church will suffer greatly.

A basic flaw in the thinking of boards, and also of pastors, is a view of power as static and limited in the total amount that may be exercised through various agencies of the church. Power is not static. It is always in flux, moving from one place of influence to another. Likewise, power is not a fixed item. It is dynamic; it grows, and it shrinks. The church does not have something like a pound of power at its disposal, so that if the board has a full pound of power the pastor has none, and if the board should decide to give half a pound of power to the pastor then the board has only a half-pound left. Power grows and expands in many directions when an organization is well run, so that a board can be made more powerful at the same time the pastor is becoming more powerful.

What we have said about power as being dynamic and expandable can also be said about weakness. When the board is weak all the structures of the church are weak. And when the pastor is weakened in influence and authority, many other structures of the church will also be weakened thereby.

Issues of trust arise when the governing board:

1. Does not act affirmatively to assure that the pastor and ministry leadership team use their delegated power and influence humanely and constructively in pursuit of the church's goals.
2. Does not monitor the operational use of power with sufficient care to be sure that power is not being misused or abused by the pastor and ministry team, or by others.

A maxim is accredited to Lord Acton: "Power tends to corrupt, and absolute power corrupts absolutely." The board is obligated to be sure that the use of power at every level of the church is carried out within a system of checks and balances so that the potentially corrupting influence of power is not realized. It is the board's responsibility to be sure that the use of power is carried out positively so that persons who are under the influence or authority of others are helped, and not harmed by the process. Greenleaf writes:

> The role of [the governing board] is to hold what approximates absolute power over the institution, using it operationally only in rare emergencies, ideally never. [Boards] delegate the operational use of power to administrators and staff, but with accountability for its use. . . . Furthermore, [the board] will insist that the outcome be that people in and affected by the institution will grow healthy, wiser, freer, more autonomous, and more likely to become servants of society. The only real justification for institutions beyond a certain efficiency is that people in them can grow to greater stature than if they stood alone. It follows then that people working in institutions will be more productive than they would be as unrelated individuals. The whole is greater than the sum of the parts.[17]

Within the church, absolutely no one, including the pastor, is to be entrusted with the operational use of power without the close oversight of an informed and effective board.

The Ambiguity of Authority in the Church

It is the very nature of the church that lines of authority are always fraught with much ambiguity. First, there is the ambiguity that is inherent in the relationship of the pastor to each staff person, to the congregation, and to every individual member within the congregation. The question always remains: Who works for whom? On the one hand, the pastor is seen as the manager and is ultimately responsible for the performance of all paid and volunteer workers. On the other hand, most of the volunteer workers are members of the church, and they exercise voting power in matters of hiring and retaining the pastor. Thus there is a real sense in which the pastor is working for them. A constant point of frustration in the church, especially in times of conflict, is over who works for whom.[18]

Second, the church, in order to remain growing and effective, must have within it a significant perception of stability, and at the same time be open to much change. The church is both timeless and timely. Indeed, the survival pattern of the growing church is to have a stability about it that gives a general sense of direction and rightness and calmness, while at the same time being an organization that is entrepreneurial, innovative, and risk-taking. Balancing stability and change is never easy. Together these ingredients provide an environment in which persons feel at ease within the structures of the church, while also keeping the eyes of the church open to the essential responsibilities and opportunities of its mission within the community.

The ambiguity of board and pastoral roles in providing stability and change must be worked through in order for a congregation to navigate its future. In too many cases, the church board expects the pastor and staff to plan the goals of the church and to advocate for them. While the pastor must lead in this in order to bring about the necessary changes for continual effectiveness of the church, it can be expected that many people within the congregation will resist the change. They resist not because the change is wrong, but because there are always members of the congregation who resist change simply because it is change.

When the board does not own the goals and does not advocate for them, that resistance focuses on the pastor. Too often in the mix of this, the board does not advocate for the pastor, but becomes politely neutral or disavows any involvement or implication in the goals or the changes the pastor is advocating. The result can only be that the congregation is thrown into a high level of confusion. At this point distrust for both the pastor and the board begins to escalate. When the congregation is not clear as to who is steering the ship, or when members believe the board and the pastor are attempting to steer the ship in opposite directions, distrust and resistance are to be expected.

The Ambiguity of Specialization Versus Generalization in the Church

A third ambiguity in the church is the specialization that goes along with the competence of the pastor and pastoral staff. Today people demand quality. A so-so quality of ministry will not attract new members, and will lose more than few who are already there. The time was when the pastor of a small church needed to do several things fairly well, but was not expected to do anything with outstanding competence. Today, however, in order for the small church to attract new members, and to carve out a niche for itself in the community, it must do one thing better than any other church in the community. And in the larger church, because of the complexity within the congregation, it becomes critical that the senior pastor exercise unusual competence in certain areas and that every staff member be seen as highly skilled in at least one area of ministry.

In order to achieve high competence, an associate pastor or staff member must develop something of a tunnel vision. He or she must dedicate heart and soul to one or, perhaps for exceptional people, two areas of professional work. It is to be expected, therefore, that each person on staff will tend to see the ministry of the church from his or her own perspective and want to structure that area of the church around his or her own limited spectrum of professional competencies.

The whole business of stability and change, referred to earlier, remains an abstract thought until the church comes into a crisis that requires a change of goals or behavior if it is to avoid disaster. The task of determining new ministries and directions now becomes an essential function of the board, because only they are not burdened with the necessarily narrow view that comes with specialized competence. Therefore, only the board is able to examine and objectively evaluate the assumptions that guide those persons on staff who must of necessity have high operating competence—and therefore a myopic vision.

Only the board can help the pastor, staff, and congregation decide which assumptions are still valid, which need to be discarded or modified, and what the new operating assumptions should be. This is a big order for the board, one they will never be able to fulfill satisfactorily unless they have a full understanding of the ministries and goals of the church, unless they own them, are willing to advocate for them, and also have the freedom to change them when necessary.

The Ambiguity of Belief Versus Criticism in the Church

A fourth ambiguity necessary in the church is that there must be a healthy tension between belief and criticism. It is this tension that makes for a superior institution. The pastor and staff must believe—in their programs, in their competency, and that what they are doing is right. The board, on the other hand, needs to be mostly critical, holding all things up for review.

The pastor and staff can be much more relaxed and free in pursuing their course of ministry if they have the assurance that alongside of them is a board fully dedicated to the life of the church, providing a careful and critical watch, to be sure that change does not come too fast, that innovation is well conceived, and that the resources of the church are not being expended in a nonproductive manner.

The word *critical* is difficult to use with church boards. Altogether too many people on church boards are not informed, who do not own the goals, who do not advocate openly for the staff and the ministry of the church. These persons are ill-equipped to provide *critical insight*, and yet they are more than willing to offer *negative criticism* at the drop of a hat.

The difference between critical, clear insight and criticism that is negative and unproductive behavior must clearly be drawn by the board. There is in too many churches an insidious snipping away at the pastor, or at members of the staff, until they become disheartened and languish at their task. In such cases the congregation almost invariably will become polarized for or against the pastor and staff.

The Pastor's Role with the Board of Directors

Pastors, through sometimes hard lessons, eventually recognize that the effectiveness of their ministry depends on the effectiveness of the governing board. A major role of the pastor, therefore, is to equip the board, helping them become competent and effective in their leadership. One of the most important areas in which a pastor can equip the board and help them become more effective is in spiritual discernment in their decision making. The decision-making process used most often in boards is the parliamentary model that is by its very nature controlling (chair and secretary have much power), competitive (creating winners and losers), and analytical (thinking versus intuition and feeling). Is the board limited to voting in order to understand "what the Spirit is saying to the church"? Does a group vote to determine God's will? If this is a universal process, then Joshua and Caleb would have lost the vote ten to two.

It is also probably necessary to train the chairperson of the board to be a *primus* leader. The governing board is not a support group, prayer group, or Bible study group, even though all those can take place. The governing board is a leadership body with equal status and singular responsibility to "keep a hand on the reins," ensuring that pastor, staff, and people are all going in the same—and right—direction.

The bottom-line responsibility for the governing board is to create broad-based trust for the pastoral staff and the directions in which the church is going. Trust is the simple belief of individuals that the board and church are capable of, and dedicated to, serving the needs and interests of the individual. Distrust is a belief that the church is not interested in serving *my* needs, that the board is primarily interested in its own needs as individuals or as a board. A simple, and yet important, guideline for the board in carrying out its work should be: *If we do this, will it create trust?*

In order to reach its legitimate leadership role in the church, the governing board must:

1. Continuously deal with the philosophical questions of power, authority, and ambiguity.
2. Deal with the operational processes of setting the goals and determining the ministry directions for the congregation.
3. Design the top ministry management structures and select the persons to fill leadership positions.
4. Measure the satisfaction level of the various constituencies and carry out performance reviews of personnel and of programs.

5. Monitor the rate and scope of change necessary to ensure the future of the church.
6. Provide for the professional growth and spiritual development of every member of the staff.

The board that does these things is almost certain to be an effective board, qualified to lead and worthy of trust.

The bottom-line responsibility of the pastor is to train and equip the board to do its work well. This is a responsibility so crucial that even the youngest and most inexperienced pastor should not avoid it. Equipping the board, we think, falls in the category of Paul's words to the young pastor Timothy: *Lead in such a manner that no one will despise your youth.* If you, as pastor, do not possess the skills to train your governing board, then bring the training from the outside. However you do it—do it!

A crucial part of leading and equipping the board is to nurture the spirituality of the group. If the board members are not disciplined in making themselves available to the means of grace, then grace will be lacking in the board sessions, and the decisions made will be lacking the sense of the Spirit's leading.

This chapter is written to highlight the many areas in which governing boards need leadership, guidance, and training. A place to begin thinking about what stance you should take with your board is to "locate" your group in this chapter, list the action and training areas we have suggested—and then work on these areas.

Chapter Fourteen

Don't Forget to Fly the Plane

Unfortunately . . . we often mistake a part for the whole.[1]

Max DePree

The leader must pay attention to many functions. And he or she must pay attention to these things all at the same time. Everyone else in the church has the luxury of specializing in one area, doing one thing. The leader, however, must hold all things together in his or her consciousness.

Peter Drucker tells a delightful story about leadership and flying an airplane:

> In many flight procedures manuals on small planes, after every three items is written in big letters, "Don't forget to fly the plane." Back in the mid 1980s, the pilot of a small plane was flying over Lake Michigan in a heavy fog. Unable to see any landmarks or the sky, the pilot intently kept his eye on the "level" and compass to be sure he was flying level and in the right direction—until he flew into the lake. The pilot survived the crash to tell FAA officials that, "I was so engrossed in flying in the right direction that I forgot to check the altimeter." Thus, in small plane flight manuals are the words after every three procedures, "DON'T FORGET TO FLY THE PLANE!"

Pilots of large aircraft are also not immune to the tendency to become engrossed in one thing, and forget to fly the plane. Some years ago, a 747 jet landed in the middle of the Everglades in Florida. As the plane was beginning its preparations for landing, a red light came on in the cockpit indicating that the landing gear had come down. The pilot and co-pilot became so occupied with trying to understand if and why the landing gear would have come down that they failed to notice the craft had strayed far off course and finally crashed into the waters. The pilot survived to tell the FAA officials,

"We were all so concerned about the red light that we forgot to fly the plane."[2]

Congregational Myopia

Just as the pilot and cockpit crew are the only ones who can keep an eye on all the gauges, lights, warning systems, and procedures at the same time, so also only the pastor and leadership team are in a position to keep an eye on the entire congregation, with its many operations—to view and understand all the procedures and activities at the same time.

Organizational myopia, is a terminal disease that afflicts the leaders first, then spreads throughout the entire organization.[3] Leaders who experience organizational myopia lose the ability to view the congregation as a whole entity. They fail to understand the interrelation of all the discrete structures and processes that comprise the church. They are unable to foresee the results one action or decision will have on all the other attitudes and operations going on. With the complexities and demands of everyday activities, it is very easy to lose sight of the big picture. Every squeaking wheel or "red light" is screaming, "Pay attention to me!" Nonetheless, the leader must develop the capacity to read the entire script as one scene, or else he or she will never know where the church is headed. Not only is organizational myopia an affliction of local congregations, but it has long afflicted denominations also.

The governing body of The United Methodist Church is a prime example of the single-theme phenomenon. For almost twenty-five years, every four years it has legislated a quadrennial priority and bent every effort to have its general agencies and congregations pump up the theme. Then four years later the emphasis is abandoned, and soon forgotten, in favor of the next quadrennial priority with all its promise to do what the previous emphases failed to accomplish—to renew the Church. At the time of this writing, the "theme" is *Celebrate and Witness,* but for all intents and purposes, few are paying attention to it. Like an unformed world, it is without form and void. Yet when the denomination's General Council on Ministries proposed the theme it was readily endorsed by the Church's General Conference. We recently asked one of the delegates to the General Conference why the body accepted the theme since, apparently, no one has much interest in it. He said, "Well, it's nice. Who could say no to it?" He then went on to say, "By and large, all quadrennial themes are like that. They are nice and ignored; perhaps the last quadrennial emphasis that had any effect upon the Church was the *Fund for Reconciliation,* in 1968–72. Apart from that, the one-theme approach to unifying or invigorating the Church has never had the ability to mobilize the denomination."

Whether for a denomination or local congregation, the leaders must develop the capacity to understand and influence the entire picture at the same time. Simply focusing on one condition at a time is tantamount to staring at a single red light in the cockpit of a 747.

The United Methodist Church is not the only organization with a tendency to look at one red light at a time. The leaders of the Assemblies of God have long shown signs of moving toward the slews of focusing on one thing at a time. In 1990, the Church, already showing signs of flying into turbulent air, took the big plunge by announcing that in the decade of the 1990s the Church would focus on "church planting." This announcement drew immediate criticism from much of the grass roots, two of whom asserted that the problems of the denomination were complex and would not be solved by focusing on a single theme. As a matter of fact, a single issue approach would not produce growth but only hasten further decline.[4]

Most segments of the North American Church have long attempted renewal by focusing on one program or theme, each emphasis lasting roughly for a decade or two. In the early 1900s the theme was "revival," and the program was revival crusades. In the 1940s the focus was "Sunday school." For the 1950s the focus was building new church buildings and church planting. In the 1960s the church sought to renew itself through social action. The

1970s saw the church turn to a decade of introspection and small groups. The emphasis of the 1980s was the baby boomer. The 1990s is yet to be decided.

Through all these single-minded efforts, the church has never been able to renew itself. Why then does the church continue to play one string at a time? There are perhaps two explanations for this. First, individual leaders often confuse their personal investment in a single approach or program with the systemic needs of the congregation and assume that the organization must mirror their single-strength approach. Second, religious leaders are trained to be managers, and as such are conditioned to deal with one organizational unit at a time. Again, we emphasize that only the leaders are in a position to see the entire picture. All other workers are in a position to view only one program or condition at a time.

No one expects the Sunday School Superintendent to spend much time understanding the environment and operations of the finance committee. Indeed, the Sunday School Superintendent will do his or her job best by focusing time and energy exclusively on the Sunday school. By like manner the church janitor is not expected to be concerned with the work and responsibilities of the choir director. By the very nature of their jobs, program managers and workers do their best work when they take a specialized and narrow view of things—when they stick to their knitting. However, unless the leaders are looking at all of the programs and conditions as a whole, as a single entity, all sense of direction is lost, all sense of common mission is lost, systemic problems are not resolved, and there is no common volition to hold the many entities together.

The Leader's Instrument Panel: A Systems Approach

The leader, like the pilot of a plane, must learn to read the entire instrument panel, and not see only one indicator at a time. To keep an eye on the instrument panel requires a holistic approach to understanding congregational life and ministry. The systems approach[5] is the most helpful "instrument panel" for the leader, and it is made up of three major components, as illustrated in Figure 14.1.

Figure 14.1

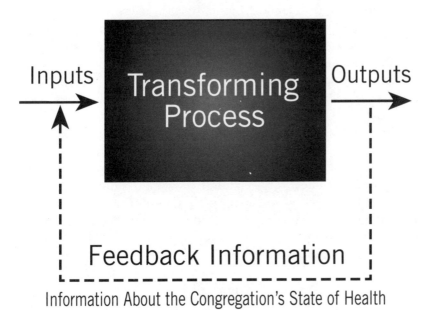

Information About the Congregation's State of Health

Inputs into Congregational Life and Ministry

> Inputs are those influences and resources that make their way into the organization, whether known or unknown, wanted or unwanted.

These inputs enter the organization from outside—from the organization's environment. Without any inputs from the environment, the congregation becomes entropic; it deteriorates, runs down, and eventually dies. So every congregation must learn how to bring into itself the resources it needs in order to survive and to keep out influences that are threatening its survival.

The *input system* is comprised of all the efforts the congregation puts together in order to bring in from the environment the resources it needs to achieve its mission. Four major inputs that a congregation seeks to import from its environment include human inputs (e.g., new

people and their skills, values, humor, experiences, politics, brokenness, enthusiasm), technical inputs (e.g., a new computer system),
organizational inputs (e.g., hired personnel, leadership style), and
social inputs (e.g., local, state, and federal laws, societal trends).[6] The
leader must consistently ask, "What inputs need to be addressed in
order to provide the energy needed to keep the congregation vigorous—to keep this plane flying?"

Transforming Inputs into Energy

The fundamental purpose of the transforming system is to transform the inputs into energy—energy the congregation needs to survive and to carry out its mission. The leader's instrument panel of the
transforming system is composed of four major components: the congregation's mission, its organizational structures and policies, its
human relations, and its spirituality, as illustrated in figure 14.2:

Figure 14.2

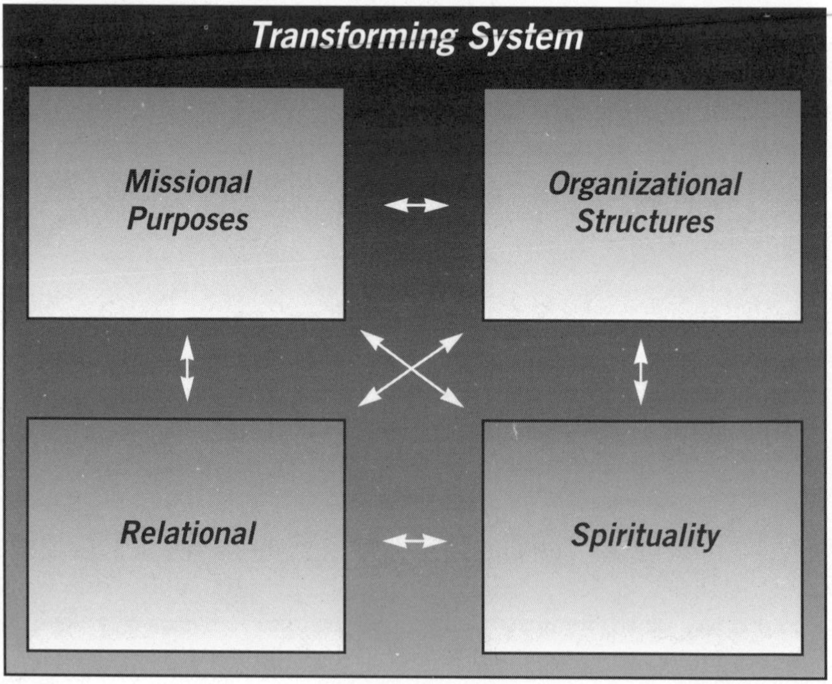

> The missional component of the transforming system is the congregation's understanding of its purpose and reason for being.

This component includes the congregation's theological beliefs and values that give the organization its unique identity as well as its sense of "call" to be God's people in the community and in the world. The mission of the church is a matter of both **being** and **doing.** Mission clarification is the effort of the congregation to discern God's calling—exploring what they must be in order to do God's calling.

God's calling is always to a specific people, in a specific time and place. It is foolish for the congregation to say "Our mission is to reach the world" when it does not have the resources or will to reach the community it lives in. Better to focus on a five-square block area, or on one specific ministry to the community than to dissipate the system's energies trying to be all things to all people.

Therefore, the congregation as a system must decide its being and doing with an eye to the *timeless* understandings of the Christian faith and tradition, and also with an eye to its own *timely* environment. Because each congregation has its own unique environment, each must have its own unique understanding of its mission. The mission of one Presbyterian church in town will not be the same as the mission of another Presbyterian church in town—it can hardly be, since they exist in different environments. The two sources for church mission may be diagrammed as follows in figure 14.3.[7]

It is a fundamental understanding of systems theory that the missional component and the environment are the two aspects that exert the most influence on the system's character and reason for being. As such, the leaders must pay close attention to them—and yet many pastors pay virtually no attention to them at all. In a rapidly changing environment, missional opportunities are also changing rapidly. Again, the congregation that does not change to meet the changes in its environment (paradigm shifts) will soon find itself cut off, irrelevant, lost.

Figure 14.3

Components of Church Mission

Biblical images & imperatives

Environmental realities

Timeless truths every church must regard as axiomatic

The needs of society, community and congregation our local church can and should do something about

Universal
Never change
Timeless
General
  responsibilities

Local
Always shifting
Timely
Particular
  opportunities

MISSION STATEMENT

- 125 words or less
- Reflects both vertical and horizontal relationships
- Deals with aspirations while being realistic
- Meaningful, simple language without clichés

The **organizational component** of the transforming system is the combination of human endeavor, organizational policies, and structures that the congregation puts together in order to achieve its mission.

The organizational structure is the skeletal system that the congregation constructs in order to hold the various parts of the system together. How will the congregation organize itself—divide and coordinate its tasks—in order to accomplish its mission?

The **relational component** includes the quality of human relationships within the congregation, the morale of the people. To what extent do people live together in covenant community? To what degree do persons share in one another's lives? Does the organization cause people to grow or to shrink?

Relationships in the congregation do not develop in a vacuum. If persons live and work in effective and growing structures, they experience a sense of growth, self-actualization, and worth. If the structures are inappropriate and ineffectual, persons experience themselves as disempowered, shrinking, and frustrated. These personal reactions to the congregation's missional understanding and organization, whether positive or negative, are expressed in the relationships people have with one another.

The **spirituality component** of the transforming process includes the programs, covenants, and disciplines by which the congregation seeks to so order its life that the people might live in a continual awareness of the presence of God in their lives.

The spirituality component focuses on the spiritual formation of the members, and groups, within the congregation.

The congregation's spirituality and its vision are closely related, for vision is born out of the congregation's experience of God and its life together.

These four components, then, are *gauges* to which the leaders must attend. They are like gauges on the instrument panel of an airplane, providing the pastor with crucial information for keeping the congregation in good shape and going in the right direction.

214 / Leading the Congregation

Outputs of the Congregation

Outputs are the influences and resources the organization wants to put out into its environment—in order to carry out its mission and to make society more reflective of its own values.

Outputs, therefore, are often expressed as goals, programs, missionary efforts, and the like. Because no organization operates at 100 percent effectiveness, there always tends to be a gap between the congregation's desired outputs and its actual outputs. This gap is like a warning light on an instrument panel, signaling potential breakdowns. The leaders must learn how to measure the gap and understand what the gap signals regarding the life and working of the church's operations. The gap between what the congregation *desires* to accomplish and what it *actually does* accomplish is more often than not a *symptom* of problems that are present in the relationships between the congregation's missions, structures, relationships, and spirituality. For example, "financial problems" in a congregation are usually not problems at all. Rather, the gap between what is desired and what the congregation is actually contributing is a symptom of an unclear mission, frustating structures, lack of spirituality, and the like. To treat a gap as though it is the problem when, in fact, it is a symptom, is bound to make matters worse—never better.[8]

Feedback Information

Feedback information is generated within the organization by the mere fact that it is operating. This information is generally cast off and lost, because the organization pays no attention to it.

Feedback information is different from other types of information that must be generated by such means as evaluation (e.g., structured conversations, questionnaires). Feedback information requires no process or effort to generate since it is constantly being generated as the congregation goes about its life and work. This is the purest and least ambiguous information the congregation can possibly have—and it costs nothing to generate, because it is always there, waiting to be picked up.

For example, the congregation is constantly generating the geo-demographic trends of the congregation, the average attendance as compared to last year's attendance, financial patterns, growth patterns, staff and membership morale, average length of tenure of its professional workers, the number of social ministries it is carrying out, and the percentage of first-time visitors who visit a second time.

Feedback information may be the most beneficial input the congregation's leaders can receive. If this information is so important, and so obviously easy to collect, why do most congregations ignore it completely? The best answer probably is because feedback information is so certain it cannot be argued, and sometimes painful, yet it cannot be denied. Nonetheless, it is a gauge of the congregation's health and direction, and the leader who learns to read its signals and act on them is bound to lead the congregation into greater effectiveness—and will shrink the gap between desired and actual outputs.

To prevent a congregation from slipping ever so slowly into myopia and/or entropy, a major requirement of leadership is to be able to collect the varied interests and energies of people toward the accomplishment of a common volition. If the leadership team—pastors and board—do not take this view, it is highly unlikely anyone else will, or can. No one can get into the leaders' skin to look at the organization through their eyes. Virtually every other person in the organization is proscribed to focus on a single program or problem. It is required, therefore, of a leader that he or she possess an organizational acumen not obligatory of others. It is imperative that leaders become increasingly skilled in viewing, understanding, and relating to the congregation as a whole entity. And so we say to you, even as you find the Golden Thread and your charism and give yourself to these, don't forget to fly the plane.

So far in this book we have focused the discussion on the leader as a person, and the unique contributions the leader brings to the life and ministry of the congregation. In Part Three we will approach the subject of change and how it affects the leaders and the congregation they serve. Then we will give attention to two paradigm shifts that are even now happening—which will affect the way effective leadership and ministry will be done in the future at a congregation where you serve.

PART THREE

PARADIGMS FOR CHURCH LEADERSHIP

PART THREE

Paradigms for Church Leadership

Introduction

Perhaps all people living in different periods of history have the same perception, but the events and technologies of our time do appear to be accelerating at a more rapid, unpredictable pace than ever before. We have witnessed the collapse of governments, the realignment of world power, and the obsolence of large institutions—many of which never recognized what was taking place or refused to do anything about it. Most organizations live primarily in the past and are not able to keep up with the unprecedented change.

With the decline of large institutions comes the decline of personal trust in them. Individuals no longer look to large institutions to provide answers and solutions. This institutional malaise has not left the church and its leaders untouched.

However, with the tension and turmoil comes potential opportunities. Peter F. Drucker has identified three areas of concern when looking at the major shifts taking place in the environment of religious organizations.

The first concern is the *eternal verities* of the church that never change. These timeless values are the same in Botswana as they are in Boston, the same in the first century as they will be in the next century.

Second, the *needs and opportunities* arising out of the culture change constantly. For example, the needs and opportunities for the church are different in Los Angeles than they are in Peoria. They are also different in Peoria in 1993 than they were in Dallas in 1953.

219

Third, the *currently available tools* also change constantly. These include new tools such as the FAX machine and computers—all of which make for new performance capabilities, fresh consumer expectations, and novel competitive threats.

For the church some things never change. However, for the church some things are in rapid and radical change. It is these sweeping changes that we will discuss in Part Three of this book, because they are almost certain to have significant effects on your ministry as a leader. We will approach these changes for what they are—paradigms (see chap. 15). While the term *paradigm* often seems overused, it is, nonetheless, the best way to decribe changes at societal or individual levels. Two of the major paradigm shifts affecting the American church are the rapid shifts in cross-cultural population statistics (see chap. 16) and the involvement of women in leadership (see chap. 17).[1] These emerging shifts will affect the ministry of virtually all churches that are on the brink of experiencing a new set of expectations for pastoral leadership. The story of WhaJa Hwang embodies a leadership paradigm of exemplary ministry that is making a big difference is the lives of many (see chap. 18).

Chapter Fifteen

Paradigms for Church Leadership

With each change of paradigm, roles and relationships change and power shifts. New structures develop. New directions emerge. Things that were of great value in one age become useless in the next. Times of transition between ages and paradigms are times of confusion and tumult.[1]

Loren Mead

The pastor is meeting with the church board to discuss a plan for assimilating new persons into the congregation. The pastor begins by saying: "We have already had good success in reaching singles. I think we could target the unchurched singles in our community and bring more into the church."

A board member responds: "I think this is great! I've wanted us to reach out to the singles and younger adults for a long time."

A second board member's thoughts: "This church is way out of line with my family's needs. Maybe it's time for us to leave."

A third board member's thoughts: "I hate to see this happen. What this church doesn't need is more singles; their morality will affect our youth."

A fourth board member's thoughts: "I hope they don't expect me to spend time and energy in getting to know any new people. I've got enough problems of my own."

A fifth board member's thoughts: "How can you say we should target a particular group? Doesn't God want us to bring everyone into the church? Don't people come on their own, the way God leads them to come? This sounds too much like a business, not a church!"

---

222 / Leading the Congregation

Saint Augustine said, "Know thyself, and then thou wilt know thy God." Forsooth if a pun be permitteth we say unto thee, "In order to know thyself, thou must know thy paradigms."

New ideas and new language are all the time accepted, or resisted, because of paradigms. Our paradigms exert tremendous influence on the way we respond to new ideas, new opportunities, or unanticipated changes—whether in our home, our church, or in the world around us. This is true for individuals, for committees, and for the entire congregation.

Thomas Kuhn, in studying how scientists develop and alter their paradigms, describes a paradigm as an interpretive framework for observing reality patterns and making sense of those patterns.[2]

> A paradigm is a set of deeply held rules and regulations surrounding the way people see and do things, and how they find reason to continue doing the things they do in the same way.

Paradigms act as boundaries that filter in the information that is perceived to support a person's ideas and filter out the information that is perceived not to agree with a person's position. As such, everyone has paradigms. Whether it is the pastor fresh out of seminary with newly developed prescriptions for "doing" congregational ministry or the lay leader who has been actively involved in the church for many years; the expectations for church ministry through the eyes of the married "buster" or the newly divorced "boomer;" the way the Sunday school teacher wishes to arrange the classroom or the way the women's group thinks the church kitchen should be used—we all have our paradigms. And, of course, (because they are our paradigms) we all think *our* paradigm is the *best* paradigm—if not the *only* paradigm.

Paradigms function to cause persons to see only what they expect to see, or want to see—and they want to see only what fits their paradigm. Information that fits into one's paradigm is easily recognized as valid. Information that does not fit, however, is difficult for that person to comprehend or accept. It is easier to disregard such information, or to distort the information to make it "fit" the person's existing paradigm. In such cases, "The way we see the problem is the problem."[3]

From the beginning of this country, the small pastoral church has been the paradigm for Protestant churches—200 persons or less in Sunday worship, one pastor, all volunteer workers. After World War II, another paradigm began to emerge: the congregation with up to 500 persons in Sunday worship, a multiple staff, and volunteers managed by professionals. In the last fifteen years an entirely new paradigm has emerged: the large pastoral church; 800 or more persons attending the "weekend services," multiple services targeted to specific segments of the populace, large staffs composed of ordained and nonordained professionals, and volunteers carrying out much of the ministry of the church.

The large pastoral church paradigm has so challenged the "rules and regulations" about how a church is supposed to be that many seminary professors, "church professionals," and laypersons, have dismissed the large pastoral church out of hand, as being untrue to the gospel, cold and impersonal, a slick production, or not concerned about social needs and ministries. The constituents of the large pastoral church, however, report that their church is friendly, biblically based, interconnected by small groups in which members care for one another, and an open, expansive ministry for the laity at all levels of the organization. Such differences of perception in viewing the same phenomenon are the paradigm effect: what is clear to one person with his or her paradigm is totally imperceptible to another person with a different paradigm.[4]

Paradigms Lost; Paradigms Forged

Two major paradigms characterized Christianity in the Western world for its first 1,900 years, according to Loren Mead in *The Once and Future Church*, the church of the late twentieth century is between paradigms—the old paradigm is breaking apart, but it is too soon to predict with much credibility what the third paradigm of Christianity will look like.[5]

The two paradigms that prevailed from the birth of the ancient church to the present are: the *Apostolic Paradigm,* which prevailed from the founding of the Christian Church to the beginning of the fourth century; and the *Christendom Paradigm,* which displaced the earlier paradigm from the time of the conversion of Emperor Constantine in A.D. 313 and prevailed until about the mid-1900s.

The differences between the operating assumptions of the two paradigms are stark. In the first three centuries of Christianity, to be a Christian was dangerous, if not illegal. The environment was hostile toward the Christian faith, there were no cathedrals or large worship centers, no seminaries, and no religious bureaucracies. The central reality of the apostolic church was a local community, a congregation "called out" of the world, and yet called to witness to the world. To be a Christian was to engage in witness to a hostile world, to be prepared to give one's life for this witness. The apostolic Christians understood that the witness was costly, thus the Greek word for "witnessing" can be translated "martyr."

With the conversion of Emperor Constantine, however, the rules and regulations were radically altered as Christianity became the official religion of all Western empires—as the kingdoms embraced Christendom. The central reality of Christendom was that the church was identified with the empire. To be a citizen of the empire made one a member of the church. Gone was the animosity between the governments and Christianity. The environment ceased its hostilities, there became no separation between secular rulers and religious leaders, between secular government and religious government. The concept of congregation became that of the parish, a piece of territory assigned to the parish priest, and the mission of the parish was no longer to witness to one's neighbor (because all of the neighbors were already members of the church), but to Christianize those who were "afar off" in other regions outside the empire.

Now, in the late 1900s, it is clear that the Christendom paradigm is giving way. Even as these words are being written, new and large democracies are being formed that will apparently welcome the Christian faith, but will not embrace it as the "official" religion.[6] Likewise, there is gathering evidence that Christendom as the prevailing paradigm for the American church is wearing out. A new paradigm is emerging. "Neither the new age nor the new paradigm has arrived," writes Mead, "so we are pulled by the new and constrained by the old without the privilege even of knowing fully what the new will be like. But as the new has begun to reveal itself, it has made us profoundly uncomfortable."[7]

The old hand-holds are weakening. The once sure and certain ways to lead a congregation or a denomination are no longer sure and certain. Almost daily we're finding out more about what won't work any longer—but what will work seems less obvious. One thing is certain: In such times it is important that we understand the paradigms that institutional Christianity is laying down, and that we carefully look for the new paradigms that are coming. For this reason the study of leaders and their qualities has emerged as a popular focus among persons who make decisions about ministry.

Paradigms Help Us to Understand Denominations, Congregations, and People

Paradigms are the key to understanding why people think and behave as they do. The question is not whether you and/or your congregation operate out of an accepted pattern, an adopted set of rules and regulations about how things ought to be done. Rather, the question is this: What are the paradigms you and/or your people use to interpret what you see around you, and to guide your responses to it? Paradigms may be practical, commonsense interpretations acquired through experience, or they may be more theoretical and theological. Define a congregation's paradigms, and you will more fully understand the reasons behind the attitudes and behaviors that characterize the response of the group to new ideas, new challenges, and opportunities.

Chris Argyris and Donald Schön take the discussion of paradigms a step further when they highlight the difference between one's *espoused theory* (prescribed paradigm) and one's *theory-in-use* (actual behavior).[8] A leader's espoused leadership theory is what that person believes he or she would do, or wants to do, in a particular situation.[9] However, the theory that actually governs the actions of the leader is his or her theory-in-use. Not many pastors, for example, would exclude "servant leadership" from their espoused theological paradigm for ministry. In reality, however, their actual leadership behaviors (their theology-in-use) may not remotely resemble servant leadership.

A gap may occur between our publicly stated paradigms (espoused theory) and our actual leadership behavior (theory-in-use). The leader who has not examined his or her espoused theory and theory-in-use may well demonstrate such a gap—and not be aware of it. The followers will be aware of it, however, because they are much more convinced by his or her actions than by any amount of words spoken. Recall the adage, "What you do sounds so loud in my ear, that I cannot hear a word you are saying."

In addition to individuals in the church who have their personal paradigms, the congregation also has a corporate paradigm for interpreting its realities. Even denominations have prevailing paradigms. In fact, a denomination may be defined as a set of congregations and agencies held together around a commonly accepted cluster of paradigms that are theological and social in nature.

Paradigms are essential to the life of the church. The major problem with paradigms held by religious organizations, however, is that once adopted by the group, no matter how much theological and biblical exposition went into the discernment process at the beginning, the paradigm is quickly baptized with a seal of divine correctness. "We do it this way, because this is the way God wants us to do it—forever and ever, world without end. Amen." Therefore, religious paradigms tend eventually to be the least examined, the most tenacious, and, in a rapidly changing society, the most out-of-date. Congregational paradigms can keep members stuck, unable to see new opportunities for ministry. This is because we often "try to discover the future by looking for it through our old paradigms . . . paradigms have the power to keep us from seeing what was [and is] really happening."[10]

There is something of singular importance to all leaders of denominations, agencies, and churches who have come to rely on their past successful performance as a barometer of their future. Barker calls it the *going back to zero rule.*[11] Highly successful institutions have missed great opportunities, or collapsed, because their formerly successful paradigms had blinded them to change. No matter how large or powerful an organization is, no matter how good you are at the old paradigm, according to Barker, "With the new one you go back to zero. *Your past success guarantees nothing.*"[12]

When a new paradigm shift takes hold everyone is on a new playing field; there are new rules, new players, and more competition—everyone goes back to zero. The organization, which assumes that what has been effective in the past will continue to be effective in the future, is headed for trouble. In the sixteenth century, Machiavelli reflected upon the effects of a paradigm shift on the "successful" when he said to Prince Lorenzo:

Therefore, those of our princes who had held their possessions for many years must not accuse fortune for having lost them, but rather their own remises; for they have never in quiet times considered that things might change (as it is a common fault of men not to reckon on storms in fair weather) when adverse times came, they [were not prepared to defend themselves]. . . . I conclude then that fortune varying and men remaining fixed in their way, they are successful so long as these ways conform to circumstances, but when [the circumstances change those who are fixed in their ways will fail].[13]

Machiavelli understood why success is relative to the context.

Paradigms of the Ancient Church

One way to read Christ's ministry and the history of the ancient church is to see it as a story of clashing religious paradigms. It was no secret to the Jewish religious leaders that Jesus was announcing a faith and practice that did not fit the old rules and regulations. Christ fits the model of "Paradigm Pioneer" (Joel Barker's term), while the Pharisees model those who have "Paradigm Paralysis." Resistance of the established religion to the new paradigm is seen in the number of times it is recorded that the keepers of the old paradigm planned how to silence Christ—because his message was dangerous to "correct religion" and to the society they desired.

The Acts of the Apostles demonstrates just how tenacious old paradigms can be—even among some who had left the old way for the new Way. Paul, the apostle, ministering in the Gentile world was fashioning a paradigm based on freedom and grace, but some of the converted Pharasees wanted the old rules and regulations along with the newly developing paradigm. Theirs was a paradigm with far more stringent rules and regulations than Paul thought necessary for righteousness.

Even as Jesus was seen as an insurrectionist by the religious establishment, so also Paul's message of freedom and grace was viewed by some as heresy. For the Pharisaic sect of believers, it was intolerable that the Gentiles might be part of God's vision for the church, unless, of course, they were "circumcised and ordered to keep the law of Moses" (Acts 15:5*b*).

Paradigms of the Reformers

When Martin Luther nailed the ninety-five theses to the door of the Wittenberg Church, he announced a new paradigm for the Roman Catholic Church, and he wasn't exactly loved for it. When John Calvin attempted to establish a city-state governed by grace and the Word of God, he fashioned a new paradigm of society that combined the sacred with the profane. John Wesley was a highly respected Don of Oxford University, and a renowned preacher and theologian; yet when he launched a renewal movement within the stagnant Church of England, he was rewarded by being barred from all the pulpits in the land. Each of these great reformers proved that paradigm pioneers are never popular in institutional church circles. Is this any less true today?

As Jesus, Paul, Luther, Calvin, and Wesley were pioneers, so there are presently new paradigm pioneers in the church.[14] The church is in the throes of change, and many of the old religious paradigms are already being replaced by new ones. As leaders of the present and future church, we should at least examine the new paradigms with an open mind and a will to learn whether there be "a more excellent way."

Paradigms of the American Oldline Churches

The most pressing topic of conversation among many church leaders is the paradigm shifts that are now apparent within the North American religious scene. William McKinney, a seminary Dean and sociologist, observes:

> The oldline denominations . . . are in a deep funk. . . . [They] are no longer at the center of things as they once were. . . . They no longer own the stadium—and it is unlikely they will ever do so again. . . . We cling to the days when it was possible to speak of a "cultural mainstream" and to the times when local clergy and national church leaders were among the most important interpreters and custodians of that culture. . . . We want desperately to believe that while we may be temporarily out of step with the religious or political views of our fellow citizens, in time *they will catch up with us.*[15]

In the 1950s and 1960s, the mainstream denominations assumed that they had all the major intersections of every village and city blanketed with beautiful sanctuaries and Christian education facilities. Who believed there was any serious competition? "Matters seem far different than just a few decades ago," writes Craig Dykstra. "Through the 1950s, a cluster of Protestant denominations still wielded a cultural and social authority that gave it *establishment status.* . . . But the former establishment no longer reigns. What was 'main' stream is now one stream alongside many others—with significant consequences for American culture as a whole and for these churches."[16]

It seems obvious, and in some circles fashionable, to point to the oldline churches as examples of what happens to established institutions when there is a paradigm shift. More graciously and with appeal for less bitterness, however, we recall that the oldline churches enjoyed a central position and vital ministry in America for nigh onto two centuries before paradigmatic changes on the North American religious scene found them unaware and/or unable to respond. One hundred and fifty or two hundred years of service is a long and worthy record.

Paradigms of the Younger American Churches

It is also sobering that many churches outside of the oldline Protestant traditions are being, or will be, put back to zero by paradigmatic shifts—and these churches will not have the luxury of 150 or 200 years before finding themselves in an entirely new game. Indeed, many younger denominations are already there. Some of the so-called growth churches are no longer growing, or have seen their growth ratios severely eroded.

For example, Pentecostal groups supposed that they had the "corner" on the works of the Holy Spirit, assuming that new freedom and experiences in worship were lacking in the "formal" mainstream churches. Then, without much warning, the charismatic renewal started during the 1960s in the mainstream Protestant churches and Catholic churches, surprising most everyone, including the Pentecostals themselves. Paradigm shifts often surprise even the persons who are leading the way.

Paul B. Tinlin and Edith Blumhofer, both participants and observers in the Assemblies of God Church, recently wrote of the paradigm shifts that apparently are putting the church back to zero.

American Pentecostals have not found the courage that mainliners have shown in subjecting their faith communities to critical scrutiny. . . . But even a cursory review suggests that the AG suffers from a numerical and spiritual stagnation more typically associated with mainline Protestantism.

. . . Still widely perceived as a rapidly growing, vibrant denomination, the Assemblies of God is in fact facing problems far deeper than those suggested by the Bakker and Swaggart scandals. . . . The Assemblies of God needs to examine itself critically if it hopes to regain momentum.

. . . Sunday schools and related activites are faltering, as they are in many denominations. Sunday evening services, once the most popular, have experienced substantial declines in attendance; some Assemblies of God churches have canceled them completely. Wednesday evening adult services, once set for prayer and teaching, attract far smaller crowds than they did a generation ago. Altar services and prayer meetings have virtually disappeared. Pentecostals once yearned for a spiritual formation that they believed took some discipline and effort.[17]

Many of the younger denominations—the Assemblies of God, The Baptist General Conference, the Church of the Nazarene, The Evangelical Free Church—while slowing in America, are finding their missionary efforts to be flourishing in other parts of the globe. This might indicate that the paradigms that made them initially so successful as they started up in America may work again in other "start-up" situations. Or it might mean that the foreign, indigenous leaders have intentionally decided not to transport the paradigms of the American mother church.

Paradigms of the Large Pastoral Ministry Church

One of the new paradigms emerging for the twenty-first century, according to Peter F. Drucker, is the development of the large pastoral church, which may be the most important paradigm shift of our time.[18] Lyle E. Schaller demonstrates in *The Seven-Day-A-Week Church* how these large churches are organized around pastoral, caring, and supporting ministries for their own congregation and the community. As the federal, state, and local social service agencies become less capable of caring for social, human needs, Drucker believes it will be the large pastoral churches, with their multiple resources and ministries, that will pick up the slack. While many have disparaged the large pastoral church phenomenon, no one can argue its growing influence on the American religious scene. Presently, 50 percent of the churchgoing population of the United States attends 14 percent of the churches.

Organizational Learning

To be effective in the global context the church must be cognizant of its paradigms regarding leadership and ministry. This is true for the ruling boards, committees, and workers. Church leaders, therefore, have a responsibility to define and test their paradigms—and to lead the congregation to do likewise. Difficult as it is to get people to review and revise their paradigms, the leader must get it done. Failure to accomplish this will almost certainly conscript the congregation to frustration in its ministry results, and ultimately to ruin.

In order to do this, religious organizations must be *learning organizations*. Leaders must help organizations develop the capacity to critically assess their operating assumptions and activities. They must learn how to scan the environment for coming trends, changes, and paradigmatic shifts that will influence their future success. The organizations that excel in the future, according to Peter M. Senge, will be those "that discover how to tap people's commitment and capacity to learn at all levels in an organization."[19] Many organizations are too busy going about their business, and, therefore, have not developed the capacity to learn. As a matter of fact, most American institutions suffer from a "learning disability," and live only half as long as a person. Even when there is clear evidence that the congregation is in trouble, and the pastor is aware of it, such alarms often go unheeded. This is no accident. The learning disabilities of an organization, according to Senge, "operate despite the best efforts of bright, committed people."[20]

By the early 1970s Argyris and Schön warned of the learning disabilities in all American institutions, including religious bodies. Their substantial research indicted two types of "theories-in-use" by American organizations, which they pedantically identified as "Model I Organizations" and "Model II Organizations."

The organizational paradigm that makes Japanese industries so successful is not a "Japanese" model at all. The Japanese paradigm pioneer was an American, W. Edwards Deming,
who first introduced his new paradigm to American automobile
companies. They would have nothing to do with it. It just didn't
fit their rules and regulations. Deming subsequently presented
his new ideas to the Japanese. Having no recent successful paradigms to protect, they bought his proposal, hook, line, and
sinker. The rest is history.[21]

Model I Organizations

Model I Organizations, they say, have never developed the ability to
learn for the future. Rather, "[Operating] in primary inhibitory loops,
members of an organization respond to conditions for error in ways
that reinforce conditions for error."[22] Model I organizations approach
problems in such a way as to make matters worse, not better.

Argyris and Schön describe four operating norms that characterize
Model I organizations:

1. *Each person (or group) attempts to define the goals of the
organization and works to have others support them.* Group members rarely try to work with others to develop a mutual definition of
purposes; nor are they open to considering any information that
might cause them to change their minds or alter their perceptions.
Rather, they attempt to design and manage the environment unilaterally. They feel that they know everything necessary in order to
plan for (never with) others.

2. *Each person (or group) tries to maximize his or her winning
and minimize his or her losing.* People think that once they have
decided the goals, changing them would be a sign of weakness.
Therefore, they try to unilaterally manage the task assignment.
There is little helping others, or allowing others to help them.
Whenever they are in relationship with others, they will play the
game so that they win and the others lose.

3. Minimize generating or expressing negative feelings. People avoid expressing their true feelings and work to keep others from doing so by declaring that generating negative feelings shows ineptness, incompetence, and/or lack of diplomacy.[23] To protect themselves from garnering negative reactions, individuals (and groups) speak with inferred categories that define little or no directly observable behavior.

4. Be rational. The pressure is on to always be rational and objective, and to suppress feelings. Permitting or helping someone to express his or her feelings is seen as poor strategy. In order to avoid any show of feelings, people will withhold information and create rules to censor information and behavior.[24]

Organizations that build for themselves operative paradigms such as those described above, say Argyris and Schön, are not equipped to learn and tend to make dysfunctional responses to internal problems and external changes. Argyris and Schön suggest that about 95 percent of American institutions operate out of the Model I paradigm. These include religious organizations.

Model II Organizations

Model II organizations are those that have developed the capacity to integrate continual learning in all that they do. Model II organizations have the ability to test their assumptions and progressively learn about organizational effectiveness. There are three central governing variables of Model II organizations:

1. Valid and Useful Information. The organization works to maximize valid information—and presents this information to persons in a manner they can understand and use to make better decisions. Efforts are made to gather information from as many sources as possible—inside and outside the organization.

2. Free and Informed Choice. All persons who will be affected by the decisions that are made are given participation in deciding the decision. To ensure that each person is making quality judgments, everyone is given the information that has been gathered regarding the issue at hand.

3. Internal Commitment. Efforts are made to enlist persons' commitment to the decisions, and constant monitoring is carried out to provide continuing information regarding the results of the organization's work. The organization understands that when persons are fully involved in steps 1 and 2, the result is that they are committed to the decisions.[25]

Organizations that build for themselves Model II paradigms are learning organizations. They are equipped to respond to internal problems, and to learn from them. Also, they are equipped to respond effectively to changes in the environment in such a way that they continually renew themselves. They remain vital and effective—not in spite of the changes, but *because of the changes* that provide opportunity for continual learning and adjustment. Argyris and Schön speculate that perhaps no more than 5 percent of American institutions operate on the Model II paradigm—including religious organizations. The importance of organizational learning cannot be stressed too strongly. As a leader, you must work to create organizations that value continual learning.

Paradigms, Organizational Learning, Effectiveness

Is there any good news for us, as we consider the tenacity of paradigms as operative models in religious organizations? Yes. The good news about paradigms is that the same pressures that cause persons to tenaciously hold to their old paradigms may become the necessary impetus, when the pressure is sufficiently increased, for the people to open themselves to new operating assumptions.

The ancient church did opt for a paradigm that opened the gospel to the entire world, free of constrictive, cultural religious laws.[26] When the church had become benighted by conventions of convenience, and evil of many sorts, Martin Luther did announce a set of propositions that sparked the Reformation (an entirely new religious paradigm). Calvin did succeed in creating an awareness that societies, as well as individuals, should be governed by truth, love, and justice.

Wesley did succeed in launching a renewal movement, the effects of which have been felt around the world to this day.

As you reflect on the paradigms discussed in this section of the book, keep in mind that:

1. These paradigms may compete with many other paradigms you already hold: denominational, educational, spiritual, social, and personal. While the paradigms discussed in this section may not provide you with specific answers for your situation, they will offer you something to consider when interpreting the realities in which you live and minister.

2. The paradigms described in this book are our best understanding of leadership and the church. However, we do not wish to fall into the disorder that Barker calls "Paradigm Paralysis." Eventually, other paradigms will replace them, those that we have attempted herein to articulate. Times will change, and with the changes will come new realities of church leadership and ministry.

3. People can choose to change their paradigms. Barker uses a "paradigm shift" question in order to challenge persons to think about their paradigms. An application of Barker's question is this: "What today is impossible to do in your congregation—but if it could be done, it would fundamentally change what you do?"[27]

Chapter Sixteen

Church Leadership in a Multi-cultural Context: An Emerging Paradigm

Gerardo J. de Jesus *

> *They sing a new song:*
> *"You are worthy to take the scroll*
> *and to open its seals,*
> *for you were slaughtered and by*
> *your blood you ransomed for God*
> *saints from every tribe and*
> *language and people and nation;*
> *you have made them to be a*
> *kingdom of priests serving our God,*
> *and they will reign on earth."*
> (Rev. 5:9-10)

Imagine that you are newly called or appointed to a congregation comprised of persons of several races or has multi-lingual programs and worship services. Do not dismiss this idea as something that could only happen along the immigrant coasts in North America. In the next ten or twenty years, a congregation made up of Koreans, Hispanics, Whites, and African Americans in some proportion is just as likely in Athens, Georgia, as it is in New York or San Francisco.

* Gerardo J. de Jesus is an American Baptist pastor at My Friend's House in California. He is also a Ph.D. candidate in Theology and Personality, The School of Theology at Claremont.

The multi-cultural congregation is to be desired and not feared. Revelation 5:9-10 makes no pretense concerning God's intention for the future of the worshiping community and for all humanity. From the perspective of the eschaton (the future age), the multi-cultural community is reconciled. Yet from the reality of the present, the church community is far from being God's true intention for humanity. Nevertheless this eschatological hope gives us a glimpse into the futures.

The debris of broken lives and alienated communities and nations in the history of humanity will not have the final word regarding the destiny of humankind. The final word is *reconciliation* among people of different races and cultures! And that reconcilation is best implemented in the midst of a worshiping congregation.

To become the leader of a multi-cultural congregation is to become an advocate for building bridges among people who live outside the mainstream due to the color of their skin, their accents, or their gender. If the church in a multi-cultural world is to become "the first fruits" of God's *telos* for all humanity, as described in the vision of John, then the church must first become a community that is reconciled with itself. There is no justification—neither on natural grounds nor on historical premises—for discrimination, segregation, alienation, or state-sponsored apartheid within our denominations or congregations.

Furthermore, if the leader and the church in a multi-cultural world is to be a witness of Jesus Christ by living out its faith within a multi-ethnic community, then the leader and the church must be willing and ready to count the cost of discipleship by providing the kind of leadership necessary for the church's vision of such a community within itself. Church leaders must be informed by a vision of the future which will help them understand how far we have yet to go before we become the kind of community God intends for us to be.

Multi-cultural church leadership is yet to become a topic of serious consideration by many pastors who assume that because of their social or geographical location they will not likely be thrust into a diverse, multi-cultural congregation. Indeed, most congregations do not yet realize that the next generation of church leaders presently in training will be much more diverse in race and gender. Furthermore, seminaries and institutions of pastoral training are ill-equipped in curriculum development, policy making, and faculty personnel for preparing persons to "partner" with God toward this future.

The very nature of "leadership" within the multi-cultural church is difficult to define. While there is much to learn about ministering to a multi-cultural, multi-ethnic congregation, there are three perspectives that can be discussed if we are to be effective in working with diverse congregations or denominations.

For congregations and individuals to remain faithful in providing leadership to a multi-cultural church in a multi-cultural world, they must: (1) appreciate different faiths and their symbolic categories of learning; (2) understand alienation; and (3) be willing to share power with unpredicatable and uncontrollable persons who are different.

Appreciate Different Faiths

Multi-cultural leaders must have the temperament to appreciate the faith-experience of those outside their normal gates.[1] The effective leader will know how to embrace the symbols created by others in their faith-journey. Jesus shows those with a static view of God how others, from the multi-ethnic community, respond in faith from within their own social-symbolic systems and cultural traditions. Jesus is the Way to God for all people. Yet, how we experience the "Way to God" is accommodated to our own respective sociocultural experiences. His "way" prevents us from making "our way" the absolute criterion for describing or understanding God. His "way" frees us to experience the reality of God in our day-to-day living, within our own space and time, and within our own "symbolic" universe. His "way" prevents any attempt on the part of any group to dominate the scene on the "way" to knowledge and experience of God.

Understand Alienation

The multi-cultural leader is self-consciously driven to understand the severe alienation experienced by persons of minority cultures. This understanding must be anchored in the God who comes to us in the humanity of Jesus Christ. Jesus shows us the Truth about God, his inclusive love, and appreciation for diversity. He does so by exposing the distorted, idealistic, and fallacious images we have created about the nature of God. These images help secure our own ideals and agendas, creating "insiders" and "outsiders" within the church. The Truth of God in the humanity of Christ provokes us to reorder our social relationships, demanding that we embrace and love our neighbor who is different. Jesus sets us free from the alienated condition that we create for ourselves in society, culture, and gender, breaking "down the dividing wall, that is, the hostility between us" (Eph. 2:14).

Learn to Share Power

The leader of a multi-cultural community must have a desire for abundant life. In practical terms, to have life, and have it more abundantly, means that those who hold the reigns of power in a given institution must learn to share the overflowing sources of power, submitting their own ego and agenda to God's intended future. Most of us do not prefer to share power unless we can ultimately control the outcome or the persons appointed to tasks. We often lack the will to offer resources or authority to persons who are apparently unpredictable (from our point of view) or who have the capacity to operate in ways that we cannot control.

The leader of a multi-cultural congregation will learn to effectively share power with the team and the board and take the risk that the outcomes are not exactly as the leader envisioned, because now the leadership team owns and implements the plan.

How We See Ourselves

To create a Christian community that reflects the vision of a new humanity in Revelation 5, the leader of a multi-cultural congregation must be enlightened by how those in the multi-ethnic Christian community understand themselves, how they arrive at their "inner logic," how their self-understanding relates to their faith-formation, and the symbols they create in the process of their life experience.

> I recall feeling different among my Anglo brothers and sisters at the Christian liberal arts college I attended. As often as I tried to remind myself that we're all "one in Christ," I couldn't

about 110,000 new immigrants are streaming into the city each year. In California, ethnic minorities already make up more than 40 percent of the state's thirty million people.

And what's already true for California and Los Angeles will be so for much of America by the beginning of the twenty-first century. The multi-cultural tide is moving across the nation, from west to east, from east to west, from south to north. In the midst of this reality, the Anglo Americans are rapidly becoming a minority group. In keeping with this, *American Demographics* says, "You'll know it's the 21st Century when everyone belongs to a minority group" (Judith Waldrop, "You'll Know It's the 21st Century," *American Demographics* [December 1990]: 23-27).

These changes already hold tremendous implication for religious leaders. At the least in a multi-cultural city or community, monolingual pastors are culturally disadvantaged and ill-equipped to minister to the segments of the population that are growing most rapidly—thus being cut off from ministry in the most fertile areas.

Recently Shawchuck & Associates had opportunity to consult with a ten-year-old congregation composed of an Anglo group and a Korean group. Each group carries on its own program, while certain administrative and ministry activities are carried out jointly. The church was founded by the coming together of an Anglo congregation and a Korean congregation. The new congregation has always been served by two pastors—one Anglo American and one Korean American. Both of the founding pastors (Anglo and Korean) are now gone, and two other pastors have come to serve the congregation. The two Korean pastors are both bilingual, speaking both English and Korean, while both of the Anglo pastors speak only English.

The inability of the Anglo pastors to speak Korean has proven a tremendous handicap in the blending of the two groups, and it has led to much distrust and hostility. The Korean pastor knows so much more about what is going on in the congregation because he can communicate with all the members. While the Anglo pastor has difficulty communicating with the Korean people, the Korean pastor can attend to the pastoral needs of the entire congregation; the Anglo pastor can attend only to the English-speaking person's needs. Therefore, the Korean pastor appears to be more concerned with the congregation's pastoral needs than does the Anglo pastor.

Further, the Korean pastor can more easily work with all of the ministry and administrative units, because no matter what language is being used or what questions are being asked, he understands and can respond in a helpful manner. Also, the Korean pastor can read all of the church's official minutes and documents, with the Anglo can comprehend only those of the Anglo groups. Therefore, there is great distrust of the Korean pastor and lay leaders on the part of the Anglo leaders (none of whom speak Korean, yet many of the Korean leaders speak English) because they fear that since many of the Korean laypeople know what the Anglos are thinking, there must be power plays going on that the Anglos do not know about.

This is an example of how monolingual pastors will find themselves culturally and professionally disadvantaged in the future. The good news for this particular congregation is that the Anglo pastor is taking Korean language lessons, and in a few years he will be equipped to serve the entire congregation, and not merely half of it. The fact is that multi-cultural and multi-language congregations are springing up all over the country. Seminaries and denominational agencies responsible for ministerial training must prepare future ministers now for these opportunities.

Another implication these new realities hold for the American church is that for the first time the predominant denominations are being forced to compete for "these new peoples," as ethnic pastors and non-American agencies seek to establish churches and/or denominations that are not related to the North American churches. Already, this phenomenon has led to situations that serve to accentuate how difficult it may be for the North American church to share any of its territory with immigrant pastors and churches

The Korean Methodist Church of Korea recently announced its intentions to send Korean missionaries to the United States to establish Korean congregations that were to be related to The Korean Methodist Church in Korea, and not The United

Methodist Church. At issue here is the founding of another Methodist denomination in the United States, having no structural accountability to the United Methodist bishops and conferences.

The Council of Bishops of The United Methodist Church raised strong objection, saying if The Korean Methodist Church was to send missionaries to America, then the missionaries and their works must become a part of The United Methodist Church, and not a new denomination. Currently, The Korean Methodist Church has at least temporarily backed off its plans, but the tension still exists.

This example illustrates a paradigm shift regarding the long-accepted relationship of the American denominations to the rest of the world. For the past 150 years or so, the American denominations have sent its missionaries around the world, with the intent to evangelize the peoples and to establish churches based on the North American church model. These efforts were funded and supervised by North American church agencies. Only in the past thirty years have any serious steps been taken to establish indigenous churches. The Korean Methodist Church is proposing a complete turn of events. They propose sending missionaries to America to establish a denomination based on the Korean church model.

This did not fit the old rules and regulations that the North American church has so long held as the only rules to be followed. So the North American bishops responded out of the only paradigm American denominations have ever known—the Christendom paradigm: "America is our parish. All the people who live in our parish belong to us. Missionaries don't evangelize in our parish. But we evangelize the peoples outside our parish."

The Korean Methodist Church, however, was operating out of a different paradigm, a set of rules and regulations much nearer to that of the Apostolic Church paradigm. The world is everybody's parish, and the Korean people are our people, wherever in the world they are. Operating out of their paradigm, it made perfect sense that they should send their pastors to establish Korean Methodist churches—even in America.

It does not matter how we settle this tension between the bishops of The United Methodist Church and The Korean Methodist Church. More to the point is the fact that the old Christendom paradigm and the power positions of American denominations are giving way to forces they cannot possibly withstand. Though American denominations may, for a while, resist the establishment of indigenous churches on American soil, they cannot stem the tide of the historic changes that are rushing toward us.

Such inabilities of the Anglo, English-speaking Methodist church to accommodate other cultures or languages is not unique to the Korean situation. The founding of the Evangelical and United Brethren Churches was in large part due to the inability of the Methodist pastors to communicate with or understand the cultural differences of the German-speaking Methodists.

The above examples could be multiplied, with examples given from many denominations and congregations. These, however, should be sufficient to illustrate the problem and opportunities (many of which may be missed) that will come rushing toward the North American Church as America, itself, continues its migration from a once single dominant culture and language to many cultures and languages.

Chapter Seventeen

Women in Church Leadership: An Emerging Paradigm

Carol E. Becker*

A middle-level manager in a major denomination was recently up for a promotion to senior management, a measure that had to be approved by the denomination's Board of Directors. Her supervisor told her in advance that he would recommend her and indeed, she did receive the promotion. But immediately after the board meeting, the supervisor called her to his office to report that "a substantial number of board members had voted against her promotion." The supervisor surmised this was in part because she was "too aggressive." When the woman objected, citing examples of her male colleagues who were far more aggressive in similar situations, the supervisor readily agreed. He even sympathized. But he added, "That's just the way things are."

Women moving into leadership positions in the church receive many mixed messages about themselves and their work. This scenario illustrates at least three, all of which would be confusing to a thoughtful woman. First, of course, is the compelling message that women long to hear from the church: "We want you here. We know you have something to contribute." The second message is a bit more

*Carol E. Becker was Director of Communications for the Evangelical Lutheran Church in America from 1987 to 1992. She is an author and communications consultant to religious organizations.

problematic, and it goes something like this: "If you are going to be here, we want you to act in a way that will be comfortable for us [men]." The implication of this second message for the intelligent woman is, of course, that the men are not really sure that they *do* want her there after all. But the third message is the real clincher. It's simple: "This is the way things are [in this case, women aren't supposed to be assertive], and you have to fit in." This message makes no sense to women because it does not fit the paradigm out of which they live and work.

A Paradigm for Women in Leadership

Women do work out of a different paradigm. Judy Rosener hails a new generation of women leaders making their way into top management "not by adopting the style and habits that have proved successful for men, but by drawing on the skills and attitudes they developed from their shared experience as women." They are succeeding, Rosener says, "because of—not in spite of—certain characteristics generally considered to be 'feminine' and inappropriate in leaders."[1] Rosener characterizes the leadership style of this new breed of women as interactive because they "encourage participation, share power and information, enhance other people's self-worth, and get others excited about their work.[2] Men, of course, can work by these principles. Some actually do. But in order to do so, men must have healthy feminine aspects.

Sally Helgesen pictures women as *weavers*. It is not so much the goal reached that is the point of satisfaction for women in leadership, she points out. It is as much the connections and the process used to reach the goals. And in making connections, women weave a "web of inclusion" in the workplace. The point of authority in the web is *the heart*, not the head.[3] In "emphasizing interrelationships, working to tighten them, building up strength, knitting loose ends into the fabric, it is a strategy that honors the feminine principles of inclusion, connection" and it "betrays the female's essential orientation toward process, her concern with the means used to achieve her ends."[4] Helgesen stresses that "the strategy of the web is guided by *opportunity*, proceeds by the use of intuition, and is characterized by a *patience* that comes from *waiting* to see what comes next."[5] These are principles for leadership that come more naturally to women, because they come from the feminine within us.

Other recent writers concur. Deborah Tannen asserts that the goal of men in conversation is power, whereas for women it is establishing relationships.[6] In comparing women's style to a dominant white male system, Ann Wilson Schaef identifies the prevailing system of our culture as white male, and she describes male managers typically as "being in front," having the information and the answers, presenting an all-knowing image, and female leaders as facilitators—finding people, nudging them, encouraging.[7] Alicia Johnson adds that women bring a balance to the workplace, tending to work as consensus managers, rather than tough leaders.[8]

Women working in the church demonstrate these differences just as much as do women in the corporation. They want power in order to share with others and get the job done by collaboration. They may have trouble accepting their own power and acting powerfully, as men do, but "because their bodies give them graceful lessons in letting happen what needs to happen, women sometimes show a paradoxical strength as they embrace their vulnerability."[9] Men, on the other hand, tend to want to act powerfully in order to influence others, and they may avoid their vulnerability.

These observers are describing the fact that women prefer to work from experience. Fundamental to the feminine approach is experience. Tied closely to experience, of course, are relationships, process, change, interaction, and waiting.

These are the very principles of leadership that are increasingly affirmed in management literature, by Deming's total quality management movement, by the call for more team building in management, by relational management, and by this very book. Such affirmation predicts that the principles of the feminine paradigm should be legitimized as an important component of effective leadership in the executive suite. As this happens, the white male system should give way to a more integrated model of leadership that will embody the best of what both the masculine and feminine styles have to offer. Will this happen in the church? And when and if it does, will the contribution of women even be recognized?

An Invisible Paradigm

At the same time that much is written about the need for more person-centered management, much is also written about the fact that women know how to manage in this way. Savvy leaders will agree that person-centered management is needed. But there is little agreement on how much women have contributed to the changes that are needed and are beginning to come about. This, says Schaef, is because the white male system is still the norm in management circles, and why: "Women frequently go along with the expectations of the white male system in order to win acceptance" either by being "proper" women or by trying to be "like men." The latter choice, she says, is common among professional women, who "believe that the only road to success is to act like men and beat them at their own game."[10] In Schaef's words of a decade ago, she predicted what we experience today.

The idea that women lead from a different paradigm is rejected in many quarters today even by women because they fear it will be used against them. Rosener's article prompted not only widespread affirmation from women, but also vociferous protest from both men and women who apparently perceived that it is either threatening or dangerous. Rosener herself points out the downside of identifying a feminine style. The feminine paradigm has to be accepted, she stresses, or else there is great danger for the woman manager, who will seem weak if judged by the masculine paradigm of leadership.[11] Tannen agrees and warns that clarifying differences can be used to justify unequal treatment of women.[12]

On the other hand, women who demonstrate masculine traits in their leadership style can't win either. Schaef warns that women who "are too successful" by white male system standards are punished.[13] They are admonished for being "too assertive, direct, goal oriented, visible, or powerful." It happens to women working in the church as well as those in the corporation.[14]

This, of course, is exactly what happened to the hapless female leader whose story we used to introduce this chapter. The board of directors had nearly denied her the promotion, in part because she was "too aggressive." It was not because she was ineffective. In fact, a man in her position, behaving the way she did, probably would have been affirmed. She was evaluated and found wanting because she did such a good job of adopting a masculine style of assertiveness in her work. But she was a woman and wasn't supposed to be so assertive! Had she been compliant and possibly accomplished less, she would have been judged ineffective in her job. Furthermore, even though her supervisor did see that the female leader was being judged unfairly by a masculine paradigm, he accepted the paradigm as a "given."

This leader realized, only after several months of pondering, that she was not to blame. Successful female leaders must remind themselves of this fact over and over again. What's wrong is not women. Male systems cannot embrace the feminine paradigm. It is not enough to bring women into leadership. In fact, it is violence against women when they are brought in and then "set up" by an alien system. On the one hand, they are expected to stop being "like women." On the other hand, when they do try to "act like a man would," they are judged harshly.[15]

Women themselves verify this message. Though it is widely believed that women lack staying power in top management ranks because they have overriding childcare or other family concerns, new surveys are showing a different problem. Women are no more likely than men to cite concerns about family or children as reasons for leaving. Nor do they leave over excessive job stress. Women leave leadership posts, in some cases "giving up" on their careers entirely, because they have fewer advancement opportunities.[16] Carol Hymowitz and Timothy Schellhardt sum it up this way: "The biggest obstacle women face is the most intangible. Men at the top feel uncomfortable with women around them."[17] Women come up against what is popularly called "the glass ceiling." A more appropriate metaphor, says Schwartz, is a cross-sectional geological diagram. "The barriers to women's leadership occur when potentially counterproductive layers of influence on women—maternity, tradition, socialization—meet management strata pervaded by the largely unconscious preconceptions, stereotypes, and expectations of men. Such interfaces do not exist for men, and tend to be impermeable for women."[18] The most critical barrier for women is the inability of the white male to recognize and value the feminine paradigm for leadership.

The stated reason for not advancing a woman might be that "she wouldn't want this overseas assignment"; or "she doesn't have the right kind of experience for this promotion"; or "her family concerns will not allow her to devote her time to this assignment"; or "she's not tough enough for this." Underlying all of these reasons is the real reason: "We [men] are uncomfortable [or unfamiliar] with her style." Men will make this mistake often without malicious intent, because they do not even recognize the feminine paradigm of leadership.[19]

Statistics show that in traditional organizations, it is very difficult for new paradigms (outside the accepted white male norm) to be recognized and valued. Nearly thirty years after Betty Friedan called upon women to join men in the world of work, only 3 percent of top executive jobs in the largest companies in the United States are held by women.[20] Though Rosener claims there is no pay gap for women at the top, she acknowledges that women in mid-level management make roughly $12,000 less than men in comparable jobs.[21] Furthermore, more women than men report that they are unlikely to remain in their present jobs, and that they are looking for jobs that will provide them with more career opportunities.[22]

Feminine Paradigms in the Church

The church may rightly be judged a good candidate for success in embracing the feminine paradigm of leadership. The Christian faith itself is based on the feminine principle of paradox.[23] Furthermore, within congregations and church management circles there seems to be a higher level of comfort with the feminine paradigm, and a higher percentage (than in other non-profit organizations or in business environments) of men who themselves embrace the feminine paradigm in their leadership style. According to Neuchterlein and Hahn, "Clergymen are not necessarily representative of men in our culture: some clergymen do want power in order to influence and persuade, but other clergymen want power in order to help empower others."[24] They cite one study in which more than 50 percent of male and 80 percent of female clergy "preferred having power in order to have and share resources with others."[25] Furthermore, they add, "men and women in ministry tend toward psychological androgyny; that is, they experience the integration of both masculine and feminine qualities."[26]

This kind of healthy blending of the masculine and feminine is expected in the church. People say: "This is the church, and things are different here." In making comments like this, those who work for the church are stating their expectation that work will be more participatory, person-centered, and networked rather than power-based. In other words, they may be stating their expectation that leadership will embrace the feminine paradigm. Unfortunately, what we often hear from clergy and lay staff, after a time of working in the church, is less comforting. They say, "This is the church, and things should be different here. But they aren't." Church leaders (both male and female) cite disillusionment over this issue as one of their hardest adjustments.

Numbers alone warn us that women are still having difficulty breaking into leadership in the church. Though the ordination of women is not new in most Protestant denominations, a study conducted by the National Council of Churches in 1988 put women at only 7.9 percent of the ordained clergy among denominations ordaining women in North America. This percentage is an increase of 4 percent during the period 1978 to 1988. In more recent years, the number of women attending theological schools has risen sharply. It is yet unclear whether women will have an easier time entering the clergy pool, and moving within the system, as their numbers increase.[27] It is also unclear how successful women are in moving into senior leadership positions in denominational ranks. At the time of this writing, no studies have been done to evaluate these trends.

Why is the church not succeeding better? First, though the church does embrace the feminine paradigm of leadership better than many institutions, and certainly radically better than the business world, it does so within a system that is in other ways religiously hierarchical and theologically grounded in prevailing white male thinking about organizational systems.[28] In order to remain grounded in white male thinking, the church actually casts off the feminine principles that are at the heart of the faith, de-values experience as a grounding for theology or practice, and hotly debates the value of diversity in its ranks. All of this happens not because the people of the church want it to happen, or are cavalier about the fundamental values of the faith. It happens because the prevailing system of our culture has no theology of differences.[29] The result is that men and women working together in the church get caught trying to be collaborative in systems that remain hierarchical.[30]

A second barrier for the church is even more difficult. There is significant evidence that the very presence of women in the church is deeply troubling to the psychic imagination of men. Janette Hassey points out that this has been true at least since the Middle Ages: "Dominating the medieval era, St. Augustine's theology grounded the inferiority of women in creation, before the Fall." God, he said, "intended women's subordination by making Eve's physical body dependent on that of Adam."[31] There is significant current debate about exactly what St. Augustine meant by his remarks. He may well have been misunderstood. Nevertheless, his words and the centuries-old posture of discomfort that the Christian tradition shows to women has had profound effect on our collective unconscious. In the centuries since St. Augustine, the church has developed elaborate theological systems that remind women of their innate inferiority, based on the biological fact that they are closely tied to the physical. Women, therefore, become "standard bearers" of the sexual, living reminders that we are all sexual beings. Since the Christian tradition has long been uncomfortable with the physical, and particularly the sexual, the very presence of women is deeply troubling for the church. The fact that sexuality is a major identifying characteristic of the white male system,[32] combined with the fact that church systems and theologies are so firmly grounded in white male thinking, exacerbates this problem.

The result is that the church has institutionalized fear of the feminine. Historically, this discomfort is illustrated by the admonition that women should cover themselves (to protect men!), the stoning of the adulteress, the burning of "witches," and a host of other rules and behaviors, including our current theological justifications for keeping women out of leadership in the church.[33] On the conscious, rational level, most of us, both men and women, would deny that there is any such deep-seated psychology involved. In fact, we may be shocked by the very idea. And we would certainly deny that the rules of the white male system have anything to do with our fear of the feminine. But there are too many rules of that very system, and too many restrictions on participation and behavior of women in the church that can't be explained any other way.

The very fact that denominations still debate whether women should be clergy, governing board members, or even Sunday school teachers and choir members is the most obvious example of the influence of white male thinking about systems on the participation of women in church life.[34] To women and men who have broken out of these biases, the debate does not even make sense because it is based on a meaningless assumption: that only white men can "approach God" as intermediaries for the people. This idea, Schaef charges, is pure white male thinking, denies the feminine attributes of God, and betrays the church as idolatrous.[35]

A third barrier to acceptance of the feminine paradigm in church leadership is the nature of the theological enterprise. Until recently, when eloquent female theologians like Mary Daly, Carol Oachs, and others began publishing, the very nature of the theological enterprise was based on white male systems and ideas. Systematic theology is still typically arrived at by a very careful analysis of ideas, a construction, often in minute detail, of "what's right," and an assumption that the most important thing in one's faith is to know God or to think about God in the right way. There has been little room for experience in the mix. Women in church leadership are now challenging those assumptions, not by overt action, but simply by virtue of the way in which they go about their ministry. Increasingly, the carefully constructed theologies of the white male system are challenged by women who demonstrate that experience too is a part of theology. Men react to this in at least two ways. Some will attack. They attack the quota systems that allow women into church leadership in greater numbers. They also attack their church for "becoming less theologically sound." The implication is obvious: Now that we have women in our ranks, we can no longer construct a male system theology, and that isn't right. At the basis of their rejection is not hate for women. It is an inability to understand the fact that experience is a valid component of theology.

Women working in the church must deal with all of the biases of the business world, but in addition to that, they face the biases of the church against women in leadership. Women themselves report that when biases against their participation are covert and theologically justified, they are much harder to overcome, much more psychologically painful, and much harder to live with. It's one thing for women to hear that they "don't fit into" the business world. It's a much more difficult thing for women working in the church to hear from their colleagues that even God thinks they're second class.

Women Working in the Male Paradigm

John Naisbitt argues that women in the next century will benefit in the workplace because their style is unique and needed. Helgesen and Rosener agree, arguing that women will be able to use their unique style to transform organizations. Ann Huff disagrees. She argues that women working in a male system merely become "organizational wives," relegated to the repetitious "housekeeping" chores of administration.[36] In fact, she asserts, the very feminine leadership styles that Rosener, Helgesen, and Naisbitt claim will help women are the styles that will trap them instead—an ability to be people-centered, encouraging of others, deferential to the success of groups rather than themselves, negotiating rather than forceful, networking rather than hierarchical. Her point: "Organization wives not only exhaust themselves, they behave in ways that keep them at lower levels in their profession. They deny themselves, and are denied by their organizations, the experiences that will allow them to rise to the top."[37] Neuchterlein and Hahn describe how this happens to women in congregational ministry, citing the example of a female pastor who "recognizes that she, as a woman, has been culturally conditioned to be actively involved in service projects and behind-the-scenes church work that have called forth sociomotive roles. She recognizes that she has not been encouraged to take on masculine roles and be a leader of church groups or churches."[38]

Huff's prediction is chilling for every woman leader, in the church or out. It is based on the assumption that women will continue to work within the masculine paradigm, and therefore, their style will be used against them. Literally, it will "keep them in their place."

What does happen to women working as women in a white male system? On the one hand, they are expected to be like men if they want to succeed. But the more they do act like men, the more they are criticized. This happens because women are not judged by the same criteria, even when they adopt the masculine leadership paradigm. On the other hand, if women try to work as women, assuming they will be judged on the merits of the feminine paradigm, they are considered weak and ineffective, or as Huff predicts and Neuchterlein and Hahn illustrate, they are "relegated to the role of organizational or church wife."

The female leader who was considered too assertive by her denomination's Board of Directors got caught in the "you're too bitchy" trap. There are other traps for women working in the white male system.[39]

"What Does It Feel Like?"

> When Suzanne was elected the first female bishop in her denomination in the United States, she had only one complaint. "I wish someone would ask me about the issues." About the only thing she is asked to comment about is: "What does it feel like to be the first woman bishop?" Suzanne recognizes the need to speak for all women, she emphasizes, but adds that there are many more important issues in the church. She can talk about those as well as her male colleagues can, but she is seldom asked.

The first trap for women working in a male system is that gender is always the main issue. It is never quite possible for a woman to overcome the charge that she got the important job "because she is a woman." If her denomination has a quota system, this perception is particularly accurate. Beyond that, people always want first to know what it feels like "for a woman to work here." When she demonstrates that she is actually able to talk intelligently about other things, she surprises people.

This kind of tokenism is stressful for women because it makes them representative of all women, and not individuals. It also makes them visible targets for the pain, confusion, and grief that men and women feel over their changing roles in society at large. Finally, this trap encourages women to overachieve lest they give off the message that women "can't hack it."[40]

The Invisible Woman

In one denomination, the women have agreed to wear bright colors to senior staff meetings. In order to follow this important dress code, some of the women had to buy new suits—red or bright blue, or even yellow. All felt it was worth it. The goal for these women was, literally, to be more visible and thereby increase the number of times they would get the opportunity to speak in meetings. Early on in their experience, these women, who represent about 15 percent of the group, realized that their floor time was minimal. Their complaints led to a consultant analysis of the group dynamic, which verified what the women experienced. Their solution was to dress to be noticed.

A second trap, related to the first, is that women remain invisible. No matter how good their ideas, how often they themselves create opportunities to share ideas, or how often or how vocally they speak up in meetings, they remain invisible. Here's how this plays out: Women's ideas are not taken as seriously. Women are not asked for advice by their male colleagues nearly as often as men ask each other for advice. And often, women will experience men asking each other for further information about an idea or report that originally came from a woman. Over time, these kinds of experiences make women wonder if they are invisible to the men around them. They are not, of

Whose Idea Was It Anyway?

Some years ago, when Hannah's denomination conducted building-wide office renovations, another female manager approached Hannah with a problem. She was unable to get the all-male building remodeling team to take her office design seriously. It seemed that the remodeling in her division would never get done, because the team members were telling her what to do, and she had other ideas. Hannah's unit, on the other hand, had not only succeeded in being remodeled, but it had moved to another location in the building where the remodeling plan could be carried out better. Hannah's female colleague asked her how she had done it. "Simple," Hannah replied. When the remodeling team wouldn't listen to her, she assigned the project to one of her male staff members. The change in attitude was instantaneous, and before she knew it, all of Hannah's ideas for the new space became a reality.

course, but their leadership style is. What's really happening is that others around them, especially the men, cannot relate to the women's way of talking or interacting.

This strategy is typically embraced by women working in a white male system. It's a way of finally getting something done. And savvy women know that they need men around them to get anything done. It's not because they or their female staff are not competent. It's because the male system thrives on the white male style. The trap is that women are forced to give up their ideas to men in order to move their organization or their objectives forward. In the end, the women lose because the men get the credit for their ideas or their work. Women will get out of this trap only when the male system breaks down enough to allow female paradigms for leadership to be recognized and appreciated.

This phenomenon may be the result of the wish of both males and females within the white male system to align themselves with the leader who has power. Kanter defines power as the ability to get things done, mobilize resources, and access whatever is needed to move ahead. In the corporation (and, Conger argues, in the church as well), effective leadership requires competence and power. Most people want to work for and align themselves with a leader who has power; furthermore, men are perceived to have more power.[41] When clergywomen or female leaders hear the complaint that "things will fall apart if we have a women in charge," they are experiencing the assumption that women lack power. Indeed, because women are working in a system that does not welcome them, it is often true that they have less access to power than do their male colleagues.[42]

Make Me Comfortable

> On her first day as a new senior leader in the national office of a major denomination, Betty had an urgent request to meet with a mid-level leader in another department. To her surprise, he opened the meeting by asking her to turn over a staff position in her department to his. "I'm sure we agree that this is the proper way to organize the staff," he said. Betty was stunned but gathered her composure quickly and replied with a firm no.

> To clarify her response, she explained how she saw the position
> in question. As a result of that meeting and her firm response,
> Betty endured five years of professional harassment from this
> mid-level manager.

Betty's mistake was that she failed to observe one of the cardinal
rules of the white male system: Men in senior positions need to feel
comfortable at all times, and it is the job of others around them,
including women above them in the system, to keep them comfortable. Said another woman manager, "I continue to get promoted not
only because I am productive. It's also because I do my work and
don't make any trouble. But you can be sure that any time I break
even the smallest rule, I am reprimanded thoroughly." Women make
men at the top feel uncomfortable when they break the rules of the
white male system. But even when they don't break the rules,
women still make men feel uncomfortable because they often lead
from a paradigm that is not recognized and validated by that male
system.

By virtue of the fact that women make male system managers
uncomfortable, women are subject to reprimand. It may be only a
warning from the boss. Often it is more. Women may be the recipi-
ents of public criticism for their work, private maneuvering to reduce
their authority, or any one of a range of other tactics. In the church
this criticism may also take a theological spin, as it did with Mary, who
was invited to give a paper at a major theological convocation hosted
by her denomination. One of three speakers, Mary followed a speech
by a well-known male theologian. Her paper effectively challenged
some of his ideas, and was interesting and engaging of the audience.
Some months later, this theologian surprised Mary by publicly claiming that she was "not fit" to be a leader in the church. Mary objected
but never received an apology. In fact, Mary was asked to submit her
paper for "review."

Women like Mary are often mystified by the vehemence of the
attack against them. It seems out of proportion to the circumstances
because they don't recognize that power over others is a fundamental
value in the white male system, and that all work is a struggle for
some kind of power.[43] For men operating within the system, however,

power is the source of their authority. They experience women like Betty and Mary as threatening their power every time they create discomfort. The response of the men is swift and brutal: Cut off her power!

Work Twice as Hard?

One denomination decided to open computer support offices and hired Susan, a highly competent, experienced laywoman to head the staff. She had a proven track record and was dedicated to her new post. Susan worked long, hard hours. Yet, she could seldom engage her male colleagues in casual conversation, and she had scant informal opportunity to get to know her male colleagues and thereby enhance the interface of her new department with existing units. After three years, Susan left, and a man was hired to replace her. Within a very short time, other male managers became excited about the "new" opportunity to "really use," the computer support department.

What Susan experienced was the trap of having to work twice as hard to get half as much done. This happens when women are not accepted by the male group, because they have not passed the loyalty tests.[44] When acceptance is not forthcoming, the work that women do is thwarted because they are denied access to influence in the organization. Furthermore, even when women are granted power, they must continually protect the access they have. Said one manager: "If you can work very, very hard, and if you can live with the charge that you got this job just because you are a woman, and if you can live with the doubts people have about your effectiveness when they observe you leading 'like a woman,' you might succeed. But you will always get reminders that you don't really belong."

These reminders take the form of statements that put women down as a category or that lift women up as an exception. They may also be insults or ridicule of women or women's incompetence, kidding, and off-color jokes told specifically because a token

woman is present. The woman is thereby tested and retested by
the dominant group to see if she will be loyal by allowing the inap-
propriateness. At the same time she is tested, she is reminded that
ultimately she is an outsider.[45] Some women find this loyalty testing too difficult to endure, and they never become part of the
dominant (male) group. They are thereby left without all-impor-
tant support from male peers. Others who pass the test are better
accepted, but run the risk of forgetting what it was like to be an
outsider, buying into the white male system and withdrawing their
support and mentoring from other women.

The Better You Do . . .

> When Harriet joined the senior staff of a major denomina-
> tion, she undertook a program to bring new technologies to
> the service of national ministry programs. This required
> approaching male colleagues in other departments, and Har-
> riet did so with the assumption that collaboration would be
> possible. She knew that she and her staff had expertise in
> technology. However, two years after starting this initiative,
> Harriet had gotten nowhere. Instead of finding her colleagues
> eager to collaborate, she found them either uninterested or
> actively thwarting her efforts.

Harriet fell into the trap of being better at a skill than a dominant male in her peer group. Women in leadership, in the church
and out, quickly find that it is deadly to "do better" at any task than
a dominant male, lest he be humiliated. Conger emphasizes that "a
humiliated or resentful dominant male does not make a supportive
peer." She cites one male manager who comments, "It's OK for
women to have these jobs as long as they don't go zooming by
me."[46] Thus women commonly remind each other, "The better you
do the worse it gets." Success may also earn female leaders the
wrath of other women who have bought into the white male system. Because some women also believe in the white male system,
they continue to think that the problems they experience are their

own fault. They direct more anger internally, against themselves, and when another woman does well, her success reinforces their own lack of self-esteem. Their internal voices tell them: "If she can do so well, why can't I? The problem must be me. There *is* something wrong with me."

Female leaders caught in this trap often find themselves holding back out of fear of retaliation or fear of visibility that might bring them criticism. In fact, Rosabeth Moss Kanter points out that fear of success in women may actually be in part fear of retaliation.[47]

Harassment

At a retreat of a senior leadership team in one denomination, the participants divided into groups to discuss a topic, and they wrote ideas on newsprint. When the groups came together, the retreat leader picked individuals to post the results. Two men were chosen from the first two groups. By the time a petite woman rose to post the results from the third group, it was obvious to everyone in the room that she would not be able to reach high enough to post her papers with the other two. There was laughter and joking as the group watched her struggle. After she sat down and the fourth and final newsprint had been posted, the leader stopped the meeting and recounted to the group what he had just seen: The only time there had been joking and laughter during this exercise was when the woman stood to post her results. Furthermore, he observed, the men had laughed and the women had been silent.

This incident is, of course, another example of loyalty testing. But it is more than that. It is harassment, as is much loyalty testing. We all know about harassment. We've read and heard about it, and we all know that sexual harassment in the workplace is forbidden. It still happens, but at least we have a high level of awareness about it. What we miss is that sexual harassment isn't always about explicit sex. It can also be about how a woman looks. What is so shocking about this example is that it was group harassment. And after the men were confronted with it, they were angry that they had been set up. They expressed little concern for the woman who had been harassed. They accused the leader of "ruining" their discussion. Harassment is wrong, demeaning, and shaming of women. Yet it happens, and it is one of the traps for women who work in the white male system.

How Do I Look?

> Lynn, a well-known freelance professional, decided it was time to take a job. She applied for a position for which she was well qualified. She knew her denomination was looking for women, and although she knew about the gender trap, she hoped this would help her receive careful consideration. Indeed, she was called back for a second interview. By this time, she knew that her main competition for the job was another woman—younger, less experienced, but better looking. Lynn knew the outcome even before she got the call. The younger, prettier woman got the job.

Women know that appearance counts. Anyone who hires knows this. But for women, it counts in ways that it should not. Sometimes being attractive helps. Most often, being too attractive hurts. And sometimes being plain is an advantage. The point is that how a woman looks is always an issue. Appearance is never a neutral factor. This is because, as Schaef reminds us, in male system thinking, everything and everyone is first and foremost defined sexually.[48] Women remind men of sex one way or another, depending on what they look like. Whether appearance helps or hurts, a woman depends on what makes the men around her comfortable. Generally, more attractive women make men feel more comfortable. Thus appearance may help land them jobs. What Lynn didn't know is that after you've got the job, the tables are often turned. Pretty women "aren't supposed to be too aggressive." So the woman who makes men feel most uncomfortable is usually the very attractive woman who is also very aggressive and direct. To a man, she looks most like a woman, but she acts least like one!

In the church, there is significant advantage to being plain. Men working for the church carry a heavy load of guilt about inappropriate sex, as we all do. Yet, because they are male system thinkers, they do tend to define relationships sexually. They are reminded of sex by women, as all men are, but they feel guilty about it, perhaps more than the average man. For these men, it is often more comfortable to work with women who are plain, women who remind them less about sex.

Be Yourself

Elizabeth is typical of Judy Rosener's interactive leader. She places high value on engaging people on her staff in decision making. Yet, her department exists within a very hierarchical system. At the same time that Elizabeth works very hard to use interactive leadership, she is pressed by the male system around her to be less interactive. It's a delicate balance, but Elizabeth has been encouraged by her staff and the many ways they appreciate her style. In fact, when she gets pressed for time and is pulled away from staff concerns, she often hears from her employees that they want her to be more caring, attentive, and connected to their concerns and tasks. This request makes sense to Elizabeth, because it fits her leadership paradigm.

Recently, however, her staff gave a different message. The department was facing a major decision, and Elizabeth set up a system that would engage people at all levels in setting direction. The staff responded by complaining that she was not decisive enough, that she didn't seem to know what she wanted to do, and that she was taking too long.

Women often get caught in the trap of being themselves. Of course, it is essential for women to lead from their own paradigm.[49] But whenever they do, there is the possibility that they will be considered weak or ineffective. When this happens, it's because the woman is leading from one paradigm and being judged by another. For women working in the white male system, there are many dangers to "being yourself." Asking for ideas might be interpreted as not having answers. Sharing information and power "allows for the possibility that people will reject or challenge the leader" or her authority. Generating enthusiasm in employees can be interpreted as cheerleading.[50] Still, it is important for women to be themselves and envision a time when the white male system will open up enough to embrace the feminine paradigm of leadership.

Models for Change

What women and men in church leadership need most is acceptance of the female paradigm of leadership. Until that happens, women will continue to be barred outright from many leadership positions, and women who do provide leadership in the church will continue to suffer the stress of working in a male-dominated system. Women report that this stress causes depression, weariness, and discouragement, and that it ranges from "mildly irritating" to crippling of their leadership on all counts.[51] For men, an acceptance of the feminine paradigm of leadership can be incredibly stress reducing. A man no longer has to have all the answers, all the power, and all the information when he realizes that there is another way to lead.

In the meantime, suggestions that are offered for women in the workplace still focus on helping them survive in an alien system. Huff suggests strategies for women. First, learn to say no so as not to become overly engaged in "secondary activities" of the organization. Next, stop trying to do everything so thoroughly and so well. Third, share relational tasks that need to be done. Fourth, expect more from men and less from women. Above all, learn to focus on the significant achievements. These are not skills that will help awareness and acceptance of the feminine paradigm. They are skills that will help women survive in the system dominated by masculine paradigms. And, she adds, they require women to resist their internal radar, and "reinforce behaviors that are more directly task related."[52] Unfocused energy and unending hope (which are both part of the feminine archetype), she says, "are perhaps the ideal combination for raising young children; they are more problematic in intimate relationships with other adults, and are absolutely disastrous in the workplace."[53]

Huff is right, so long as women continue to work in a system dominated by masculine paradigms. She does not suggest strategies that will necessarily bring about acceptance of the feminine paradigm, however. Marilyn Loden does suggest approaches that, if taken seriously, would help broaden acceptance of the feminine paradigm. First, in fact, she calls for adoption of workplace policies that value diversity and expansion of the definition of effective leadership, to include the feminine paradigm. Beyond that, she itemizes several practical and challenging steps: salary equalization, creation of executive women's councils, career tracking for high potential women, increasing the presence of women on corporate boards, workplace communication that reinforces the organization's commitment to women in leadership, and others.[54]

These strategies will accelerate changes within the male system and in small ways speed up the processes that will create a better environment for women within the white male system. However, they assume a prior step that is extremely challenging. The first step in understanding and accepting the feminine paradigm of leadership is exploding the myths of the white male system. Men particularly must accept that it is not reality. It is only a system. It is not innately superior to any other system. It is not omnipotent. And finally, the system does not make it possible for them to be totally logical, rational, and objective.[55] Though Schaef is pessimistic about the ability of men to break out of the white male system, it is the essential first step,[56] and many men take on the challenge admirably. In fact, it was a very courageous man who outlined this recipe for change: "Every man must admit to himself that, at some level, he is sexist. Only then does he have the openness to learn and value a new system." In order to do this, men must hear the statement not as an accusation, but as a statement of fact. Men are all sexist at some level because they all grew up in and benefited most from the white male system. They can't avoid it. As long as they fail to accept this fact, they will be unable to break into a new paradigm. Sexism is indeed subtle and insidious. It damages women most coming from the man who thinks he is not sexist because it's hard to get the issues on the table when there is denial at work.[57]

274 / Leading the Congregation

It's also important to recognize that men are not the only ones who have been duped by the white male system. Women have bought into the system, too. That fact is remarkably well-illustrated by the debate that still rages on the pages of management journals about whether men and women are in fact different in their leadership styles. These are the managers who think we are basically alike. The system is fine—people just need to adjust. Of course, it is true that all women do not lead by the feminine paradigm, just as it is true that all men do not lead out of the dominant male style.[58] This does not change the fact that all of us are in some way influenced and biased by a system of thinking and behaving that is so pervasive as to seem the equivalent of reality.

Once we have gotten this far, it is instructive to observe how male leaders in the church react to the news that sexism is alive and well, and they themselves are nurturing it. They seem to fall into three groups. First, there are the men who do not understand it at all. These men can participate in sexist behavior and not even recognize it, even when they are confronted with it. They will not understand this chapter. They are not callous or dumb, however. They simply cannot, under any circumstance, "get out of" the white male system. It is, therefore, impossible for them to see anything else. I do not know of any women in this group. Even if they deny it, women have experience at some level that helps them to at least see the white male system for what it is—a system with flaws like any other.

A second group of men react swiftly and decisively. They want to sit down with women, "hear all about it," and fix it. These are men who react to the sexism of the white male system in classic white male style. Do something. Do it now. Go on to something else. They are still shrouded by the white male system, though they see its flaws. The give-away is that they approach "fixing the system" in typical male dominant style. It's a task to be accomplished and nothing more. Once it's done, we'll all go back to business as usual.

A third group of men display real courage. Almost immediately upon hearing about sexism or being confronted by their participation in it, they pause and listen. They do not do anything else. Above all, they do not claim to be feminist, and they do not try to solve anything. They have some awareness that any activity they might undertake would cast them back into their own system. Thus the very act of pausing is a "first move" away from the system. It is an act alien to the white male system way of doing things, and it takes great courage and determination for a man to make this move. It is the beginning of real change. And though it is true that both men and women must undergo intense personal change in order to reach a point of working together better, it is necessary particularly for men to make this shift. They, after all, are the guardians of the white male system.

Another critical step in opening our awareness to new paradigms is in our use of language. We can each reprogram our internal "talk" on this subject in some simple ways that will have profound effect over time. After all, language defines what we believe! Next time you think, "A woman cannot lead this church," rethink it this way: "A woman's way of leading will not be accepted by this church." Next time you hear that "it is not right for women to be leaders in the church," change the beginning of the sentence like this: "Within the white male system, it is deemed not right for women to be leaders in the church." And when you hear someone say, "She's too bitchy and assertive," gently remind them that "the white male paradigm judges her to be too bitchy and assertive." Over time, the positive influence of different thinking can change our minds. It can open us up to the possibility of another paradigm.

It is a long personal and corporate struggle to bring about this kind of change. Carol Pierce and Bill Page describe in some detail the process that both men and women undergo as they come to terms with each other.[59] This process is very akin to what we will experience as we work together to open up the male paradigm for leadership and bring the female paradigm to respectability. Men must move from the extreme of controlling women through murder, mutilation, battering, rape, and coercion through intimidation, teasing, excluding, avoiding, devaluing and downplaying the role and importance of women, to role slotting, paternalism, and depersonalizing women until they get finally to their own anger and hurt. At this point, men realize that they themselves have been hurt by the narrowness of the white male system. In this journey, men move from controlling women through violence and exploitation at the extreme, to sexual harassment, to outright discrimination, to controlling women through courtesy. After they get through anger, they may still be defensive and will compete indiscriminantly with men and women. At this point, Pierce and Page say, men are ready for the decision to change. Only at this point are men able to pause and listen to women. Only at this point are men able to begin accepting the feminine paradigm of leadership. After they listen, if they truly listen, they are able to change the way they help women and become increasingly direct and stop trying to protect women. Then they may connect better with men, become more introspective, and differentiate people. They are ready now for shared leadership with women and acceptance of the best of both the masculine and the feminine paradigms of leadership.

Women go through a similar process. From the extreme of controlling men by murder, they move through suicide, addiction, self-destruction, then through helplessness, endurance, and frozen anger, to withholding, seduction, withdrawal, and control through helping men. Women may at this point come back to anger, which is still buried. In this journey, women move from controlling men through violence and psychological punishment at the extreme, to manipulation, to controlling men through deference. After they recognize their anger (though they may not yet express it), women can move on to role slotting the husband or boss, to maternalism, acting feminine, and finally to surfacing anger. Once anger is expressed, women can move to a point of questioning everything, and then to acting masculine. If they don't get stuck here—and many women in leadership do—they can move to a point of competing indiscriminantly with men and women, to overreacting, defensiveness, and finally, to a point where they are able to make the decision to learn and change. For women as for men, this point must be reached before they can accept and strive to integrate the feminine paradigm for leadership. It requires that women take responsibility for themselves and decide to "be themselves" even if there are risks. Once on this path, women will begin helping men in a different way. Women will acknowledge their own power, examine competition among women with more discrimination, become increasingly assertive, and differentiate people. They are now ready for shared leadership with men and acceptance of the best of both the masculine and the feminine paradigms of leadership.

The church is fertile ground for this change. We saw earlier in this chapter how appropriate the church is as a place where the feminine paradigm can be accepted. The fact that the church has fallen short does not absolve the church from further effort. Christ himself taught us how a man can embrace feminine paradigms. His example is a beacon for each of us in church leadership as we struggle to make the personal changes that will bring about a revolution. Only then can we hope that the feminine paradigm of leadership will enrich us all.

Epilogue

In the fall of 1992, four women were elected to the United States Senate (bringing the total number to six), and forty-seven were elected to serve in the United States House of Representatives (106 women of 435 candidates ran for office). This did not take place because of any quota system but by the will of the people in those states. The increasing involvement of women in politics, business, education, and even in the church represents obvious and irreversible changes in our time. Twenty centuries of resistance toward women in church leadership are slowly beginning to crumble in less than one century. In the same fall that so many women were elected to serve in the United States government, the Church of England began for the first time to allow women to serve the Church as ordained priests.

It has been established that women *do* work out of a different paradigm that lends itself to new ways of leading and ministering. In our work with churches, for example, we believe that some of them would not be in such severe conflict had they included women in pastoral and lay leadership positions. What was needed in preventative conflict and in the middle of the conflict situation were leaders who were interactive and discerning, who would and could share power and information and enhance the self-worth of each person. What will major institutions be like when women are well represented? We will eventually find out because there will be no turning back, nor should there be. We will know that this paradigm has fully occurred when we have included women in all levels of church leadership without being consciously aware that we have done so.

Chapter Eighteen

Leading for the Leasts: A Woman's Story

WhaJa Hwang*

[The criteria for servant leadership are twofold]: Do those served grow as persons? Do they, while being served, become healthier, wiser, freer, more autonomous, more likely themselves to become servants? And, what is the effect on the least privileged in society; will they benefit, or, at least, not be further deprived?[1]

Robert K. Greenleaf

The words that follow are those of a most reluctant writer, finally penned in surrender to our much conjoling. This is the story of the life and ministry of a Korean woman, WhaJa Hwang. Shawchuck met WhaJa Hwang in 1983 when she attended a doctoral course he taught. From that class they went on to become close friends and working colleagues, both in Korea and in the United States. Shawchuck knew, or rather felt, from the beginning that she had a story to tell, but it was not until some years later, and after he had opportunity to see the results of her ministry in Korea, that she finally told him the following account of her life as a girl growing up in the Korean culture, and as a woman called of God to minister to the poor-

*WhaJa Hwang is a Korean Presbyterian laywoman in Seoul. She earned her M.Div. in Korea and D.Min. at McCormick Theological Seminary in Chicago.

est and most marginal people of Korea's society—and as a Presbyterian laywoman working within the (patriarchal) Korean Presbyterian Church.

We include her story as a tribute to all women who today are faithfully responding to the call of God to their lives; but even more, to encourage all of God's faithful servants, men and women, who work against seemingly insurmountable odds—and never give up. Also, we tell the story as a summing up into one life the entire content of this book. We could give you no better review of the many topics, ideas, and principles discussed in this book than to tell you WhaJa's story. We have seen the fruits of WhaJa's ministry with our own eyes, and visited with many of her closest friends. Her story is true.

I grew up in the Korean countryside, under the love and care of my parents and teachers. When I was in ninth grade I asked my parents if I could attend a high school in Seoul. My mother agreed, and said that she would be very proud if I became a woman leader. But my father said that a woman should find happiness in being a good mother and taking care of her husband. A woman, he said, did not need education and should not go into the world by herself. My father was very strong willed, but this time my mother did not obey. She took me to Seoul to take the high school entrance examination.

We set out for Seoul very early on a beautiful morning. I walked quickly ahead. My mother followed behind carrying a bag she had packed the night before without my father knowing it. After much walking we stood on the steps of one of Korea's most respected girls' high schools, which I entered to take my examination. I passed with the highest score. I was so happy that I called home to tell my father, but he was not happy at all. He insisted that I come home, but I waited in Seoul, hoping he would send me the tuition. He did not send the tuition, but he called every day insisting that I come home. Finally, it seemed I had no alternative but to do so. But by now I had become acquainted with several teachers at the high school, and they had received a report that I had graduated from middle school with top honors. So they accepted me into the school without paying tuition.

I graduated from high school with highest honors and announced my intention to stay in Seoul to attend college. Again my dear father objected, saying it was not right for a woman to have so much education. But with the help of my high school faculty, I found a college that offered me a scholarship. When I graduated from college, my father surrendered and agreed I could enter the Presbyterian Korean Theological Seminary in Seoul. An American missionary to Korea provided me a full scholarship. At the time I graduated from seminary there were few women who were seminary graduates, and they were rarely hired by churches because they were felt to be "overqualified." (To this day Presbyterian women cannot be ordained in Korea, so to become a pastor is impossible, but to be a minister for Jesus is everyone's possibility.) I prayed without ceasing for an opportunity to work in a church. One of my professors recommended me to a church in Seoul. The pastor asked me to come, and thus I began my ministry.

The Sounds of Poor People Crying

One day a tattered woman in her foots (bare footed), came to me and asked, "Can a woman like me come to church?" I was surprised by this question. She told me that her son attended a mission boy's high school and brought home a copy of the Bible; she carried the Bible with her and read it while selling her goods in the street market. She felt drawn to the church, but saw herself as unworthy, for she thought churches were only for the rich people. From that time on I started asking myself, "What kind of people are welcome in the church? Is it true that people who are poor are not deserving of the church?"

I left my job at the church to teach Bible classes in a Christian middle school for boys. In my second year there, three boys were called out of my class to go to the finance office. In a few minutes they returned weeping. They told me they had been dismissed from the school because their parents had not paid the tuition. As I watched them leave, something happened inside me. I asked their friends about their living situation.

It is hard to desire littleness and nothingness, obscurity and benign respect in a world obsessed with possessions and positions. It is hard to choose a pauper's station [as a leader], when everyone around us is scrambling for upward mobility. (p. 33)

One of the students had a father who was a carpenter, but because of the rainy season, he could not work and was, therefore, unable to pay his son's tuition. Another student's mother earned the family living, but now she was sick and could no longer earn any money. By then I could not continue with the lesson. We closed our Bibles and began talking about Jesus, how he felt about the poor, and how we were to care for our poor neighbors.

The week after the incident a boy in the class came to me with an envelope full of money, which the students had gathered to pay the tuition for the three poor boys who had left the school. He told me that they had done their best, but it was not enough to pay the tuition of all three boys. I added the rest of the money for the tuition and promptly carried it to the finance office. The next day our three poor friends were back in the classroom with us. Through these experiences I realized that my ministry must be among the poor. Only there could I answer God's call to my life. I left the school to search for a way to help the poor.

> "Childlike spirituality . . . is a way to lead . . . with an attitude similar to a child's; one who opens the self to this reality as a gift, and one who lives and ministers as the least in a service to all." (p. 30)

In the early 1970s, Seoul filled with people coming in search of a better life, but without money and no help to enter into the city's society. These people could not afford to rent the poorest shacks, so they built tent homes in the hills on the edges of the city. Those who had a little money rented single rooms in run-down apartment houses near the tent cities, where an entire family would live in the one room. I spent many days and nights walking through these apartment areas and the tent cities, praying that God would show me how to help these people.

I chose an apartment area that housed several thousand poor families as my mission field. Each morning I would get off the bus and climb the several hundred stairs to the apartment area, where I would pray for a way to help these people. No one knew me or looked at me or greeted me when I went to them. I decided to try meeting someone inside the apartments. I went to the fifth floor of an apartment building and knocked on a door. The door squeaked open only enough to peek through. "Go away," was what I heard, and the door slammed shut. All day long I knocked on apartment doors, always with the same disappointing result.

I gave up trying to get inside the apartments, and for three months wandered from here to there among the poor, trying to understand their interests and how I might serve them. Then a Korean women's group came into the area attempting to distribute a cooking spice called Mi-Won to the poor mothers. I decided to work with them, though few poor mothers were interested in the spice. But a few did take the spice, and this gave me an opportunity to ask them what the greatest needs of the people were. They simply answered anything that would help them care for their families on so little money.

I thought, "That's it." These mothers live in one-room apartments, only fifteen-feet square, with their entire family, and their greatest need is to live very economically. I searched my brain for an item that every household needed, no matter how poor. I also began to read about group purchasing and consumer unions.

In those days it was very difficult to purchase petroleum by-products. Soaps were essential in every household, but it was hard to find and market prices were very high; 30 percent-50 percent higher than the same soap would cost in other places. I decided to begin my ministry to the poor with laundry soap. A Presbyterian deaconess whose husband owned the MuKoongHwa Curd factory came to my mind. I told her that I would like to sell soap as a mission project to the poor people, and asked her to sell me three cases of soap at their cost. She asked me what it meant to sell soap for a mission purpose, so I told her she would know soon enough. She sold me the soap at cost. I then posted many advertisements on the walls of the apartments, announcing a one-day sale on soap at a very low price. The announcement read:

Attention!!
MukoongHwa Curd Co. Product
Laundry Soap at Wholesale Prices
2 bars per home

On the day of the sale, many women came to buy. I had 165 bars to sell, and could sell to only 82 women. However, selling the soap wasn't important to me. I wanted to investigate the needs of these 82 homes, and so I made each of the 82 women who bought my soap fill out a chart. It read:

NEEDS CHART

Name _____

Address _____Tel. No. _____

Next items needed:	*Number wanted:*
sugar	
tooth paste	
beauty soap	
etc.	

Through the chart, I was able to get not only their names and addresses, but a list of the items they needed most. I knew the people would not speak to me if I went to their doors, so I called everyone who listed a phone number and said I was the woman who had sold them soap, and asked them what they thought I should sell next. Just about all of them said sugar. So I found a sugar wholesaler who agreed to give me sugar at his price. Then I sold it to the poor at the wholesale price; one package to each woman. Again I made each woman fill out the Needs Chart. Then I called all the women who listed a phone number and asked what I should sell next.

Eventually, all I had to do was make a couple of phone calls to get women to put up the advertisements instead of doing it myself. This meant that community organization was beginning to happen. Then I began to organize the women in each apartment to decide what items were needed, and to advertise and arrange for the sale day. I continued to look for products at the manufacturer's cost and sell the products at that price. After a while I organized a number of apartments into a purchasing union, and they began to operate their own purchasing, at wholesale prices. This was the beginning of a number of group purchasing unions.

Many people gave me their trust and became members of the purchasing union. After a few months, the unions began charging a little more than they were paying for the products. When they had enough money, they would help a family move out of the tent city or a crowded one-room apartment into a better apartment.

In a few months, about 500 homes belonged to our organization. Eventually one of the members asked me, "Why are you doing such hard work for nothing?" I realized the time had come to tell the women my story. I told them that I had come to serve them for Jesus Christ, and I witnessed the words of God. Now the people who once did not trust me listened to my story, and began to tell others. After that, a man told me that he used to be an elder in the church, but had moved his family into this poor area when he failed in his business, and now he could not go to church. Then others came who once were deacons or elders or Sunday school teachers in churches where they used to live. I talked to pastors near the poor areas, and soon many of these people were attending church again.

One day a parent who had no money to enroll his son in school came to me and asked if I could establish a night school for the students who were unable to go to school. After a few months of planning with the poor parents, I gathered college volunteers for the night school programs. About twenty students came after a hard day's work to study under the volunteers, who were like older brothers and sisters to them. They studied hard and prepared for the school entrance exam. The volunteers wanted no pay. Instead, they brought note books, pencils, and other supplies for the students.

Sometime later, a man from the apartments came to me and said he did not have enough money to pay for a doctor for his sick children.

His words seemed like the voice of God telling me it was time to start a clinic for the poor.

> God asks all that we have —nothing more, nothing less. (p. 61)

I went to one of the medical doctors who belongs to the Christian Medical Association of Seoul. I explained to him the need for a clinic to heal the poor sick people, just as Jesus did. He discussed the idea with the members of the Christian Medical Association, and they all agreed to help. Soon they came to the GeumHwa Apartment area to start a clinic on Saturday afternoon. At that time, Korea did not have an insurance system. If the people went to the doctors, they had to pay a great amount, and this made the poor people think that all doctors were thieves. Rather than pay, the people would endure their pain until they could no longer stand it. Finally they would go to the pharmacy to buy medicine without a prescription. When they heard of the famous Christian Society doctors, they came in hordes, sometimes as many as sixty patients a day. The doctors were hard-working, patient, and sincere. Soon a Christian women's association heard of the doctors' work and began volunteering money to pay for medicine and other medical needs.

Together we were able to do all of these things. For God's work, there are enough human and material resources. The problem is finding a way of involving people in deciding their own needs, and involving them in obtaining the resources to meet their needs. The doctors, student volunteers, and church women were all sincere and were not absent for even a day. All of them took their responsibilities seriously. Through these programs, I was able to meet and talk with these poor people easily. The volunteer teachers, the doctors, the faithful women, and myself were welcome in every home, and the people heard our witness of Jesus' love for them gladly.

The Sounds of WhaJa Crying

I married in 1967 while in my second year of studies at the seminary. My husband never understood why I wanted to study for ministry. Nor did he understand my concern for the poorest and least noticed people. He owned and operated a salt refinery. In 1973 he was seriously injured in a train accident and lived in a coma for thirteen years, before he died in 1986. I was thirty-two-years-old at the time of the accident, and we had two small children. For one year the salt factory sat idle, while I waited and prayed for him to recover from the coma. The machines were rusting into a state of uselessness. After a year I knew I could not go on hoping for his recovery, and decided to reopen the business, though I had no experience whatsoever in operating a salt refinery.

I gathered together as many of my husband's workers and associates as I could. Once again the salt factory was operating. For three years, I concentrated on nothing but my employees, business partners, and the business itself. It was becoming a solid business. In 1977 the

Korean government asked me to provide salt for the Army, Navy, and Air Force. I knew this was more than I could manage, so I declined. However, the government kept insisting until I committed our factory to produce salt for 600,000 soldiers.

Then something happened to me. I wanted to produce even more salt and make even more money. I decided to expand the facilities in areas I knew nothing about, and I installed new machines in the factory. But by the time the new machines were installed the price of salt had fallen sharply. The new machines did not function properly. Our production fell to the point that we were hardly able to honor our contract with the military. We lost all of our other markets. I could not save my company, and went bankrupt in 1979. By the time I sold my factory to clear my debts, I had nothing left. These were dark days. I cried alone with a thousand pains. In tears, I searched for God's answer, "Why have you given me such a big pain? Why? Why?"

> Out of one's deepest failures and pain arise the possibilities for the most effective ministy. (p. 62)

During the six years I operated the salt business, I was introduced to a new world of suffering. I saw it first in the lives of those who worked the graveyard shift at my refinery. I wanted to know them, so I often worked alongside them through the night. Also, I often prepared nice dinners for them and their families. Through these means I learned of their hard lives, and through them I met many of their neighbors who labored in the fields and in other factories. Every mother and father worked from the early morning until after dark, while their small children were left to care for themselves. In the rural and fishing areas, little children would play too near the sea and be swept away. Others would play on the irrigation ditches and fall into the water and drown.

During the time I operated the salt refinery I worked as a volunteer in a local church where the pastor was developing a ministry to the poor. I saw a great need to do something for the care and education of the children. We began by organizing the parents to help us prepare a place for a school and day-care center. Women from the local church cared for and educated the children. The congregation also purchased

> Congregations expect competent church leaders, but they also want pastors who possess inner character and integrity—a congruency between what they profess and what they do. (p. 37)

the supplies and school materials. When this school and day-care center was opened, we organized another and another until we had six day-care centers in this large community. The centers required more money than the local congregation could give. We prayed for help, and then began searching for it. Our search took us to Germany, where after much going from here to there we succeeded in obtaining enough grants from Kindernothilfe e.V. Duisburg (KNH) to support the day-care centers. My business collapsed at the very time we had the six centers in full operation.

The Dark Night Ends, a New Mission Is Given

After some months, as I yet sat in dark sorrow over the loss of our factory, I received a booklet and a letter from the KNH in Germany. It told the story of the children who suffer in poverty all around the world. The letter said that the German KNH had decided to help me start more schools and day-care centers in Korea. I read this little book all night, prayed, and thought about what it said, over and over again. I felt the pain and sorrow of the children in the undeveloped countries who were cold, hungry, and neglected.

That night everything became clear to me. Then I knew that God did not want my factory, buildings, or rice paddies. God wanted me. I decided to go back and serve the poor children with open and empty hands, and to give my emptied life into Christ's care, believing he could work through me, poor as I am. At last, I gave thanks to God for giving me another chance to serve him, this time with faith alone.

As soon as I awoke the next day,

> All along the way; through our successes and our failures, our victories and defeats, our saintliness and sinfulness, our acceptance and resistance, God is at work to make us what we are, but not yet. (p. 67)

I wrote to Mr. Luers of the KNH to tell him I wanted to work for poor children in Korea. In June 1980, I became coordinator for KNH children's ministry in rural and fishing villages, and urban industrial areas in Korea. I now left my dark night behind and began moving across Korea, organizing schools and day-care centers. I always involved the poor mothers whose children would come to the center. This way each center was "owned" by the families whose children came to the center. They saw the center as their center.

I would also try to involve the local congregation in helping me plan and launch the schools. I wanted the congregations to view the schools and day-care centers as their own field of ministry to the poor in their communities. And I counted on the women's organization in each church to provide the necessary volunteer teachers and workers to operate the program.

The major problems I experienced in opening these centers across Korea came from the local pastors, who did not share the same burden for the poor children as I did. Many of them wanted me to open a center in their area, but do it cheaply, not providing much care to the children, and then give the rest of the money to the pastors to support programs they felt were more important than the day-care centers. I never gave in to them for a single moment. I was determined to let them know that my responsibility

> Without resistance our ministry remains weak, diffuse, and unsure. (p. 65)

was to give the programs to the children. These differences in perspective were perhaps caused because I was a woman, and I was not ordained. After trying long and hard to reach a workable understanding with the male pastors, I gave up hope of working with them and organized only with the parents and the volunteers I recruited in each area.

At first we used the educational materials developed by the National Ministry of Education Department. However, we soon discovered that the government materials did not recognize the desperate condition of these children's lives, and therefore did not meet the educational needs of the children. From then on we developed our own educational materials, which were more suited to the needs of the children caught in poverty.

The Mission Is Joined by Others

The Reluctant Pastors

After the center program became well-known across Korea for its capable ministry to the poor, many of the local pastors who had previously ignored my ministry began to visit the centers, offering their support. Thus the day-care center program was able to develop a strong relationship with the congregations, the parents, community people, and the Korean government. Because of this strong relationship, the centers were able to mobilize personnel and educational resources for the children's program.

The Korean Government

After working with the day-care program for one year, the Korean Government took notice that children's care and education were being provided in the most needy areas, and the government began to open day-care programs in the poor areas of Seoul. The government established seventeen day-care centers in Seoul. Catholic, Buddhist, Chundo Kyo, and Christian denominations participated with the government in this mission. I volunteered to manage one of these centers while I continued my responsibility as coordinator of the schools we were starting with the help of the German church. By volunteering to serve in the government's program I had opportunity to consult with the government officials regarding the programs they were establishing.

A Young Pastor

One day a young pastor who worked in an urban industrial area came to me saying he had rented second-floor space in which to start a new church. He ministered for two months from this space, but no one came. I asked him about the situation of the community. He said, "The men and women go to work at the factories during the day. Their children are left at home alone. Sometimes parents come home during lunch hour to share a meal with their children and then leave their children locked up in their rooms. At night parents bring their overworked bodies home to rest, or the women do the laundry and clean the house. Therefore, there is no way to convince these people to attend church." I shared with him my experiences of ministry in the apartment areas. I stressed the

> The desire to serve others must be stronger than the desire to lead—so that leadership becomes a means of serving. (p. 35)

importance of opening up the eyes of mothers for child care. And then I explained how he could begin his work. After he finished listening to my story, he put up a sign, "X X X Day Care Center" next to the church sign board.

Within a few days mothers came to the day-care center to ask questions about cost, hours, and so on. It was truly good news for the parents to have their children taken care of at such a small cost while they went to work. Within a month, forty children had been enrolled in the center. Parents felt that this was a real church ministry because it met their needs and expectations. The program this pastor started spread throughout the large urban industrial area and coal mining areas in which the church was located.

I was very happy when others showed care for the poor children. This greatly encouraged me to carry on my own work. In the years from 1980–1984, with the support of many people, I opened forty day-care centers and schools across Korea. The centers continue to this day, offering care, education, food, medicine, and much love to thousands of children. These schools and day-care centers are now funded and managed by the Korean Presbyterian Church.

> The quality, character, and results of our ministry are a reflection of our spirituality, projected on the screen of the organization we lead. (p. 56)

God Leads in New Directions

From 1980 through 1983 my entire life was consumed with working with the poor families, the poorly educated teachers, and local pastors who did not understand the children's ministry. I worked from early morning until midnight, trying to mobilize the communities and resources; visiting homes, local government offices, and marketplaces to buy toys, supplies, and foods; and I always studied about educating children in order that I might develop a stronger, more meaningful educational and care program.

Then, in 1983, a new invitation came to me. McCormick Theological Seminary in Chicago invited me to study for a doctorate at the school. However, Mr. Luers, General Secretary of the Evangelical Mission work in Germany, which was funding the day-care centers I had organized, strongly insisted that I remain at my work. "You cultivated and planted the seeds. Therefore, you, yourself, should harvest the grains." However, I was badly in need of rest, and I longed for more studies, so I placed my work into the hands of the Korean Presbyterian Women's Organization and enrolled in the Doctor of Ministry program at McCormick Theological Seminary.

The Leasts Movement

"Truly I tell you, just as you did it to one of the least of these who are members of my family, you did it to me" (Matt. 25:40).

I finished my studies in the spring of 1985. Then I fasted while praying and crying to the Lord. I wanted to know what God's plans were for me. What would I do when I returned to Korea? What kind of work would I pour my life into?

After some days of fasting and prayer, I dreamed that God came to me and lifted me up into the air to a well of water surrounded by trees. Water poured over a mountain waterfall. I drank the water for a long time, and then I awakened from the dream. I lay in my dormitory bed, wondering what the dream might mean. After some time I fell asleep and the dream continued. I was again at the well where God had brought me. God did not say a word to me, and I stood there happily. God took my hand, and we flew into the sky and came back to my place. I awoke, and it was morning.

I faced God and looked for the meaning of the dream. Out of the long silence, God answered me as I bowed low on my knees. He assured me that I would be safe and would be provided with all that I needed when I worked in God. He showed me that drinking the fountain of water meant receiving from the Lord, and when the dream showed that I came back to where I was, it meant that I had to go back to the same work I had been doing. I reassured myself of this precious dream, fasted, and returned to the work I had left in Korea.

By now my position was taken over by an assistant to the General Secretary of the Society Department of the Presbyterian Church in Korea. I was, therefore, easily able to resume my place.

When I returned at the end of 1985, the Korean Presbyterian

> The encounter with God means coming to an interior attitude of complete openness. . . . Such encounters with God change our perception of realities—our rules and regulations about what can be done and how it can be done. (p. 75)

> Mission is the waking dream, embodied in the life of the leaders and the congregation. (p. 73)

churches were in their one hundredth year, and the people were looking for new mission direction. At the same time, the industrialization of Korea created vast urbanization on a scale never before experienced. People gathered in the cities without any specific plans and no jobs, only to fall into deep poverty. Many pastors came to me and talked about the poor children and women living in the slums of this newly modernized society. While listening to these stories, my passion grew, and I became determined to hear and to see these realities for myself.

> The madness of the call is that it most often takes us along paths we do not prefer, and assigns duties for which we feel most ill-equipped. (p. 66)

I looked, and I saw. The reality was that the conditions of the poor had grown worse, not better. Now more poverty ridden families than ever were living in the slums of the cities and in the rural and fishing areas, with no hope. Families headed by mere children could find no way to meet their needs. Elderly and disabled persons were completely cut off from any help.

I began going everywhere, preaching and conducting special lectures in churches and church organizations, particularly with the

women, to make persons aware of the very great need. I reminded
these groups of our responsibilities to care for the "least among us,"
and as mature congregations it is to the least that we are to be responsible. Wherever I went I gave opportunity for persons to give liberally
of their resources to help the poor.

Day by day, and month by month, the number of persons who
decided to be responsible to the poor increased. With this growing support we were able to care for child-headed families, high school students, and single-parent families. In providing this support, I did not
transmit the money directly to the poor. Rather I sent the funds to the
local churches near to where the poor families lived. Then I worked
with the pastors and people to learn how to work with the poor, to share
with them not only money but also their friendship and faith.

The result of all these efforts was that a new movement was born in
and through and around the church, which is called *The Leasts Movement*. It is a movement *of* the leasts, and not just for the leasts; it is a
movement in which everyone, the rich and the poor, cares for those
who have less than they. Within one year the movement that began
with only myself and the wife of an invalid husband expanded to over
200 people. As this mission grew, I named the movement after the
One who asks us to give to him through the leasts: "When you do it
for the least of these, you do it for me."

The House of the Leasts

While visiting the homes of children in need of care, I came to a
man who had worked in a coal mine. He was hit by a rock while
working and became a human vegetable. He was kept in a one-
room shack, with his wife and four children. The wife had to make
a living for the family. Every evening she would wait for her oldest
daughter to come home from school; then the woman would leave
for the night shift at the local factory. She would return at three in
the morning. As soon as she closed her eyes, it would be morning.
She would arise very early each day to send her children to school
and to take care of her husband all day long. Because her husband's injury was considered to be his own mistake, he was given
no compensation money. And because he was no longer on the job,
his medical insurance benefits were cut off. The family lived only

by the woman's earnings, day to day. They ate only what their money would buy after she had paid the medical bills and the costs to educate the children.

I thought about my husband, who lived in a coma for thirteen years. The wife's pain drilled into my bones. I prayed to the Lord who, through my dream, gave me a symbol of plenty in the water fountain, asking him to provide this family a home, and then I set about to help God do this. Land was provided at an affordable rate by one Christian community. Money to build a house for the family was collected. I was so happy when the poor family moved into a nice house in which to live and care for the invalid father. It was this poor woman who first helped me in The Leasts Movement. She became a good partner in our ministry.

At that same time, I had an opportunity to speak about the vision I had for my ministry on a program of the Christian Broadcast Station. After the broadcast I felt even more strongly about my vision to expand The Leasts Movement throughout Korea's least communities. This vision began to come true when a successful Pentecostal businessman came to me to inquire about my ministry, saying he had heard the radio broadcast. He gave me 25,000,000won ($3,333,000.) to build a home for the least of the leasts: those who had no one to care for them, and no place to live.[2] Others gave fans, refrigerators, kitchen appliances, blankets, and other items. Soon a home was built for thirty persons with severe physical and mental disabilities.

The persons who live in the house live as a family, with each person taking care of the others. For example, a person who cannot use his hand is fed by a girl in a wheelchair. A person who can't wash his face is helped by those who can. The rooms are cleaned by those family members who can clean them. It is a Christian community in which everyone helps and receives help from one another. The women's mission organizations, men's mission organizations, and Sunday school classes from many congregations come to help and contribute to the supporting fund. Members of the Young Adults Association

> Vision is seeing in and for others what they cannot see for themselves. (p. 25)

come to do the heavy cleaning, bathe those who are unable to move, and help where needed. This is how the leasts live in their home.

While living here, the leasts develop their gifts. They compose their own gospel songs, translate simple English, write poems, keep diaries, and read the Bible after they learn the Korean alphabet. Seeing this, I have experienced the resurrection of our Lord Jesus Christ. Sometimes there are conflicts, but we know it is too much to ask for complete peace. The conflicts help the members of the family to grow closer to the Lord.

God has given his gifts to the needy people through the day-care center program. But now it is time to greatly expand our care for the poor through The Leasts Movement. As of April 1992, the number of leasts being cared for (shelter, food, clothing, education) was 600, through the generosity of 1,451 supporters.

A New Dream of Dawn

The Leasts Movement has been growing year by year, reaching out to more and more churches across Korea. The Pentecostal businessman who funded our home for the leasts has offered me the money to build another. I am seeking God's leading in this. The Leasts Movement is now under the care of the Korean Presbyterian Women's Organization.

God is now giving me a vision of the DAWN—Developing Asian Women's Network. I see the day when The Leasts Movement will reach out through Christian women across all of Asia, and their ministry will shine like the *DAWN* of a new day. By joining their efforts, women can change their communities and the societies of Asia.

No matter how it is emphasized, the role of the Christian leader is to meet the needs of people, in the community and throughout the society. It is not enough to preach and pray. One must go where Jesus would go and do what Jesus would do. This is our calling, and God goes with us.

The Leasts Movement is already extending into other parts of Asia. In 1991 I visited Bali, Indonesia. There I met a man who wanted to be a Christian, and thus was put out by his family. He had no place to live or food to eat. Upon my return to Korea, I told the story to the committee of The Leasts Movement. They responded by launch-ing a leasts movement in Bali, Indonesia. Thus began the spread of The Leasts Movement beyond Korea. The movement soon jumped from Indonesia to the Philippines and to other areas. In its day of need, the Korean church received much needed help. Now it is time for us to share with others.

> The vision is God's first, then to be shared with those who dare to believe against all odds. (p. 74)

> Inherent in our call to ministry is the realization that we are not by nature equipped to bear this burden of leadership that God has laid upon us— we all embrace our call-ing as paupers. (p. 33)

The only lingering sorrow I have in my ministry is that the Korean Presbyterian Church has never allowed me to be an ordained min-ister. The powerful men's organi-zation will not allow women this privilege. I will always wonder: why, why?

Epilogue

On Finishing Well

"Well done, good and trustworthy [servant]; you have been trustworthy in a few things, I will put you in charge of many things; enter into the joy of your master."

(Matt. 25:21)

Swinging on a Hinge of History

This generation of religious leaders guides a church that swings on a hinge, laying aside its aging and ebbing paradigms and marching toward new paradigms that, though not yet clearly seen, are already dimly visible to the one who has eyes to see and the courage to consider what one sees.

Loren Meade persuasively argues that the church has passed through the Christendom paradigm and stands now between the paradigms knowing only that the old has passed away, but being unable to see the new paradigm that is coming.[1] Lyle Schaller states that the small Sunday morning church, affiliated with a denomination, is giving way to the large seven-day-a-week church that is not bound by aging traditions or bureaucracy. Rather, it is market-oriented and holds as its top priority the transformation of individual lives by the power of the gospel. It is the church that focuses on serving the needs and interests of the unchurched rather than serving the interests of its members, and demands quality in all its services rather than settling for mediocrity.[2] In this same vein, Peter F. Drucker writes of the emergence of volunteerism in America as the "third sector" in American society, and highlights the emergence of the very large pastoral church as one of the most important social innovations in the twenty-first century.

Church membership and attendance have been going down quite sharply in all denominations, whether "liberal," "mainstream," "evangelical," or "fundamentalist." But membership and attendance are growing rapidly in "pastoral" churches—Protestant and Catholic, "mainstream" and "evangelical"—which concentrate on serving parishioners, their needs, their problems, their families. . . . The success of the pastoral church is a marketing success.[3] They asked, who are our customers and what is of value to them? They saw the fact that the young educated people do not go to church [as] an opportunity.[4]

The changes already rushing toward the church and ushering in the twenty-first century are not ordinary but epic. Perhaps, as far as the American Church is concerned, only four times in the history of Christianity have the changes equaled those coming toward us in the last decade of the twentieth century and into the twenty-first. Those other epochal shifts in Christian history were: (1) the genesis of the Apostolic Church, (2) the founding of Christendom, (3) the Reformation, and (4) Vatican Council II in the Roman Catholic Church.

Who among us can provide the necessary innovation, entrepreneurship, and vision to lead the church through the uncertainties of an all-pervasive paradigm shift, and into an as-of-yet unclear future pregnant with promise and opportunity? It is unlikely that the seminaries and Bible colleges and institutes can, for they are limited by their own ability to see, let alone adjust to, these changes. The mainline seminaries, for the most part, continue to be the keepers of a liberal theology and the teachers of a liturgy, from which those born after 1955 are fleeing in droves. It is unlikely that the bishops and other top judicatory officials or the general agencies of the denominations can; for they are keepers of the denomination's tradition and guardians of bureaucratic hierarchies from which those born after 1955 also flee.

Only the people and their pastors are free to change with the innovation and openness necessary to grasp the future as it rushes upon us. The necessary transformation must happen at the local level, or it will not happen at all. This is not a new thing. At least since Jesus the model for Christian transformation has been one person, one family at a time. The changes necessary for transforming a life or a congregation cannot be legislated—they can only be modeled and transmitted from one person to another. The number-one requirement for a growing and vigorous congregation is a pastor whose life has been transformed by the gospel, and who knows it and is not hesitant to give personal witness to it. In the new paradigm, the life and spirituality of the messenger are more important than the sermon. Further, this pastor must be a transforming leader who can (1) conceptualize a vision of a new tomorrow; (2) articulate that vision so persuasively that people rally in support of it; and (3) know how to turn that vision into reality.[5]

Between the paradigms we cannot see—but we are seeing. We see that 75 percent of the people who attend church in the United States are in one seventh of the churches. Put another way, only 25 percent of the people who attend church comprise 86 percent of the congregations. So, while we cannot clearly see the new paradigms that are coming, their outlines are already visible if we have the eyes to see and the courage to consider without turning away. And what we see coming toward us may seem like threats and doom, or it may seem like new and challenging opportunities—enough for a lifetime of challenge and accomplishment.

How we respond to the future is of our choosing. We may be filled with fear at facing all of the new problems and uncertainty, and bury our little talent deep in the ground out of our own despair—for safe keeping. Or we may get bored by all the monotony and trivia that push their way into our consciousness—and surrender our birthright for a mess of pottage. Or finally we may by faith stretch beyond our own little abilities—and allow God to do extraordinary things through our ordinary endowments.

The choice is ours: whether to merely finish, or to finish well.

Striving to Finish Well

We recently received a letter from the president of a small Christian college. He said, "I will be 55 in November. I would like to 'finish well.' I want to leave a better church in my trail." What will it take to finish well? The Master in the stewardship parable of Matthew 25 put the answer thus: Be faithful in a few things. Jesus again plied this theme when he said to Martha, "Martha, Martha, you are worried and distracted by many things; there is need for only one thing. Mary has chosen the better part, that will not be taken away from her" (Luke 10:38-41).

To finish well means to focus well. How we define and measure the "bottom line" is not as important as is what we do with what we have, remembering that one day each one of us will give an account of our stewardship (Luke 16; Matt. 25). But in this accounting God is not the bookkeeper. We are. As Robert Farrar Capon points out: "The only bookkeeper in the parable is the servant who decided he had to fear a nonexistent audit and who therefore hid his one talent in the ground."[6] There is no need to fear God because of our own disappointment in our own bottom line results. As Capon notes, "The servant with the little shovel and his mousy apprehension that God is as small as himself is such a nerd! He is just one more of the pitiful turkeys that Jesus parades through his parables to shock us, if possible, into recognizing the stupidity of unfaith."[7]

To finish well is to continually gaze upon, and follow closely, the One who already accomplished the bottom line for us—our Caller and Colleague. For the last time, we quote Caretto:

> I saw the altogether slick and shaky basis of my so-called apostolate and consequently my altogether rather false vision of my relationship with Him. . . . My mistake was very plain under the headlamps of divine truth.
>
> Do you think, Carlo, that history revolves around people; do you believe in newspapers, politics and the power of words and means; do you believe in yourself, in your potential for good too, in the effectiveness of your activities and your thoughts?
>
> All wrong, Carlo my boy, History revolves around me, Christ. I am the savior, not you. I am the life. . . .
>
> To sum up, my sister, to be consistent with what the light of the Lord gave me in that flash . . . there was just one thing to be done: believe that our duty is setting ourselves to listen humbly to Jesus as Mary did, with no other concern, to have no other dream than loving Jesus freely with such a love that it becomes activity, apostolate, salvation.
>
> Dolcidia, take account of the being of God. There are two masters who want you to serve them. The first one gets worked up, acts and builds, and in odd moments comes and tells you how much he has done, and asks you to help him with his plans. The other is in love with you and does nothing but love you and gaze at you, and the same thirst for the salvation of the brethren leads him to a love, from which one can never be separated. Which of the two has more truth about

him? The calculation is very simple and is just a question of being consistent.

May God give [us] the grace of being consistent. The rest is just so much smoke, indeed acrid smoke. To be forgotten, to live a hidden life and to be poor and humble—isn't that the idea of Christian . . . life?[8]

There *will be* an accounting for the charism God has given each of us in our call to ministry. But it will likely not be as we imagine. In the treasure chest of the Rabbi stories lies this anecdote: A man one day approached a Rabbi and asked, "What will the day of judgment be like?" The Rabbi gazed upon the man and said, "On the day of your judgment God will look at you and ask, 'What difference has your life on earth made? Did you enjoy the world I gave you? Did you take good care of your neighbors?' This," said the Rabbi, "is what judgment is like."

To finish well means that we must decide *today* our responses to questions such as these—and then spend the rest of our days making our responses come true.

About beginning and finishing, Paul plies two themes. First is the theme of running. He often describes the Christian life and ministry as a race, and of this he says: "Run in such a way that you may win . . . exercise self-control . . . do not run aimlessly . . . so that after proclaiming to others [you] should not be disqualified" (I Cor. 9:24-27). To the Galatians, he wrote: "You were running a good race. Who cut in on you?" (Gal. 5:7 NIV).

Second, Paul utilized the theme of forgetting. "But this one thing I do: forgetting what lies behind . . . I press on toward the goal for the prize of the heavenly call of God in Christ Jesus" (Phil. 3:13-14).

We are called to run and to win. But the race can be difficult. So we have written to encourage you, and ourselves, to keep running and forgetting. Forget the paltry failures and deep disappointments. Forget the grand accomplishments and public acclaim. Written between the lines of Paul's words is the eternal promise of God's grace ever given—that we may run well, that we may lay down the memories that keep old wounds open, past failures stinging, and willful pride unbending—that we may, unencumbered, press on toward the prize that is inherent in our calling. What is this prize? It can be nothing less or more than hearing the words of the One who called us to our vocations, "Well done, good and faithful servant! Come on in."

To run well, to discipline ourselves, to press on toward the prize—this is what it means to finish well.

Appendix

Ministry Roles

The definitions of the Roles from the Better Preparation for Ministry questionnaire.

Care Giver: Demonstrates a ministry style that is supportive and healing, providing intentional structures and programs which are pastoral in nature, and is an effective pastoral visitor.

Denominational Participant: Values, supports and relates to other churches and structures of his/her denomination; is knowledgeable in working with and through the polity of the denomination.

Ecumenist: Values, supports and relates to other religious bodies and agencies outside his/her own denomination; local ministerial groups, National Council of Churches, World Council of Churches, etc.

Evangelist/Witness: Values an evangelical belief system and gives witness to it through dialogue and litany; demonstrates sensitivity to the other's beliefs; is willing and able to plan and carry out an evangelism program, involving lay persons at all levels.

Interpersonal Skills: Is able to "read" people, respond appropriately, and treat others with unconditional positive regard; able to participate in and lead groups effectively, and to properly diagnose and intervene into interpersonal processes.

Leader for Social Justice: Values and knows how to support and organize others in efforts toward shaping local and national policies and practices dealing with matters of human rights and justice.

Manager/Administrator: Is competent in planning, implementation, administration; evaluation of resources, programs and personnel (paid or volunteer); highly values the capabilities of each person to engage in meaningful ministry, and supports them in their tasks.

Personal Integrity: Demonstrates that he/she is "at home" with oneself; is confident in his/her abilities; has integrated all facets of one's personality and experience into a coherent wholeness of one's public and private life; decides actions based upon appropriate reasons and not self-serving motives.

Personal Spiritual Renewal: Values and practices the spiritual discipline necessary to sustain an appropriate spirituality for ministry, and keep his/her existential love for, and awareness of, God alive and vital.

Personal Witness: Possesses a zeal to share his/her beliefs with others, inviting them to accept the lordship of Christ over all of life.

Preacher: Is skilled in preaching sermons that are biblically based and theologically sound; aimed toward providing practical insights for Christian living whether for spiritual nurture, prophetic challenge, or care and comfort.

Prophet: Is possessed by a vision of the Kingdom of God, is able to translate this into a vision for the church, and to communicate and advocate for it.

Public Leader: Maintains a conscious awareness of, and participates in, community and public spheres in relationship to local, national and global matters.

Resident Theologian: Assists individuals and groups to clarify thinking about ultimate meaning and eschatological values, and to make practical application to personal life and the church's organization/ministry processes; teaches the biblical, Christian, and denominational values, and integrates these into the church's experiences.

Scholar/Learner: Develops and maintains competencies in his/her area of interest; carries out research, writing, and other scholarly activities.

Sense of Call: Enters into, and remains in ministry, out of an all encompassing belief that God has called him/her to this work, to which he/she responds with a sense of urgency and dedication.

Spiritual Guide/Resource: Values and knows how to support and direct others in their quest for authentic spiritual experience and maturity; provides resources and experiences, offers spiritual direction, teaches spiritual discipline, within the frame work of the Christian and the church's tradition.

Stewardship Enabler: Values and knows how to interpret a biblical/theological base for stewardship; is equipped to support and enable laity responsible for stewardship education, budget building, financial management, and securing pledges and financial giving.

Teacher/Educator: Cares about Christian education; is willing and able to work with others to plan, implement, and manage Christian education programs; participates in Sunday School, adult and other educational programs.

Wisdom: Demonstrates good judgment based on knowledge and reflective experience; presents a "persona" which inspires trust that he/she will be truthful in all situations; is able to offer wise rule, sound advice, and appropriate support or challenge.

Worship leader/Liturgist: is able to provide a rich, enjoyable, authentic worship service; integrating faith, the church's traditions, the scriptures and sacraments.

Notes

1. Why Is It So Tough to Be a Church Leader?

1. Carlo Carretto, *The God Who Comes* (Maryknoll, N.Y.: Orbis Books, 1974), p. viii.

2. Robert K. Greenleaf, *Servant Leadership: A Journey into the Nature of Legitimate Power and Greatness* (New York: Paulist Press, 1977), p. 5.

3. With faster travel, expanding computer technology, worldwide news media, and the like the world has become a global village in which the sentiments, experiences, and opinions of civilization at the grass roots level are more compatible, if not similar. This being true, it is safe to assume that the basic distrust, lack of confidence, in leadership, will not soon be reversed.

4. Warren Bennis, *On Becoming a Leader* (Reading, Mass.: Addison-Wesley, 1989), p. 19.

5. John W. Gardner, *On Leadership* (New York: The Free Press, 1990), p. xi.

6. Ibid.

7. Henri J. M. Nouwen, *In the Name of Jesus: Reflections on Christian Leadership* (New York: Crossroad, 1989), pp. 58-59.

8. James MacGregor Burns, *Leadership* (New York: Harper Torchbooks, 1978), p. 18.

9. For example, see Mark 9:33-37; 10:35-45; John 13:1-17.

10. Dallas Willard's comments on Acts 1:6-8 during his third lecture, "Spirituality and Leadership" at the Spirituality and Community Seminar, February 13-15, 1991, sponsored by Fuller Theological Seminary, Pasadena, California.

11. Donald E. Messer makes a helpful contribution to this discussion in reconsidering the imagery of ministry:

> A need exists for rethinking the image of ministry in our time, reappropriating the central biblical and theological understandings in contemporary metaphors appropriate to the age. . . .
> . . . Over the centuries, symbols of priest, prophet, pastor, servant, and shepherd have been metaphors of ministry without parallel in terms of their influence and impact on Christian communities in a variety of cultures. In recent decades more secular models have accented creative dimensions of ministry—counselor, administrator, pastoral director, professional, midwife, player coach, and enabler to name but a few.
> However, each generation must review and reappropriate these portraits of ministry, finding its own contemporary images that project motivation and meaning. (Messer, *Contemporary Images of Christian Ministry* (Nashville: Abingdon Press, 1989), p. 14)

12. George Barna reports, in his 1991 annual survey of values and religious views in the United States, that 28 percent of his sample (N=1005) strongly agreed that the church was relevant to the way they live today. The breakdown of age groups was as follows: 18-25 years old (23 percent strongly agreed); 26-44 (25 percent strongly agreed); 45-54 (31 percent strongly agreed); 55-64 (29 percent strongly agreed); 65 years plus (49 percent strongly agreed). See Barna, *What Americans Believe: An Annual Survey of Values and Religious Views in the United States* (Ventura, Calif.: Regal Books, 1991), pp. 185-87.

13. Derek J. Tidball, *Skillful Shepherds: An Introduction to Pastoral Theology* (Grand Rapids: Ministry Resources Library, 1986), pp. 314-15.

14. The desert fathers, and some mothers, were a large group of persons who fled the cities after Christianity was adopted as the state religion in the third century, and it was no longer dangerous to be a Christian. Seeing how this change of status brought new temptations in the lives of Christians and churches, the desert fathers and mothers fled to the desert in order to con-

front the powers of evil in the desert. Their warning was "swim for your life," and with this, they began a movement of men and women fleeing to the desert that lasted approximately 1,000 years.

15. For additional reading, see *Philokalia* (collection of the Desert Fathers), Urban T. Holmes, *Spirituality for Ministry* (San Francisco: Harper & Row, 1982), pp. 42-43, 47, 54.

16. Gale D. Webbe, *The Night and Nothing* (San Francisco: Harper & Row, 1964), p. 80.

17. For a reflection on the temptations of Jesus and church leadership, see Nouwen, *In the Name of Jesus*.

18. Saint John of the Cross, *Dark Night of the Soul* (Garden City, N.Y.: Doubleday, 1959), pp. 88-89.

19. Ibid., p. 89.

20. Holmes, *Spirituality for Ministry*, p. 43.

21. Warren Bennis and Burt Nanus have defined the difference between leadership and management as follows: " 'To manage' means 'to bring about, to accomplish, to have charge of or responsibility for, to conduct.' 'Leading' is 'influencing, guiding in direction, course, action, opinion.' The distinction is crucial. Managers are people who do things right and leaders are people who do the right thing. The difference may be summarized as activities of vision and judgment—effectiveness versus activities of mastering routines—efficiency." (Warren Bennis and Burt Nanus, *Leaders: The Strategies for Taking Charge* (New York: Harper & Row, 1985), p. 21.

22. Ibid., p. 92.

23. James M. Kouzes and Barry Z. Posner, *The Leadership Challenge* (San Francisco: Jossey-Bass Publishers, 1987), p. 27.

24. Gardner, *On Leadership*, p. 4.

25. See Dietrich Bonhoeffer, *Life Together* (San Francisco: Harper & Row, 1954). Bonhoeffer strongly asserts the importance of seeing God as the source for our vision in fellowship because of Jesus Christ. He writes: "Innumerable times a whole Christian community has broken down because it had sprung from a wish dream. The serious Christian, set down for the first time in a Christian community, is likely to bring with him [or her] a very definite idea of what Christian life together should be and to try to realize it. But God's grace speedily shatters such dreams. . . . God hates visionary dreaming; it makes the dreamer proud and pretentious" (p. 26). When a person fashions a community from their own vision, become the law and judge over others, "he acts as if he is the creator of the Christian community, as if his dream binds [others] together. When things do not go his way, he calls the effort a failure. When his ideal picture is destroyed, he sees the community going to smash. So he becomes, first an accuser of his brethren, then an accuser of God, and finally the despairing accuser of himself" (pp. 17-39).

26. George S. Odiorne further illustrated this point: "Churches become enmeshed with covered-dish suppers and basketball leagues—activities generating little other than indigestion and flat feet. . . . Service clubs spend more and more time exhorting members to 'support this activity' with no hint of a worthwhile payoff." Odiorne, *The Human Side of Management by Integration and Self-Control* (Lexington, Mass.: D.C. Heath and Company, 1987), pp. 56-57.

27. See Bennis and Nanus, *Leaders*, p. 21.

28. Stanley Hauerwas and William H. Willimon, *Resident Aliens* (Nashville: Abingdon Press, 1989), pp. 112, 115-16.

PART ONE

The Leader as a Person

1. Michael E. Cavanagh, *The Effective Minister* (Harper & Row, 1986), p. 1.

2. C. Welton Gaddy, *A Soul Under Siege* (Louisville: Westminster/John Knox Press, 1991), p. 30.

3. Michael E. Cavanagh, *The Effective Minister*, pp. 2-3.

4. James M. Hoppin, *Pastoral Theology* (New York: Funk and Wagnalls, 1885), p. 8.

2. The Interior Attitudes of the Leader

1. Thomas Moore, *Care of the Soul: A Guide for Cultivating Depth and Sacredness In Everyday Life* (New York: HarperCollins, 1992), p. xi.

2. For an excellent discussion, see Louis Beirnaert, "Childlike Spirituality and Infantilism," in Robert W. Gelason, ed., *Contemporary Spirituality* (New York: Macmillan, 1968), pp. 270-77.

3. Michael Quoist, *Prayers for Life* (Dublin: Gill and Macmillan, 1954, 1963), p. 3.

4. A. B. Bruce, *The Training of the Twelve* (Edinburgh: T & T Clark, 1888), p. 195.

5. Carlo Carretto, *Letters to Dolcidia* (Maryknoll, N.Y.: Orbis Books, 1991), pp. 39, 56-57.

6. Dietrich Bonhoeffer, *The Cost of Discipleship* (New York: Macmillan, 1937, 1973), p. 118.

7. This was probably the Scripture that prompted the layperson (and thousands of others) to pray, "O Lord, we know you want our pastor to be poor and humble, so you keep him humble, and we'll keep him poor."

8. Richard Foster, *Freedom of Simplicity* (New York: Harper & Row, 1981), p. 81.

9. Carlo Carretto, *Letters to Dolcidia* (Maryknoll, N.Y.: Orbis Books, 1991), pp. 36, 50-51.

10. See Henri J. M. Nouwen, "The Selfless Way of Christ," *Sojourners* 26 (July 1981): 26.

11. Rupert Hart-Davis, *Hugh Walpole: A Biography* (New York: Macmillan, 1952).

12. Henry David Thoreau, *Journal,* Sept. 2, 1951. In Odell Shephard, ed., *The Heart of Thoreau's Journals* (New York: Dover Publications, 1961).

13. Robert K. Greenleaf, *Servant Leadership: A Journey into the Nature of Legitimate Power and Greatness* (New York: Paulist Press, 1977), p. 13.

14. Ibid.

15. Ibid., pp. 13-14.

16. Carlo Carretto, *Why, O Lord?* (Maryknoll, N.Y.: Orbis Books, 1987), p. 45.

17. W. K. C. Guthrie, *Socrates* (Cambridge, England: Cambridge University Press, 1971), p. 151.

18. After Gideon's successful victory over the Midianites, the people of Israel wanted him, his son, and his grandson to "rule over" them. Gideon replied that neither he nor his son would "rule over" them, because only God should "rule over" them. However, Gideon did make a request of them to give him a portion of their booty—43 pounds of earrings and royal garments and camel collars—from the conquest (see Judg. 8:22-28). The biblical judges, including Gideon, usually were leaders during a particular crisis and, afterward, leadership would return to tribal leaders. While Gideon did not respond to an invitation from the people to rule over them for three succeeding generations, he did choose gifts from the booty that became idolatry for him. Perhaps power was not Gideon's weakness, but material possessions were.

19. See Theodore G. Tappert, ed. and trans., *Luther: Letters of Spiritual Counsel* (Philadelphia: The Westminster Press, 1955), pp. 124-30.

20. John T. McNeill and Ford Lewis Battles, eds., *Calvin: Institutes of the Christian Religion* (Philadelphia: The Westminster Press, 1960), pp. 35, 37.

21. See Steve Harper, *Devotional Life in the Wesleyan Tradition* (Nashville: Abingdon Press, 1983), pp. 18-27.

22. See Gary L. Harbaugh, *Pastor as Person: Maintaining Personal Integrity in the Choices and Challenges of Ministry* (Minneapolis: Augsburg, 1984), p. 9.

23. See "Celebrating Community: An Inside Look at the Early Years of Willow Creek Community Church" in *Willow Creek Magazine* 2, 2, November/December, 1990, p. 35. Also, see Bill Hybels, *Too Busy Not to Pray: Slowing Down to Be with God* (Downers Grove, Ill.: InterVarsity Press, 1988).

24. Thomas Oden, *Becoming a Minister* (New York: Crossroad, 1987), p. 12.

25. See C. Welton Gaddy, *A Soul Under Siege* (Louisville: Westminster/John Knox Press, 1991), p. 11.

3. The Leader's Spirituality

1. Nouwen, *The Living Reminder: Service and Prayer in Memory of Jesus Christ*, p. 12.
2. Ibid.
3. Henri J. M. Nouwen, *Gracias! A Latin American Journal* (San Francisco: Harper & Row, 1983), p. 44.
4. William R. Nelson, *Ministry Formation for Effective Leadership* (Nashville: Abingdon Press, 1988), p. 19.
5. Eugene H. Peterson, *Working the Angles: The Shape of Pastoral Integrity* (Grand Rapids: Wm. B. Eerdmans, 1987), pp. 1, 4.
6. John Wesley, *Standard Sermons* (London: Epworth, 1967), vi, as quoted by Steve Harper, *Devotional Life in the Wesleyan Tradition* (Nashville: Upper Room, 1983), p. 29.
7. John Telford, ed., *The Letters of the Rev. John Wesley* (London: Epworth, 1960), p. 103, as quoted by Steve Harper, *Devotional Life in the Wesleyan Tradition*, p. 11.
8. See Dallas Willard, *The Spirit of the Disciplines* (San Francisco: Harper & Row, 1988), p. 4.
9. John Chrysostom, "Homilies on Ephesians." Cited by Thomas C. Oden, *Becoming a Minister* (New York: Crossroad, 1987), p. 16.
10. Henri J. M. Nouwen, *Gracias! A Latin American Journal*, p. 21.
11. See ibid., p. 40.
12. Willard, *The Spirit of the Disciplines*, pp. 7-8.
13. Ibid.
14. Carretto, *Letters to Dolcidia*, p. 116.
15. John Wesley found the Lord's Supper so important to the minister's life and work that he taught that every pastor should take the Lord's Supper as often as possible, at least twice a week. And he taught that every Christian should eat the meal as often as possible, at least once a week.
16. Carretto, *Letters to Dolcidia*, p. 88.
17. Dietrich Bonhoeffer, *Life Together* (New York: Harper and Bros., 1954), pp. 77-78.
18. Walter Brueggemann, "Covenantal Community," *New Conversations* 2, 3 (Winter 1977): 4-9. Published by The United Church Board for Homeland Ministries.
19. See J. H. Jowett, *The Preacher: His Life and Work* (Garden City, N.Y.: Doubleday, Doran & Company, 1928), p. 103.
20. Henri J. M. Nouwen, *Creative Ministry* (Garden City, N.Y.: Image Books, 1971), p. xix.
21. Much of our thinking on this subject is from George A. Aschenbrenner, "Consciousness Examen," *Review for Religious* 31 (1972): 14-21.
22. At first this practice of one or two fifteen-minute contemplative prayers each day may seem sterile or artificial. Integrating ourselves into a process of discernment is not always easy. It takes time and practice.
23. Fredrick C. Gill, *Through the Year with Wesley* (Nashville: The Upper Room, 1983), p. 48.
24. George A. Aschenbrenner, "Consciousness Examen," *Review for Religious* 31, 1 (1972): 15.
25. Aschenbrenner identifies the dangers of empty or unhealthy introspection. However, "a lack of effort at examen and the approach of living according to what comes naturally keeps us quite superficial and insensitive to the subtle and profound ways of the Lord deep in our hearts. The prayerful quality and effectiveness of the examen itself depends upon its relationship to the continuing contemplative prayer of the person. Without this relationship examen slips to the level of self-reflection for self-perfection, if it perdures at all." Aschenbrenner, "Consciousness Examen," p. 15.
26. Ibid., p. 17.
27. Ibid.
28. John Wesley listed general questions that a serious Christian may propose before evening devotions: "1. With what degree of attention and fervor did I use my morning prayers, public or private? 2. Have I done anything without a present, or at least a previous perception of its direct or remote tendency to the glory of God? 3. Did I in the morning consider what particu-

lar virtue I was to exercise, and what business I had to do, in the day? 4. Have I been zealous to undertake, and active in doing, what good I could? 5. Have I interested myself any further in the affairs of others than charity required? 6. Have I, before I visited or was visited, considered how I might thereby give or receive improvement? 7. Have I mentioned any failing or fault of any man, when it was not necessary for the good of another? 8. Have I unnecessarily grieved anyone by word or deed? 9. Have I before or in every action considered how it might be a means of improving in the virtue of the day?" (p. 79). Wesley offered the following questions on Monday morning: "Did I think of God first and last? Have I examined myself how I behaved since last night's retirement? Am I resolved to do all the good I can this day, and to be diligent in the business of my calling?" (p. 82). Frank Whaling, ed., *John and Charles Wesley: Selected Prayers, Hymns, Journal Notes, Sermons, Letters and Treatises* (New York: Paulist Press, 1981), pp. 79, 82.

29. Aschenbrenner, "Consciousness Examen," p. 19.

30. Whaling, *John and Charles Wesley*, p. 80.

31. David L. Fleming, *The Spiritual Exercises of Saint Ignatius: A Literal Translation and a Contemporary Reading* (St. Louis: The Institute of Jesuit Sources, 1983), p. 3.

4. The Leader's Call

1. See Dietrich Bonhoeffer, *The Cost of Discipleship* (New York: Macmillan, 1937, 1973), p. 105.

2. Ibid., p. 41.

3. Soren Kierkegaard writes: "What a tremendous paradox faith is, a paradox which is capable of transforming a murder into a holy act well-pleasing to God, a paradox which gives Isaac back to Abraham, which no thought can master, because faith begins precisely there where thinking takes off." (*Fear and Trembling: The Sickness Unto Death* [Garden City, N.Y.: Doubleday Anchor Books, 1954], p. 64.)

4. Bonhoeffer, *The Cost of Discipleship*, p. 87.

5. Macrina Wiederkehr, *A Tree Full of Angels* (San Francisco: Harper & Row, 1988), p. 18.

6. Bonhoeffer, *The Cost of Discipleship*, p. 99.

7. Nikos Kazantzakis, *The Saviors of God: Spiritual Exercises*, trans. Kimon Friar (New York: Simon & Schuster, 1960), pp. 107-8.

8. J. Pelikan and H. T. Lehmann, eds., *Luther's Works* (St. Louis: Concordia, 1953). pp. 12-13.

9. Evelyn Underhill, *The Spiritual Life* (Harrisburg, Pa.:, Morehouse, 1937, 1938, 1955), pp. 29–30.

10. James E. Dittes, *When the People Say No: Conflict and the Call to Ministry* (New York: Harper & Row, 1979), p. vii.

11. Carlo Carretto, *Letters to Dolcidia* (Maryknoll, N.Y.: Orbis Books, 1991), p. 36.

12. See Edmund Colledge and James Walsh, trans., *Julian of Norwich Showings* (New York: Paulist Press, 1978), from The Classics of Western Spirituality series.

5. The Leader's Vision and Ensuing Mission

1. To understand just how unthinkable one's vision and mission may seem to others, and how resisted, imagine a fourteen-year-old girl in your congregation who reveals that she is pregnant, and who then claims that the father of her unborn child is God. How long would it be before well-intentioned people suggested the names of psychiatrists to the parents? Imagine how Mary's neighbors must have reacted to her vision, Luke 1:46–55.

2. Ibid.

3. David L. Fleming, *Modern Spiritual Exercises: A Contemporary Reading of the Spiritual Exercises of St. Ignatius* (Garden City, N.Y.: Image Books, 1983), pp. 48-49.

4. Based on the poem "Pilgrim's Prayer" by John Donne, *The Gatepost*, January 1, 1991, p. 6.

6. Managing Your Own Effectiveness

1. The subject of managing one's own effectiveness of necessity centers upon working with and through people. Building relationships is an important part of the leader's effectiveness. This subject deserves a much longer discussion than is allowed in this book. Therefore, we are preparing a sequel to this book, which will deal extensively with the concerns of the leader as a manager of ministry and a manager of people.

2. Robert R. Updegraff, *All the Time You Need: The Greatest Gift in the World* (Englewood Cliffs, N.J.: Prentice-Hall, 1958), p. 5.

3. See, for example, Arthur F. Miller and Ralph T. Mattson, *The Truth About You* (Berkeley, Calif.: Ten Speed Press, 1977, 1989). Lloyd C. Douglas, *The Minister's Everyday Life* (New York: Charles Scribner's Sons, 1926): "Ascertain as early as possible what features of your ministry are most effective; what things you do best, and with the finest results; what things are most rewarding to your sense of duty fulfilled—and concentrate on these things," p. 32.

4. Peter F. Drucker, *The Effective Executive* (New York: Harper and Bros., 1966, 1967), p. 19.

5. The above discussion is influenced by notes taken of a lecture of Peter Drucker, at a conference of clergy in 1989.

6. James Glasse, *Putting It Together in the Parish* (Nashville: Abingdon Press, 1972).

7. Douglas, *The Minister's Everyday Life,* p. 17.

8. Drucker, *The Effective Executive,* pp. 25-26.

9. Ibid., pp. 47-51.

10. Stephen R. Covey, *The 7 Habits of Highly Effective People* (New York: Simon & Schuster, 1989), pp. 150-56.

11. See ibid., p. 151.

12. Henri J. M. Nouwen, "Time Enough to Minister," *Leadership Journal* (Spring 1982): 105.

13. See Updegraff, *All the Time You Need,* p. 3.

7. The Dark Side of Leadership

1. Thomas Oden, *Becoming a Minister* (New York: Crossroad, 1987), p. 12.

2. Lloyd C. Douglas, *The Minister's Everyday Life* (New York: Charles Scribner's Sons, 1926), pp. 219-20.

3. George Aschenbrenner, S.J., "Consciousness Examen," *Review for Religious* 31, 1 (1972):14-21.

4. For an excellent introduction into discernment, see chapter 12, "Guidance," in Richard Foster, *Celebration of Discipline* (San Francisco: Harper & Row, 1988).

5. Marie M. Fortune, *Is Nothing Sacred?* (San Francisco: Harper & Row, 1989), p. xii.

6. Paxton Hibben, *Henry Ward Beecher: An American Portrait* (New York: The Press of the Reader's Club, 1927, 1942), pp. 188-89.

7. C. Welton Gaddy, *A Soul Under Siege* (Louisville: Westminster/John Knox, 1991), pp. 56-57.

8. The difference between neurotic and normal is one of degree as on a continuum. There are many types of organizational and leadership dysfunctions. Kets de Vries and Miller point out that their theory is, at present, speculative in attempting to integrate psychoanalytic theory with organizational life. See Manfred F. R. Kets de Vries and Danny Miller, *The Neurotic Organization: Diagnosing and Changing Counterproductive Styles of Management* (San Francisco: Jossey-Bass Publishers, 1984); *Unstable at the Top: Inside the Troubled Organization* (New York: New American Library, 1987); Manfred F. R. Kets de Vries, *Organizational Paradoxes* (London: Tavistock Publications, 1980); Manfred F. R. Kets de Vries, *Prisoners of Leadership* (New York: John Wiley & Sons, 1989).

9. Kets de Vries, *Prisoners of Leadership,* p. 9.

10. Kets de Vries and Miller, *The Neurotic Organization,* p. 22.

11. See Kets de Vries and Miller, *Unstable at the Top.*

12. Ibid., p. 13.

13. Kets de Vries, *Prisoners of Leadership*, p. 93. In this chapter (pp. 91-114), Kets de Vries describes how a narcissistic personality develops and the differences among reactive narcissism, self-deceptive narcissism, and constructive narcissism in relation to leadership.

14. See Kets de Vries and Miller, *Unstable at the Top*, p. 199.

15. Kenneth Blanchard and Norman Vincent Peale, *The Power of Ethical Management* (New York: Ballatine Books, 1988), p. 20.

16. See Kenneth Prior, *Perils of Leadership: Overcoming Personal Battles* (Downers Grove, Ill.: InterVarsity Press, 1990).

17. Urban T. Holmes, *Spirituality for Ministry* (San Francisco, Harper & Row, 1982), pp. 42-43.

18. Gaddy, *A Soul Under Siege*, p. 56.

19. See Gary L. Harbaugh, *Pastor as Person: Maintaining Personal Integrity in the Choices and Challenges of Ministry* (Minneapolis: Augsburg Publishing House, 1984), p. 9.

20. John T. McNeill, ed., *Calvin: Institutes of the Christian Religion*, Library of Christian Classics, vol. XX (Philadelphia: Westminster Press, 1960), p. 35.

PART TWO:
What the Leader Brings to the Congregation

8. The Changing Roles of Today's Pastor

1. Donald E. Messer, *Contemporary Images of Christian Ministry* (Nashville: Abingdon Press, 1989), p. 68.

2. Leadership Network is a private foundation devoted to equipping and networking pastors of large churches—churches with 1,000+ in attendance at their major worship services. Focus groups of pastors of large churches were conducted in Phoenix, Arizona; Minneapolis, Minnesota,;Denver, Colorado; and Portland, Oregon. See Norman Shawchuck, "Compiled Report, Nominal Group Technique, Focus Groups: Pastors of Large Churches for Leadership Network," Tyler, Texas. Following the focus groups, Dr. Richard Olson surveyed 1,000 pastors as a major part of his Ph.D. dissertation at Northwestern University, see *The Largest Congregations in the United States*, 1988.

3. Following the focus groups, Leadership Network commissioned a survey of pastors and lay leaders in large congregations, designed to test the validity of the focus groups' information. The survey was mailed to 50 percent of the large congregations in the United States. The survey results substantiated the conclusions drawn from the focus groups.

4. The Better Preparation for Ministry Project (BPMP) was initiated by the Board of Trustees and the administration of McCormick Theological Seminary (a United Presbyterian school) as a means gathering data to use in a review of its Master of Divinity curriculum. Presently, the school's M.Div. curriculum reflects an effort to prepare persons for ministry in the 1960s, in a context of social unrest and change of that era. Twelve focus groups were used to provide information that would inform the construction of a questionnaire, which included specific revisions in the language of various denominations to be sampled: American Baptist, United Church of Christ, United Methodist, and Presbyterian. Eight modules of the questionnaire included the following: (1) Role items of clergy; (2) Critical incident items dealing with the best and worst pastors experienced by the respondent; (3) Demographic items; (4) Student service items; (5) Seminary setting items; (6) Educational process; (7) Instructional area; and (8) Open-ended items. The McCormick Theological Seminary sample included faculty (30), trustees (33), advocates (80), students on the president's list (160), other students (530), alumni

(3,345), donors and friends (1,188), and spouses of donors and friends (453). The church samples included ABC (963), UCC (562), PCUSA (2,275), and UMC (1,867). Also included were seminary presidents (167) and their list of graduates. Adding to the sample were 457 megachurches (800+ in Sunday worship attendance). The total universe sample of this study was 14,291. Of this total, 3,251 questionnaires were returned, which was 23 percent of the total sample. The average age was 51 (standard deviation of 12.9); 657 females and 2,539 males participated in the study. The ethnic/racial groups included the following: African American (433), African-Other (3), Asian-Korean (10), Asian-Other (18), Caucasian (2,625), Hispanic (33), and Native American (31). Academic degrees included: Bible school degree (78), BA/BS (2,569), MA/MS 9,767), Ph.D. (207), M.Div. (2,474), and D.Min. (627). The denominations represented were Baptist (155), Disciples of Christ (16), Episcopal (25), Lutheran (93), United Methodist (320), Orthodox (1), Pentecostal (7), Presbyterian (1,324), Roman Catholic (33), and United Church of Christ (110). The nature of ecclesiastical involvement included ordained (2,340), pastor (1,873), ruling elder/lay leader (232), paid staff (442), volunteer worker (300), national/regional staff (392), national/regional board member (130), ecumenical staff/board member (97). The average Sunday worship attendance of the respondents' places of worship was 299. See Norman Shawchuck and Gustave Rath, "A Report of the Better Preparation for Ministry Project: A Research Project of McCormick Theological Seminary," Chicago, Illinois, March 13, 1991.

9. The Congregation's Spirituality

1. Richard J. Hauser, *In His Spirit: A Guide to Today's Spirituality* (New York: Paulist Press, 1982), p. 11.
2. Ibid., p. 12.
3. Dietrich Bonhoeffer, *Ethics* (New York: Macmillan, 1955, 1967), p. 88.
4. Ibid., pp. 80–85.
5. Ibid., p. 81.
6. Ibid., p. 82.
7. It is easier to write about a spirituality of religious leadership than it is to give oneself to that spirituality. In this chapter, you may appropriately ask whether we are really serious about the things we say. We would not say to you what has not already been accepted by us. This is not to say we have arrived. We are not there yet, but we are on the way. Our hope in writing this chapter is that we might say the one thing needed to encourage the reader who has not yet set forth on the journey—and it is a journey, a life-long journey.
8. Carlo Carretto, *Letters to Dolcidia* (Maryknoll, N.Y.: Orbis Books, 1991), pp. 45-46.
9. Mother Teresa, *Words to Love By* (Notre Dame: Ava Maria Press, 1983) p. 15.
10. Eugene H. Peterson, *Working the Angles: The Shape of Pastoral Integrity* (Grand Rapids: Wm. B. Eerdmans, 1987), pp. 2, 10.
11. See Henri J. M. Nouwen, *The Way of the Heart* (Minneapolis: The Seabury Press, 1981). The idea of spirituality as a journey is another concept that differentiates the Western model from the scriptural (neo-Western) model of spirituality. The Western model sees spiritual formation much more as a fixed condition than as a journey toward spiritual maturity.
12. The themes and colors named here are suggestive and vary from denomination to denomination.
13. For a more in-depth discussion of the seasons of spiritual experience and the "journey" aspects of spiritual formation, see Norman Shawchuck, *What It Means to be a Church Leader: A Biblical Point of View* (Leith, N.D.: Spiritual Growth Resources, 1984), and *How to Conduct a Spiritual Life Retreat* (Nashville: The Upper Room, 1986).
14. Carlo Carretto, *Why, O Lord?* (Maryknoll, N.Y.: Orbis Books, 1986).
15. Dietrich Bonhoeffer, *Life Together* (San Francisco: Harper & Row, 1954), pp. 77-78.
16. Ibid., p. 23.
17. Henri J. M. Nouwen, *Making All Things New* (San Francisco: Harper & Row, 1981), p. 32.

18. See Wayne A. Meeks, *The First Urban Christians: The Social World of the Apostle Paul* (New Haven, Conn.: Yale University Press, 1983).

19. M. Scott Peck uses this term to describe those who attempt to form a community. Often they will try to "fake it. The members attempt to be an instant community by being extremely pleasant with one another and avoiding all disagreement. This attempt—this pretense of *community*—is what I term 'pseudocommunity.' It never works." See M. Scott Peck, *The Different Drum: Community Making and Peace* (New York: Simon and Schuster, 1987), pp. 86-87.

20. Bonhoeffer, *Life Together*, pp. 110-11.

21. Ibid., p. 88.

22. See Richard J. Foster, *Celebration of Discipline: The Path to Spiritual Growth*, rev. and exp. (San Francisco: Harper & Row, 1988, p. 7.

23. Dallas Willard, *The Spirit of the Disciplines* (San Francisco: Harper & Row, 1988), p. 157.

24. Ibid., p. 158.

25. Ibid., pp. 175-76.

10. The Leader as Guardian of the Corporate Vision

1. John W. Gardner, *On Leadership* (New York: The Free Press, 1990), p. 131.

2. See Richard R. Broholm, *The Power and Purpose of Vision: A Study of the Role of Vision in Exemplary Organizations* (Indianapolis: The Robert K. Greenleaf Center, 1990), p. 6.

3. John W. Gardner, *On Leadership* (New York: The Free Press, 1990), pp. 130-31.

4. Warren Bennis and Burt Nanus, *Leaders: The Strategies for Taking Charge* (San Francisco: Harper & Row, 1985), p. 28.

5. For more on the three types of congregations, see Lloyd Perry and Norman Shawchuck, *Revitalizing the 20th Century Church* (Glendale Heights, Ill.: Spiritual Growth Resources, 1991), pp. 13-17.

6. Warren Bennis, *On Becoming a Leader* (Reading, Mass.: Addison-Wesley, 1989), p. 194.

7. From a lecture by Wayne Shabaz, faculty orientation at Southern California College, Costa Mesa, Calif., September 1, 1992.

8. See "The View from Above: An Interview with Terry Fullam," *Leadership* (Winter 1984): 12-22.

9. Ibid.

10. Peter M. Senge, *The Fifth Discipline: The Art and Practice of the Learning Organization* (New York: Doubleday Currency, 1990), p. 212.

11. "The View from Above: An Interview with Terry Fullam," pp. 17, 19.

12. For an excellent discussion on ministry in different congregational/organizational structures, see Roy M. Oswald, "How to Minister Effectively in Family, Pastoral, Program, and Corporate Sized Churches," *Action Information* (March/April 1991): 1-7.

13. Richard R. Broholm, *The Power and Purpose of Vision: A Study of the Role of Vision in Exemplary Organizations* (Robert K. Greenleaf Center, 1990), p. 4.

14. "The View from Above: An Interview with Terry Fullam," p. 21.

15. Gordon Cosby, *Handbook for Mission Groups* (Washington, D.C.: The Potter's House), pp. 58-59.

16. Chris Argyris, *Integrating the Individual and the Organization* (New Brunswick: Transaction Publishers, 1990), p. 7.

17. Henry Mintzberg, *Mintzberg on Management: Inside Our Strange World of Organizations* (New York: The Free Press, 1989), p. 122.

18. Martin Luther King, Jr., is not the only compelling example of how a leader may communicate a vision to others—so that the personal vision becomes the foundation for an even larger corporate vision. Such examples abound all around us. As an example of this we have included in this book the story of Whaja Hwang, a Korean lay woman whose vision to serve the poor has captured the hearts and energies of hundreds in Korea and around the world (see chap. 18).

19. This principle holds true in all great movements of social change. Historically, at least four ingredients have been required for any social movement or change: (1) a small group; (2) thor-

oughly committed to a single cause [or vision]; (3) with a leader who can articulate the cause with clarity and passion; and (4) a slogan that emotively reminds the group of their history and cause.

20. See Raymond J. Bakke and Samuel K. Roberts, *The Expanded Mission of "Old First" Churches* (Valley Forge: Judson Press, 1986).

21. Robert K. Greenleaf, *Servant Leadership* (New York: Paulist Press, 1977), p. 88.

22. Adapted from James M. Kouzes and Barry Z. Posner, *The Leadership Challenge* (San Francisco: Jossey-Bass, 1987), pp. 125-29.

23. Frances Westley and Henry Mintzberg, "Visionary Leadership and Strategic Management," *Strategic Management Journal* 10 (1989): 20.

24. Two sources of organizational energy, according to Senge, are fear and aspiration: "The power of fear underlies negative visions. The power of aspiration drives positive visions. Fear can produce extraordinary changes in short periods, but aspiration endures as a continuing source of learning and growth." A congregation may be motivated by a "negative vision" over a short term when its survival is threatened. But when the threat is over, so is the vision. In a fear-oriented congregation, energy is focused primarily on what the congregation does not want to happen. See Senge, *The Fifth Discipline*, p. 225.

25. A leader or a congregation may have a vision, but it may not be worthwhile. Some congregations are obsessively driven and ambitious to the point of being pathological; their vision is not from God. "Thus says the LORD of hosts: Do not listen to the words of the prophets who prophesy to you; they are deluding you. They speak visions of their own minds, not from the mouth of the LORD" (Jer. 23:16).

26. Senge, *The Fifth Discipline*, pp. 219-20.

27. Ibid., p. 218.

28. Bennis, *On Becoming a Leader*, p. 186.

29. Chris Argyris describes the sources of energy for organization. The psychological energy of individuals comes about through psychological success. He states, "Under a climate of trust, the individuals may increase their opportunities for psychological success." See Chris Argyris, *Integrating the Individual and the Organization* (New Brunswick: Transaction Publishers, 1990), p. 31.

30. See Stephen R. Covey, *The Seven Habits of Highly Effective People* (New York: Simon and Schuster, 1989), pp. 220-22.

31. Greenleaf, *Servant Leadership*, p. 88.

32. Kouzes and Posner, *The Leadership Challenge*, p. 151.

33. Greenleaf, *Servant Leadership*, p. 330.

34. Senge, *The Fifth Discipline*, p. 227.

35. Ibid., pp. 227.

36. Ibid., p. 228.

37. Ibid., p. 229.

38. Ibid., p. 230

39. Ibid., pp. 227-30.

11. Understanding the Congregation's Life Cycle

1. Burt Nanus, *The Leader's Edge: The Seven Keys to Leadership in a Turbulent World* (Chicago: Contemporary Books, 1989), p. 149.

2. Atrophy is the wasting away of a body part or tissue; it may also mean the arrested development of a part or organ that may be incidental to the normal development of an organism.

3. Robert K. Greenleaf, *Servant Leadership* (New York: Paulist Press, 1977), pp. 174-75.

4. Adapted from marketing theory in Philip Kotler and Alan R. Andreasen, *Strategic Marketing for Nonprofit Organizations* (Englewood Cliffs, N.J.: Prentice-Hall, 1987), pp. 396-419. Also see Ichak Adizes, *Corporate Lifecycles: How and Why Corporations Grow and Die and What to Do About It* (Englewood Cliffs, N.J.: Prentice Hall, 1988).

5. Excerpted from Richard Phillips, "Silent 'Church of Good Cheer' Awaits Auctioneer's Gavel," *Chicago Tribune,* July 20, 1978, section 7, pp. 1-2.

12. The Leaders' Role in Congregational Renewal

1. Loren B. Mead, *The Once and Future Church* (Washington, D.C.: The Alban Institute, 1991), p. v.

2. James A. Belasco, *Teaching the Elephant to Dance* (New York: Penguin, 1991), p. 2.

3. *Newscope* 20, 37, September 18, 1992.

4. Joel Arthur Barker, *Future Edge: Discovering the New Paradigms of Success* (New York: William Morrow and Co., Inc., 1992) p. 11.

5. For a brief, but instructive, introduction to discernment as a decision-making method, see *Studies in the Spirituality of the Jesuits,* "A Method for Communal Discernment of God's Will," vol. III, no. 4, September 1971; "Toward a Theological Evaluation of Communal Discernment," vol. V, no. 5, October 1973; "Communal Discernment: Reflections on Experience," vol. IV, no. 5, November 1972; and "Trust Your Feelings, but Use Your Head: Discernment and the Psychology of Decision Making," The American Assistancy Seminar, 3700 W. Pine Blvd., St. Louis, MO 63108. For a story (a novel) account of a congregation that decided to use discernment, see Bob Slosser, *Miracle in Darien* (Plainfield, N.J.: Logos International, 1979).

6. For examples of helpful literature regarding the future, see Russel Chandler, *Rushing Toward 2001* (Grand Rapids and San Francisco: Zondervan and Harper copublication, 1992); Stan Davis and Bill Davidson, *2020 Vision* (New York: A Fireside Book, 1991); Loren Meade, *The Once and Future Church* (Washington, D.C.: The Alban Institute, 1991); John Naisbitt and Patricia Aburdene, *Megatrends 2000: Ten New Directions for the 1990s* (New York: William Morrow, 1990); Faith Popcorn, *The Popcorn Report* (New York: Doubleday Currency, 1991); William Strauss and Neil Howe, *Generations: The History of America's Future 1584–2069* (New York: William Morrow, 1991). For studying the cultural and socio-demographics of your community, contact Church Information and Development Services, 151 Kalmus Drive, Suite A-104, Costa Mesa, California, 92626.

7. For a complete text on innovation, see Peter F. Drucker, *Innovation and Entrepreneurship: Practice and Principles* (New York: Harper & Row, 1985).

8. Ibid., p. 152.

9. See Ray Bakke, *The Urban Christian* (Downers Grove, Ill.: InterVarsity Press, 1987), pp. 19-20.

10. Raymond J. Bakke and Samuel K. Roberts, *The Expanded Mission of "Old First" Churches* (Valley Forge, Pa.: Judson Press, 1986), p. 15.

11. Ibid., pp. 15-16.

12. Ayn Rand, *Atlas Shrugged* (New York: Random House, 1957).

13. For a more in-depth discussion of excellence in the workplace, see Joel Barker, *Future Edge*; Tom Peters, *A Passion for Excellence: The Leadership Difference* (New York: Warner Books, 1985); Tom Peters and Robert Waterman, *In Search of Excellence: Lessons from America's Best-run Companies* (New York: Harper & Row, 1982); Robert Waterman, *The Renewal Factor: How the Best Get and Keep the Competitive Edge* (New York: Bantam Books, 1987); and Craig Hickman and Michael Silva, *Creating Excellence: Managing Corporate Culture, Strategy, and Change in the New Age* (New York: New American Library, 1984).

14. See George S. Odiorne, *Management and the Activity Trap* (New York: Harper & Row, 1974) and, by the same author, *The Human Side of Management: Management by Integration and Self-Control* (Lexington, Mass.: Lexington Books, 1987).

15. Odiorne, *The Human Side of Management,* p. 56.

13. The Leadership Team of the Congregation

1. Our thinking about the role and function of the congregation's governing board, and the relationships that must exist between the governing board and the pastor have been most deeply influenced by Robert Greenleaf and Peter F. Drucker. The chapter that follows is a summary of their approaches to leading an organization's board. We commend to you all of the insights these two have penned on the subject of the organization's board of directors.

2. Peter F. Drucker, *Managing the Non-Profit Organization* (New York: HarperCollins, 1990), p. 178.

3. Robert K. Greenleaf, *The Institution as Servant* (Peterborogh, N.H.: Center for Applied Studies, Window Row Press, 1972, 1976), p. 2.

4. Jerome, *Dialogus contra Luciferianos*, ch. 21: PL 23,175 as quoted in Edward Schillebeeckx, *Ministry: Leadership in the Community of Jesus Christ* (New York: Crossroad, 1981), p. 1.

5. For example, those appointed as deacons in Acts 6 included Philip, the "evangelist," who did everything the apostles did. It was also the Greek-speaking Jewish Christians who fled to Samaria and Syria and, while on their way, founded many communities of faith.

6. See Schillebeeckx, *Ministry,* pp. 5-37.

7. We are using "governing board" as a generic term to identify the group charged with the oversight of the congregation's affairs. Depending on the ecclesiastical tradition of the congregation this group may be called deacons, trustees, council, elders, consistory, vestry, session, and the like.

8. Peter F. Drucker, *Management: Tasks, Responsibilities, Practices* (New York: Harper & Row, 1974), p. 628.

9. Peter F. Drucker, "It Profits Us to Strengthen Nonprofits," *The Wall Street Journal,* Thursday, December 19, 1991, p. 14.

10. Richard T. Ingram, *Making Trusteeship Work* (Washington, D.C.: Association of Governing Boards of Universities and Colleges, 1988), pp. 1-2.

11. For an imaginative and sobering essay on the leaders' temptation to reward and protect incompetency, see Peter Drucker, *The Temptation to Do Good* (New York: Harper & Row, 1984).

12. See Robert K. Greenleaf, *Servant Leadership* (New York: Paulist Press, 1977), pp. 61-69.

13. See Greenleaf, *Servant Leadership,* p. 83. According to Greenleaf, the pyramid principle established by Moses and Jethro did not work precisely because of the abuse of power. He writes, "In the end the Lord sacked Moses. Why? Because in that dramatic incident of drawing water from the rock he acted as if he were God. . . . Missing was the necessary guardianship of strong trustees and an astute chairman. . . . The abuse of power is curbed if the holder of power is surrounded by equals who are strong, and if there is close oversight by a monitoring group, trustees who are not involved in the daily use of power" (see pp. 84-85). In addition Greenleaf identifies the flaws in the concept of the single chief: "To be alone at the top is abnormal and corrupting" (p. 63). There are no colleagues at the top, only subordinates. The pyramid weakens information links, drying up channels of honest feedback. Second, there is a self-protective image of omniscience, which comes about from the filtered communication. Third, those at the top suffer from real loneliness and are overburdened. Fourth, there is a major interruption when that person leaves. Fifth, the single chief prevents leadership by persuasion because there is too much power and what he or she says will be taken as an order. Sixth, the prevalence of the lone chief places a burden on the entire organization and society because it gives control priority over leadership (see pp. 63-66).

14. The sentient boundaries are comprised of the deeply held norms, values, traditions, secrets, stories, etc., which are in the deep memory of the congregation and give it its unique sense of identity, "who we are."

15. David Hubbard's interview with Peter F. Drucker in "The Effective Board." In Drucker, *Managing the Non-Profit Organization,* pp. 171-72.

16. Greenleaf, *Servant Leadership,* p. 82.

17. Ibid., pp. 103-4.

18. For a more complete discussion of this matter, see Norman Shawchuck, "The Local Church: Who Works for Whom?" *Leadership: A Practical Journal for Church Leaders* 1, 1 (Winter 1980).

14. Don't Forget to Fly the Plane

1. Max DePree, *Leadership Is an Art* (New York: Dell Publishing, 1989), p. 142.
2. As told by Peter Drucker in March 1989 to the Leadership Network conference for pastors.
3. Myopia is a condition whereby the visual image focuses in front of the eye's retina and, thereby, results in defective vision of distant objects.
4. See Paul B. Tinlin and Edith Blumhofer, "Decade of Decline or Harvest? Dilemmas of the Assemblies of God," *The Christian Century*, July 10-17, 1991, pp. 684-87.
5. Organizational systems theory was spawned with the advent of the space age, when for the first time in human history the problems at hand were too complex to be understood or addressed with a linear planning model. Systems planning was devised to help understand tremendous complexities in an uncertain and rapidly changing environment. With its commitment to working with the organization as a whole, rather than as a collection of separate entities, systems leadership is as much an art as a science. The artist views the whole scene in order to understand it, while the scientist breaks the specimen down into its smallest divisible parts in order to understand it. For an excellent discussion in its application for the church, see Alvin J. Lindgren and Norman Shawchuck, *Management for Your Church* (Leith, N.D.: Organization Resources Press, 1977).
6. See John A. Seiler, *Systems Analysis in Organizational Behavior* (Homewood, Ill.: Richard D. Irwin, Inc. and The Dorsey Press, 1967), p. 28.
7. Lloyd Perry and Norman Shawchuck, *Revitalizing the 20th Century Church* (Schaumburg, Ill.: Spiritual Growth Resources, 1982) p. 22.
8. For a complete discussion of systems symptoms and problems, see Alvin Lindgren and Norman Shawchuck, *Management for Your Church: A Systems Approach* (Leith, N.D.: Spiritual Growth Resources, 1977, 1984).

PART THREE:
Paradigms for Church Leadership

1. These two paradigm shifts are not confined to the North American church; rather, they represent societal changes. As such they will certainly affect the entire American church in the next decade or two, because the church tends to follow the basic societal shifts by about twenty-five years—or fifty or five hundred. A friend told us of listening in on a recent discussion with Pope John Paul II in which persons were pressing him for statements as to when the American Roman Catholic Church will change its position on married priests, abortion, and so on. Our friend said the pope listened to the demands for immediate change and, laying a finger on his cheek, he mused, "Yes, it has been a rather turbulent century, hasn't it?"

15. Paradigms for Church Leadership

1. Loren B. Mead, *The Once and Future Church* (Washington, D.C.: The Alban Institute), p. 8.
2. See Thomas S. Kuhn, *The Structures of Scientific Revolutions* (Chicago: University of Chicago Press, 1970). Kuhn described the limitations of a paradigm when he wrote: "To be accepted as a paradigm, a theory must seem better than its competitors, but it need not, and in fact never does, explain all the facts with which it can be confronted" (pp. 17-18). Furthermore,

Kuhn suggested that once paradigms are accepted, it may take a major upheaval to replace the existing one. Ultimately, a person must have faith in the new paradigm for it to succeed.

3. Stephen R. Covey, *The 7 Habits of Highly Effective People* (New York: Simon and Schuster, 1989), p. 40.

4. Transcript of Joel Barker's video, *The Business of Paradigms: Discovering the Future* (Burnsville, Minn.: Charthouse Learning Corporation, 1990), p. 67.

5. See Mead, *The Once and Future Church.*

6. An example of Christianity existing within a new paradigm is seen in South Korea, where within the past forty years Christianity has grown to encompass about one third of the nation's forty million people, alongside two other religions of equal size, the Moslem faith and Buddhism.

7. Mead, *The Once and Future Church,* p. 22.

8. See Chris Argyris and Donald A. Schön, *Theory in Practice* (San Francisco: Jossey-Bass, 1974), p. 7. Also see Chris Argyris, *Increasing Leadership Effectiveness* (New York: John Wiley & Sons, 1976); Chris Argyris and Donald A. Schön, *Organizational Learning: A Theory of Action Perspective* (Reading, Mass.: Addison Wesley Publishing Co., 1978).

9. This is part of the blind spot of a person—those thoughts, feelings, and motivation known to others but not to oneself. See Joseph Luft, *Group Processes: An Introduction to Group Dynamics* (Mountain View, Calif.: Mayfield Publishing Company.

10. Transcript of Joel Barker's video, *The Business of Paradigms: Discovering the Future,* p. 68.

11. Transcript of video by Barker, *Discovering the Future: The Business of Paradigms.* Barker uses an illustration of watchmaking. In 1968, the Swiss had 65 percent of the world market share in watches and more than 80 percent of the profit. Ten years later, they had less than 10 percent of the market share and had to release 50,000 of the 65,000 workers. The paradigm shift here was the quartz movement, invented by the Swiss themselves but developed for mass markets by the Japanese.

12. Ibid., p. 79.

13. Nicolo Machiavelli, *The Prince* (New York: New American Library, 1952), pp. 119, 122-23. Machiavelli also said that more kingdoms collapse because of their success than ever fail because of failure.

14. Paradigm pioneers are always on the fringes, seldom even noticed by those who operate out of the established paradigms. See the transcript of Barker's video, *The Business of Paradigms: Discovering the Future,* p. 83.

15. William McKinney, "Sidelined Protestantism: What Should Its Churches Do Now?" *In Trust* (Autumn 1989): 14-20, italics added.

16. Craig Dykstra, "Publisher's note," *Progressions: A Lilly Endowment Occasional Report 2,* 1 (January 1990): inside cover page. This entire issue deals with examples of "rough waters" for mainstream Protestant churches—paradigmatic issues such as baby boomers, decline of the Presbyterians, the changing leadership role for the pastor, the changing roles of women in the church, and the fading of denominational distinctiveness.

17. Paul B. Tinlin and Edith Blumhofer, "Decade of Decline or Harvest? Dilemmas of the Assemblies of God," *The Christian Century,* July 10-17, 1991, pp. 684-87. The Decade of Harvest is a ten-year plan for growth and expansion within the Assemblies of God throughout the 1990s.

18. See Jean Evangelauf, "The Father of Modern Management Nurtures the Human Element," *The Chronicle of Higher Education* (February 10, 1988). See also Lyle E. Schaller, *The Seven-Day-A-Week Church* (Nashville: Abingdon Press, 1992). Schaller examines this cultural shift in terms of Sunday morning churches and seven-day-a-week churches.

19. Peter M. Senge, *The Fifth Discipline: The Art & Practice of the Learning Organization* (New York: Doubleday, 1990), p. 4.

20. Ibid., pp. 17-18.

21. See Mary Walton, *The Deming Management Method* (New York: Perigree Books, 1986).

22. Argyris and Schön, *Organizational Learning,* p. 60.

23. See Argyris and Schön, *Theory in Practice,* p. 86.

24. Argyris and Schön, *Organizational Learning,* p. 61. See also Argyris and Schön, *Theory in Practice,* pp. 63-84.

25. See Argyris and Schön, *Organizational Learning*, p. 137, and *Theory in Practice*, pp. 85-95.

26. See the struggle of factions within the early church to expand their existing paradigms in Acts 15.

27. See the transcript of Joel Barker's video, *The Business of Paradigms.*

16. Church Leadership in a Multi-cultural Context: An Emerging Paradigm

1. "Christ Outside the Gate" is the title the late Orlando E. Costas gave to one of his greatest works. This term describes the place, or location where Jesus situated himself as a victim who identifies with the suffering of those who themselves are "outside the gates" of power. In having died outside the gate Jesus "changed the place of salvation and clarified the meaning of mission." Costas adds, " No longer can I see God's saving grace as an individual benfit, a privileged possession, or a religious whitewash that enables me to feel good and continue to live the old way because my bad conscience had been soothed and my guilt feelings washed away. On the contrary, because salvation is to be found in the crucified son of God who died outside the gate of the religious compound, to be saved by faith in him is to experience a radical transformation that makes me a "debtor" to the world (Rom.1:14) and calls me to share in his suffering by serving, especially, its lowest representatives: the poor, the powerless, and the oppressed." Orlando E. Costas, *Christ Outside the Gate: Mission Beyond Christendom* (Maryknoll, N.Y.: Orbis Books, 1982) p. 194.

2. Piri Thomas, *Savior, Savior, Hold My Hand* (Garden City, N.Y.: Doubleday, 1972), pp. 19-21.

3. "Praxis" is the dynamic tension between the *practice of ministry* and the *reflection on ministry*. See, for example, Juan Luis Segundo, *The Liberation of Theology* (Maryknoll, N.Y.: Orbis Books, 1976).

4. Ray S. Anderson, *The Praxis of Pentecost: Revisioning the Church's Life and Mission* (Fuller Theological Seminary, 1991) pp.10-11.

5. John De Gruchy, *Dietrich Bonhoeffer: Witness to Jesus Christ* (San Francisco: Collins Liturgical Publications, 1988), p. 54.

6. Todd H. Spiedell, "Incarnational Social Ethics," published in *Incarnational Ministry: Essays in Honor of Ray S. Anderson: The Presence of Christ in Church, Society, and Family*, p. 140.

7. Gerardo J. de Jesus, "Toward a Theology of the Barrio: Reflections of an Urban Pastor," published article in *Theology, News and Notes*, Fuller Theological Seminary, June, 1992, p. 8.

8. Ray S. Anderson, "The Humanity of God and the Soul of a City," published article in Theology, News and Notes, Fuller Theological Seminary, June, 1992, p. 15.

9. Eldin Villafane describes this issue of "Triple Consciousness" as psycho-social plight which the second and third generation Hispanic encounters in the Anglo-White society. They feel themselves "in the role of" insiders" and" outsiders" to the dominant Anglo-White group, but also" insider" and" outsider" to the first mestizaje group (first generation Hispanics)as well. They are "insiders"-totally accepted and affirmed-only among themselves(the second mestizaje group). For an in depth discussion on the issue of the "Triple Consciousness" see, Eldin Villafane, *The Socio-Cultural Matrix of Intergenerational Dynamics: An Agenda for the 90's, Apuntes,* (Mexican American Program, Perkins School of Theology, Southern University, Dallas, Tex.), Spring, 1992.

10. James H. Cone, *God of the Oppressed* (New York: Seabury Press, 1975), p. 124. See also Justo L. Gonzalèz, *Mañana: Christian Theology from a Hispanic Perspective* (Nashville: Abingdon Press, 1990), p. 26.

11. James B. Torrance, "The Vicarious Humanity of Christ," in *The Incarnation—Ecumenical Studies in the Nicene-Constantinopolitan Creed, A.D. 381,* Thomas F. Torrance, Editor (Edinburgh: Handsel Press, Ltd., 1981), p. 141.

12. Anderson, "The Humanity of God and the Soul of a City," p. 15.

13. Ibid., p. 22.

14. Ibid.

15. Mestizo translated means "culturally integrated, or mixed." This is also the title of Virgilio Elizondo, *The Future is Mestizo: Life Where Culture Meets* (Bloomington, Ind.: Myer Stone Books, 1988).

17. Women in Church Leadership: An Emerging Paradigm

1. Judy Rosener, "Ways Women Lead," *Harvard Business Review* (November/December 1990): 119-20.

2. Ibid, p. 120.

3. Sally Helgesen, *The Feminine Advantage: Women's Ways of Leadership* (New York: Doubleday, 1990), p. 55.

4. Ibid, p. 58.

5. Ibid., p. 59.

6. See Deborah Tannen, *You Just Don't Understand* (New York: Ballantine, 1991), pp. 24-25. Ann Wilson Schaef concurs in *Women's Reality: An Emerging Female System in a White Male Society* (San Francisco: Harper & Row, 1985), p. 134.

7. Schaef, *Women's Reality*, p. 128.

8. Alicia Johnson, "Women Managers: Old Stereotypes Die Hard," *Management Review* (December 1987): 39.

9. Anne Marie Nuechterlein and Celia A. Hahn, *The Male-Female Church Staff* (Washington, D.C.: Alban Institute, 1990), p. 25.

10. Schaef, *Women's Reality*, pp. 40-41.

11. Judy Rosener, "Ways Women Lead," p. 125. Amy Saltzman corroborates this view in "Trouble at the Top," *U.S. News and World Report*, June 17, 1990, p. 44.

12. Tannen, *You Just Don't Understand*, p. 17.

13. Schaef, *Women's Reality*, p. 41.

14. See Nuechterlein and Hahn, *The Male-Female Church Staff*, p. 32.

15. See Carol Hymowitz and Timothy Schellhardt, "The Glass Ceiling," *Wall Street Journal Special Report*, March 24, 1986, p. 1.

16. Cathy Trost, "Women Managers Quit Not for Family but to Advance Their Corporate Climb," *Wall Street Journal*, Midwest Edition, May 2, 1990, p. B1.

17. Hymowitz and Schellhardt, "The Glass Ceiling," p. 1.

18. See Schaef, *Women's Reality*, p. 68.

19. Johnson, "Women Managers: Old Stereotypes Die Hard," p. 37.

20. Saltzman corroborates this view in "Trouble at the Top," p. 41.

21. Rosener, "Ways Women Lead," p. 121.

22. Trost, "Women Managers Quit Not for Family but to Advance Their Corporate Climb," p. B1.

23. Schaef, *Women's Reality*, p. 148.

24. Nuechterlein and Hahn, *The Male-Female Church Staff*, p. 23.

25. Ibid, p. 24.

26. Ibid, p. 31.

27. See Constant H. Jacquet, "Women Ministers in 1986 and 1977: A Ten Year Review," Office of Research and Evaluation, National Council of Churches. Cited by Mary D. Pellauer in "Twenty Years after the Ordination of Women" (Chicago: The Evangelical Lutheran Church in America, 1990), p. 1.

28. Schaef, *Women's Reality*, pp. 164-67.

29. Ibid., p. 169.

30. See Nuechterlein and Hahn, *The Male-Female Church Staff*, p. 21.

31. Janette Hassey, "Brief History of Christian Feminism," *Transformation* 6, 2 (April/June 1989): 2.

32. See Schaef, *Women's Reality,* p. 114.

33. Paul G. Bretscher, in "Culture Virus," *Lutheran Forum* 26:3 (August 1992): 18, distinguishes between the biblical wisdom, which "perceives a factor inherent in maleness from God himself . . . by which man can fulfill God-ordained headship toward women." He adds: "The culture virus, by contrast perceives maleness as itself the cause of women's sense of inferiority." He asserts that "these wisdoms are incompatible." Arguments like this make sense when viewed from within the white male system. Outside that paradigm, they do not make sense.

34. Arguments by some leaders in the Lutheran Church Missouri Synod, which would remove women from teaching Sunday school and even singing in church choirs (*LCMS Reporter Alive,* May 11, 1992), make no sense when viewed outside this perspective. When understood inside this perspective, they not only "make sense" but are taken seriously. This example is only one of many that can be found in the literature of more conservative denominations.

35. Schaef, *Women's Reality,* p. 164. Anyone who denies that this idolatry is alive in the church should observe the reaction within one denomination, whose magazine cover depicted a black Christ on the cross for a recent Easter edition. It proved to be the cover that generated more protest than any cover in the history of the magazine.

36. Ann S. Huff, "Wives of the Organization" (Urbana-Champaign: Department of Business Administration), p. 3. Originally presented at the Women and Work Conference, Arlington, Texas, May 11, 1990.

37. Ibid, p. 7.

38. Nuechterlein and Hahn, *The Male-Female Church Staff,* p. 30. They credit K. R. Mitchell, in *Multiple Staff Ministries* (Philadelphia: Westminster, 1988), for this example.

39. All of the experiences recounted here are based on real experiences, though the names and situations have been changed to protect the identity of women reporting. It is important to note that men who work by the feminine paradigm of leadership also report similar experiences.

40. See Marian Conger, *Women in Parish Ministry: Stress and Support* (Washington, D.C.: Alban Institute, 1985), p. 16

41. Ibid, p. 17.

42. See Belle Rose Ragins and Eric Sundstrom, "Gender and Power in Organization: A Longitudinal Perspective," *Psychological Bulletin* 105:1 (1989): 59

43. See Marth Ellen Stortz, *PastorPower* (Nashville: Abingdon Press, 1993), which discusses the kinds of power that pastors use.

44. Conger, *Women in Parish Ministry,* p. 23.

45. Ibid., pp. 20-21.

46. Ibid., p. 21.

47. Rosabeth Moss Kanter, *Men and Women of the Corporation* (New York: Basic Books, 1977), p. 209. Cited in Conger, *Women in Parish Ministry,* p. 34.

48. See Schaef, *Women's Reality,* p. 114.

49. See Conger, *Women in Parish Ministry,* p. 33.

50. Rosener, "Ways Women Lead," pp. 122-24.

51. See Conger, *Women in Parish Ministry,* p. 19.

52. Huff, "Wives of the Organization," pp. 16-21.

53. Ibid, p. 22.

54. Marilyn Loden, "Recognizing Women's Potential: No Longer Business as Usual," *Management Review* (December 1987): 45-46.

55. Schaef, *Women's Reality,* pp. 8-10.

56. Ibid., p. 64-66.

57. See Conger, *Women in Parish Ministry,* p. 24.

58. Though Rosener ("Ways Women Lead," p. 124) points out that the white male system requires men "to appear to be competitive, strong, tough, decisive and in control," and therefore less likely to develop interactive leadership styles.

59. Carol Pierce and Bill Page, *A Male/Female Continuum: Paths to Colleagueship* (Laconia, NH: New Dynamics, 1990).

18. Leading for the Leasts: A Woman's Story

1. Robert K. Greenleaf, *Servant Leadership: A Journey Into the Nature of Legitimate Power and Greatness* (New York: Paulist Press, 1977), pp. 13-14.

2. To Americans, three million dollars to build a simple home for thirty severely handicapped people may seem like a lot of money. But the cost of land for housing and construction costs is tremendously high in Korea, beyond anything most people in America can imagine.

Epilogue: On Finishing Well

1. Loren B. Mead, *The Once and Future Church* (Washington, D.C.: The Alban Institute, 1991).

2. Lyle Schaller, *The Seven-Day-A-Week Church* (Nashville: Abingdon Press, 1992).

3. For a study of marketing in religious organizations, see Norman Shawchuck et al., *Marketing for Congregations: Choosing to Serve People More Effectively* (Nashville: Abingdon Press, 1992).

4. Peter F. Drucker, *The New Realities* (New York: Harper & Row, 1989), pp. 200-203.

5. Schaller, *The Seven-Day-A-Week Church*, p. 58.

6. Robert Farrar Capon, *The Parables of Judgment* (Grand Rapids: William B. Eerdmans, 1989), p. 167.

7. Ibid., pp. 168-69.

8. Carlo Carretto, *Letters to Dolcidia* (Maryknoll, N.Y.: Orbis Books, 1991), pp. 48-50.

Author Index

Subject Index

discerning vision and leader's heart 52, 94
Divine encounter *73-74, 144, 150*
implementation of *22-23, 152, 176*
in a turbulent environment *16-17, 170*
leader's vision *16, 23, 38, 69, 75, 93, 106, 114-15, 139, 146, 150, 296, 301*
lost vision *74, 154-55*
pursuance of vision *17, 72, 296*
renewed vision *44, 55, 69, 175*
sources of vision *93-94*
three dimensions of *70*
inward view of oneself *70-72*
outward view of circumstances *70-73*
"upward" view towards God *70-71*
total giving of oneself to God *74*
Vocation *20, 66-67*
Volunteers *16, 152, 178-80, 185, 199, 223, 299*

Waiting (spirituality of) *48-49, 55*
active *49*
vs. procrastination *48*

"walk standing still" *49*
Web of inclusion *254*
Willow Creek Community Church *37-38, 180*
Winning and losing (Model I Organizations) *232*
Women in leadership *253-77*
feminine paradigm in church *258-62*
harassment *269-72*
invisible paradigm *256-58*
models for change *272-77*
paradigm for women in leadership *254-56*
women working in male paradigm *262-269, 273*
Worship *114, 117, 124, 132, 166-167, 176, 224, 229, 2381*

Xavier *66*

Younger American churches *229-30*

Zechariah *64, 72*